The Employment Relationship

For Sue, whose patient and generous spirit is put upon every time I undertake a project like this, but whose skill I draw upon. For my mother, whose quiet pride in all her children is so appreciated but rarely publicly acknowledged.

To my mentor and close friend, Professor Sir Roland Smith, whose support and guidance in my career and in my personal life has been my rock.

The Employment Relationship
Key challenges for HR

Paul R. Sparrow
and
Cary L. Cooper

AMSTERDAM BOSTON HEIDELBERG LONDON NEW YORK OXFORD
PARIS SAN DIEGO SAN FRANCISCO SINGAPORE SYDNEY TOKYO

Butterworth-Heinemann
An imprint of Elsevier
Linacre House, Jordan Hill, Oxford OX2 8DP
200 Wheeler Road, Burlington MA 01803

First published 2003

British Library Cataloguing in Publication Data
A catalogue record for this book is available from the British Library

Library of Congress Cataloguing in Publication Data
A catalogue record for this book is available from the Library of Congress

ISBN 0 7506 4941 0

For information on all Butterworth-Heinemann publications visit
our website at www.bh.com

Composition by Genesis Typesetting Limited, Rochester, Kent
Printed and bound in Great Britain by Biddles Ltd, *www.biddles.co.uk*

Contents

Foreword

This book contains some valuable insight for employment specialists, human resource practitioners and policy makers alike. It provides a balanced analysis of what is happening inside organizations, both to the type of jobs and to the experience of working. As organizations continue to face unprecedented levels of competition, then the challenges discussed in this book will surely need serious attention. The authors draw a number of considerations to our attention. The relationship between employers and employees is in a state of change, with trade unions less relevant in the private sector. However, the pressure is on employees in other ways, especially at a time of skill shortages. Employers require new skills and competencies and high levels of commitment if they are to survive in a globalizing economy. However, in return they also have to meet rising employee expectations – demands for challenging work and more attention being given to the quality of life. We see shifts taking place in what people value at work, and pressures for young and old alike to better manage the work–life balance. Trust is a central theme to this book. We have to build trust in corporate governance, trust in business strategies, trust in the future success of work and trust in the skills, abilities and desires of the workforce. As we manage our way through the changing landscape at work, organizations will have to learn how to manage people more effectively in a world in which the nature and meaning of careers is changing markedly. Organizations will have to adopt and develop tools and techniques that allow them to capitalise on individual talent, while maintaining a sense of fairness and justice for the wider workforce. Demographic challenges, skills shortages, the need for ever better productivity, and changing values across generations all herald the need for greater flexibility. As organizations and individuals develop this flexibility, the relationship between employers and employees will evolve. This will not be an easy road to tread. I commend this book for helping to signpost the challenges that we face on this journey and the opportunities that will arise.

Digby Jones
CBI Director-General

About the Authors

Paul R. Sparrow is the Ford Professor of International Human Resource Management and Academic Director Executive Education at Manchester Business School. He graduated from the University of Manchester with a BSc (Hons) Psychology and the University of Aston with an MSc Applied Psychology and was then sponsored by Rank Xerox to study the impacts of ageing on the organization for his PhD at Aston University. From 1982 to 1984 he was a freelance consultant principally involved in projects relating to changing patterns of work. He then became a Research Fellow at Aston University and a Senior Research Fellow at Warwick Business School researching emerging human resource strategies in the computer and retail sectors. In 1988 he joined PA Consulting Group working as a Consultant and finally a Principal Consultant. In 1991 he returned to academia and took up a Lectureship in Organizational Behaviour at Manchester Business School, moving to Sheffield University to take up a Readership in 1995, and then a Chair in 1997. He returned to Manchester Business School in 2001. He has written and edited a number of books including *European human resource management in transition, Designing and achieving competency, Human resource management: the new agenda* and *The competent organization: a psychological analysis of the strategic management process*. He has also published several articles concerning the future of work, human resource strategy, management competencies, the psychology of strategic management, international human resource management and cross-cultural management. He is associated with the ESRC Centre for Organization and Innovation, at the Institute of Work Psychology; Sheffield; the Center for Global Strategic Human Resource Management, Rutgers University; and the Centre for Research into the Management of Expatriates, Cranfield University. He was Editor of the *Journal of Occupational and Organizational Psychology* from 1998 to 2003.

Cary L. Cooper is currently BUPA Professor of Organizational Psychology and Health in the Manchester School of Management, University of Manchester Institute of Science and Technology (UMIST). He is the author of over 100 books (on occupational stress, women at work and industrial and organizational psychology), has written over 300 scholarly articles for academic journals, and is a frequent contributor to national newspapers, TV and radio. He is currently Founding Editor of the *Journal of Organizational Behavior* and co-Editor of the medical journal *Stress and Health*. He is a Fellow of the British Psychological Society, The Royal Society of Arts, The Royal Society of Medicine and the Royal Society of Health. Professor Cooper is the President of the British Academy of Management, is a Companion of the Chartered Management Institute and one of the first UK-based Fellows of the (American) Academy of Management (having also won the 1998 Distinguished Service Award for his contribution to management science from the Academy of Management). Professor Cooper is the Editor (jointly with Professor Chris Argyris of Harvard Business School) of the international scholarly *Blackwell Encyclopedia of Management* (12-volume set). He has been an advisor to the World Health Organisation, ILO, and published a major report for the EU's European Foundation for the Improvement of Living and Work Conditions on 'Stress Prevention in the Workplace'. He was awarded the CBE by the Queen in 2001 for his contribution to health and safety at work.

1
Challenges Facing the Employment Relationship: Introduction

Nine key challenges

The purpose of this book is to integrate and synthesize the latest work from the fields of work and organizational psychology, organizational behaviour and human resource management (HRM), which is concerned with the changing nature of the employment relationship. We deal with nine challenges that face organizations in this new relationship.

The first challenge is *to gain insight into the changing psychological contract at work*, the way in which it is formed, the things that lead to a breach or violation of psychological contract, the consequences or otherwise of doing this, and the extent to which psychological contract change is a manageable process. This requires that we examine the processes that surround the workings of the psychological contract – a task undertaken in the next chapter.

A second challenge is *to consider what is really meant by flexibility at work*. Are we indeed facing a new employment relationship or have we been here before? We need to understand the patterns of continuity and change in the employment relationship. We do this by presenting an analysis of the employment trends associated with contingent work and identifying the managerial challenges that these data signal.

The third challenge is *to consider whether we have a social climate in organizations that makes the management of a changing psychological contract a feasible objective or not*. We examine the factors that first create and then determine the social climate within which the employment relationship exists.

The 'social exchanges' on which the employment relationship is founded – and from which the psychological contract develops – do not exist in a vacuum. Perceptions of justice and trust, among other factors, affect the health and functioning of the psychological contract. We need to explore the experience of job insecurity and examine the reactions that employees have had to the new form of capitalism that flourished from the 1980s onwards. Are people insecure? Can they and have they recovered from the experience of downsizing in the 1990s?

The fourth challenge is *to unravel the work and career transitions that are taking place*. What are the new career behaviours that are emerging, and is there a need for organizations to negotiate and contract with a more diverse workforce? Organizations in some high-change sectors have faced the challenge of having to re-engage large segments of their workforce. What is involved in this and can we identify the important factors in transitions so that they may be managed better in future?

The fifth challenge is *to identify the challenges that are created for organizations by the increasing individualization of the employment relationship*. We explore some of the managerial strategies that have been used to cope with this process of individualization. This takes us into an examination of some of the factors that are important in careers such as the role of social capital, the difficulties of fighting a war for talent, and the challenges of developing idiosyncratic deals for talented people whilst maintaining a climate of fairness, and the risks of excessive individualization.

The sixth challenge is *to understand whether the new employment relationship has had any significant impact on the most salient ways in which the individual and the organization are linked to each other*. We need to understand the challenges faced by organizations as they have to cope with potential changes in the nature of commitment, the way in which people identify with the organization, and the extent to which people will feel any sense of psychological ownership in the employment relationship. This also requires that we develop insight into some of the new behaviours that are desirable, such as the propensity to craft one's own job in the face of uncertainty, as well as insights into the problems that occur with overidentification at work, such as workaholism.

The seventh challenge is *to appreciate some of the barriers and limits that might affect the health and well-being of individuals and indeed of organizations*. This takes us into an analysis of the quality of life and some of the dysfunctions that can be created by today's employment relationship. In particular, we have to address the issue of work–life balance and the long work hours culture.

The eighth challenge is *to predict and understand the impact that the new employment relationship will have on different generations at work*. How stable are some of the work behaviours that we see today? Are there really differences between the generations? We have to understand the generational context within which images of the employment relationship are formed and the extent to which these create new patterns of behaviour.

The ninth challenge is *to consider some of the longer-term institutional changes faced by individuals and organizations alike*. As we face the future with a very different demographic profile, as the level of trust in national business models continues to erode, what are the implications for the way in which people will seek to deal with and engage with the organization?

The structure of the book

Why is such a book necessary? First and foremost it is because of the changing shape and form of organizations. This is where we begin the story. This is the context we must understand before we examine the impact on the psychology of work and organizational behaviour. Therefore, while much of the discussion in this book draws upon psychological principles, in this opening chapter we weave together the main dialogues that are now taking place in the broader organization theory literature. In so doing, we make no comment about the long-term sustainability of the new forms of organization, nor the psychological consequences of this pursuit by organizations of strategic flexibility. This task is undertaken in the later chapters when we apply a series of different 'lenses' to the evidence and build up a picture of the challenges that we face in managing our way through the new employment relationship.

In Chapter 2 we explain what is meant by the term 'psychological contract' and discuss how this contract is considered to regulate the employment relationship. We examine how this contract is typically measured and draw some parallels between its implicit nature and the implied terms of the legal contract of employment. The essential elements of psychological contracting theory are explained along with the way in which the contract is formed. We show that it is the perception and the emotional experience of the employment relationship that has the most important impact on individuals – and we highlight the challenges that these reactions will create for organizations. Clearly these challenges will vary depending on the intensity of the individual relationship with the organization.

How can we best understand the different intensities in the employment relationship? In Chapters 3 and 4 we shall consider the evidence behind claims that there has been a fundamental change in the employment relationship. We consider whether we have experienced some of the phenomena associated with a more contingent employment relationship (the end-of-jobs thesis and job insecurity thesis) before and examine whether there is indeed a new employment relationship, and if there is, whether it is more a product of demand or of supply. What is the level of individual volition? We create a picture of a slow demise in long-term attachment to the organization and explore the evidence behind the growth of non-traditional employment arrangements. In subsequent chapters we build up understanding around a series of important discussions that have taken place about the employment relationship in recent years.

In Chapter 5 we consider the social climate within which the psychological contract is now operating. We shall discuss the issues of trust, justice and organizational support and examine the experience of downsizing and of survivors in post-downsized organizations. We shall explore the evidence and ask if any important changes are taking place in the way that employees perceive their job security. In Chapter 6 we consider the issue of the career behaviour resulting from the employment relationship. We ask whether there are indeed new patterns of careers. The assumed individualization of the employment relationship has created a challenge for organizations to negotiate and engage with individuals over what they expect and will accept in return for accepting a relationship based more on employability rather than employment security. In order to understand the issues involved we consider the attempts made by organizations to re-engage their workforces. We outline the work transitions that individuals now have to cope with as they take on more individual responsibility for the employment relationship and note the importance of career transitions. In Chapter 7 we pick up this theme of individualization of the employment relationship and examine some of the challenges that this presents. These range from the need for organizations to compete for talent and create idiosyncratic psychological contracts for many of its employees, through to the price that can be paid for focusing too much on the contribution of the individual in the employment relationship and for unfair 'dealing'.

In Chapter 8 we return to some of the psychological challenges faced in the employment relationship and focus in particular on the ways in which the link between the individual and the organization is being challenged. The psychological contract captures an important way in which the individual and the organization become linked to each other, but there are other important linkages that surround the psychological contract. We discuss a series of important and related concepts such as commitment, organizational identification and the experience of psychological ownership in more detail and consider what is happening to each of these in the context of today's employment relationship. We examine some of the important individual outcomes from the new employment relationship that organizations need to manage much better, including job satisfaction, job-crafting behaviours and workaholism.

In Chapter 9 we consider the challenges that are created when the employment relationship becomes imbalanced, and examine recent evidence on work–life balance and the problems created by a long work hours culture. We consider the link between commitment and non-work obligations and also deal with the problem of reactive and dysfunctional behaviours to the employment relationship.

In Chapter 10 we tackle two of the challenges raised above together. First, we examine whether it is appropriate to assume that the new generations entering work will behave and react in the same way as their predecessors. The challenges associated with managing generational differences across the employment relationship are developed. We look at the work values of young workers and speculate on some of the theories about change. Second, we examine some of the challenges that will test these values, such as the shift towards being a consumer of the organization with increasing reward through stock options, the problems of corporate governance and the collapse of trust in business itself, the difficult choices that will have to be made to cope with demographic trends such as the trade-off between a longer working life and large-scale immigration.

The problem of hypercompetition: managing the employment relationship in times of disorder?

Why is it necessary to consider whether there are such fundamental changes taking place in the employment relationship? We would argue that it is necessary because many organizations are now managing in times of severe disorder. D'Avini[1] has coined the term *hypercompetition* to characterize the nature of the disorder, stress and unpredictability that is confronting modern organizations. Hypercompetition is not the force driving the changes. It is the response expected to these changes. A series of long-wave economic cycles are considered to have created this period of turbulence. Disorder is created at the interface between the end of a cycle of economic growth that was based on the post-war economy, and the beginning of a new cycle based on technological drivers of information, communication, and biotechnology. The economic opportunities are immense and the social disruptions will be very challenging. Academics of course disagree over the scale of this disorder. Business economists and strategic management researchers such as Porter[2] argue that these changes are constrained only to particular sectors, whilst organizational behaviour specialists and organizational analysts such as Zohar and Morgan[3] suggest that corporate anarchy will be the ultimate result of the economic and competitive forces that have been unleashed.

To resolve this issue a three-year collaborative project involving several hundred strategic management, marketing, international management and business policy specialists, organizational scientists, and social psychologists was organized by the US Academy of Management and the journal *Organization Science*. In introducing the resultant book, Ilinitch, Lewin and D'Avini[4] pointed out that:

> . . . The language and metaphors of today's managers make one point abundantly clear: they are experiencing the strongest and most disruptive competitive forces of their careers. Rather than a game, business has become war. Rather than an honourable fight with the best firm winning, the goal has become extermination of the enemy. CEOs from industries ranging from telecommunications to auto parts describe the competition they face as 'brutal', 'intense', 'bitter' and 'savage'. In the words of Andrew Grove, the CEO of Intel, 'only the paranoid survive' in a world of hypercompetition. Increasingly, managers are turning to academics and consultants to understand why the nature of competition is changing and for insights about how to compete in chaotic and disorderly times.

Few managers would disagree with this sentiment. For academics and practitioners alike, however, it raises some important challenges. A number of critical questions are now being asked. How can firms reinvent themselves as they become more flexible? What do disposable organizations really look like? How can organizations manage the employment relationship to exploit both flexibility and knowledge creation?

Clearly, both the technological revolution and globalization have transformed the competitive landscape. Volberda[5] argues that in order to cope with the demands of hypercompetition – indeed in order to survive – organizations have to build new core competences and develop their human capital and work systems in new ways that will enable them to pursue more flexible strategies. We believe that it is this pressure for strategic flexibility that will continue to challenge the employment relationship, most notably because it will require the development of new organizational forms.

New organizational forms and knowledge-based competition

Before we examine the evidence-based implications of this drive towards flexibility on employee behaviour, we therefore begin by outlining the reasons behind the demands for such strategic flexibility – the changes in organization form – as seen by organizational scientists. Commentators on organization design today, such as Bartlett, Ghoshal, Brown, Eisenhardt, Floyd, Woolridge and Nohria, all agree that organizations are experimenting with a range of new organizational forms and strategies to adapt to or manage the unprecedented levels of change generated in this period of hypercompetition.[6]

A theme that serves as the capstone for most of the issues discussed throughout this book is the attention that has been given to the topic of organizational forms designed for strategic flexibility. The term *organizational form* refers to the combination of strategy, structure and internal control and co-ordination systems that provide an organization with its operating logic, its rules of resource allocation and its mechanism of corporate governance.[7] Managers are the primary designers of this 'organizational form' through the choices they make – whether these decisions are planned and thought through or not – about the organization and the shape of jobs. Organizational forms and the structures and processes through which they are realized have traditionally emerged to protect the organization from, and create a buffer against, the sort of external uncertainty outlined above when we discussed the phenomenon of hypercompetition. Aldrich[8] therefore argues that organizational forms serve three purposes. They:

1 Help identify and disseminate the collective aims of the organization;
2 Regulate the flow of resources into and out of it; and
3 Identify and govern the duties, rights, functions and roles of the members of the organization.

Organizational theory considers that new organizational forms are generally produced by technological innovations, although other agents of organizational form creation such as social movements and collective action can also play a role.[9] There is a consensus that knowledge-based assets within an organization will form the foundation for success in the twenty-first century and will guide the way that we design organizational forms.[10] In economies based on information, competitive advantage is now presumed to result from the ability of firms to charge *economic rents* (defined as above-normal profits in relation to others in the industry). These economic rents are in turned gained only by those firms that can create new knowledge and keep it to itself. We assume today that knowledge-based enterprises are the most efficient way of gathering information and disseminating understanding because they have reduced communication costs and heightened capabilities to support individual learning and the management of knowledge.

Competitive advantage is then now considered to flow from the creation, ownership and management of knowledge and to reside within 'knowledge assets-based enterprises'.[11] Turuch[12] outlines four main reasons why such knowledge-based competition has already assumed heightened importance in the world economy:

1 The bulk of fixed costs associated with knowledge-based products and services now accrue in respect of their creation, as opposed to their dissemination or distribution.
2 As knowledge grows, it tends to branch and fragment. Rapid and effective re-creation of knowledge comes to represent a source of competitive advantage.
3 The value of investments in knowledge, whilst difficult to estimate, are more volatile and have a more direct linkage with overall business performance, with outcomes ranging from disappointment of expectations through to extraordinary knowledge development.
4 Even when knowledge investments create considerable economic value, it is hard to predict who will capture the lion's share of these investments.

However, there is a conflict between the need to operate in today's hypercompetitive environment and the current reliance on bureaucratic forms of organization. Although the structural implications of the shift towards a more information-intensive economy are clearly varied, Child and McGrath have specified some of the main conceptual elements that are influencing the design choices that are being made by organizations[13] in a Special Research Forum on New and Evolving Organizational Forms in *Academy of Management Journal*.

It is argued today that bureaucratic organizations have an inbuilt design-fault. They are designed for the efficient allocation of resources and assume that knowledge has already been codified. Codified knowledge can be treated as a commodity and can therefore be built into stable routines within the organization.[14] Control over knowledge flows has become much more difficult to exert and dissemination of insights has become much more open. At the same time, organizations are beginning to appreciate that control and reliance on conformity to core processes actually inhibits the creative process and exploratory learning. There has been much experimentation in recent years and a fragmentation of bureaucratic organizational forms. A wide variety of terminology has been used to capture the looser set of organizational forms that have evolved as part of this fragmentation. The most well-known descriptions of new organizational forms include:

- Post-bureaucratic and Post-modern organization[15]
- Re-engineered corporation[16]
- Virtual organization[17]
- Boundaryless company[18]
- Network organizations[19]
- Modular organizations[20]
- Fractol and modular factories[21]
- Atomized organization[22]
- High-performance or High-commitment work system[23]
- Knowledge-creating company[24]
- Distributed knowledge system.[25]

What is shared by these varied concepts? They all argue that tightly integrated hierarchies will be supplanted increasingly by '. . . loosely coupled networks of organizational actors'.[26] This becomes possible because greater flexibility has been built into organizational systems by developing 'modularity'. Modularity enables the components of any system to be recombined in different ways and to be tasked with different functions, with little loss of function through reconfiguration. Child and McGrath[27] summarize three common features of the above prescriptions and the differences between the conventional and emerging perspectives on organizational form that they highlight is outlined in Box 1.1.

This book concerns challenges to the employment relationship. It seems only sensible to outline from the outset the challenges that are faced by organizations. Their actions become more understandable for doing so. Child and McGrath identify four core theoretical issues or challenges associated with these new more loosely coupled organizational forms, which they call interdependence, disembodiment, velocity and power:

1 *Interdependence*: The scope and depth of interdependence prevalent in business today is at unprecedented levels. Advances in information and communication technologies, coupled with changes in regulatory regimes and control over capital flows, have made interdependent operations both more desirable and more cost-effective. The outcome for all parties in any business transaction are fundamentally entwined with the actions and outcomes of other parties. The management of interdependent systems has become more complex as authority is dispersed across several parties, and

---

Box 1.1   Common features of new organizatIonal forms

There are three common features shared by the many prescriptions for future organizational forms. As far as the employment relationship is concerned:

1 *The setting of goals, identifying and dissemination of aims, decision making and the exercise of power* stresses: decentralized rather than top-down goal setting; distributed rather than concentrated power; a preference for smaller rather than larger units; leadership roles that provide guidance and conflIct management rather than control, monitoring, exercise of formal authority and concrete objectives; vision that emerges in the organization rather than being dictated; and team and work group structures rather than formal hierarchies.

2 *The maintcnance of integrity, regulation of resources and establishment of boundaries within and between organizations* stresses: the production system or network as the primary unit of analysis, rather then the firm; permeable and fuzzy boundaries rather than durable and clearly set ones; flexibility rather than reliability and replicability; horizontal regulation rather than vertical regulation; relationship-based rather than rule-based integrity; and structures that are independent of assets rather than assets being linked to particular organizational units.

3 *The differentiation between rights and duties, functions and roles* stresses: general and fuzzy role definitionc, not specialized and clear ones; adaptation rather than the attempt to absorb uncertainty; impermanent rights and duties rather than permanent ones; and an orientation on innovation rather than efficiency.

Source: Child and McGrath.[27]

---

coordination of changes has become more unpredictable. The presumption that there is some advantage to the organization in controlling resources within its own boundaries is being challenged.

2 *Disembodiment*: The traditional link between ownership and control of assets and performance has been broken. It is not necessary physically to own an asset to utilize it and as a consequence the definition of what should be core activities for the firm has shifted. Large hierarchical entities have been replaced by loosely interconnected organizational components with semi-permeable boundaries. The locus of production occurs at the nexus of relationships between these parties rather than within the boundaries of a single firm. The presumption that efficient production is more valuable than inefficient innovation is challenged.

3 *Velocity*: From product development down to internal communications, forces such as trade liberalization, deregulated capital movement and new communication technologies have accelerated the velocity at which the organization has to function. This has led to hypercompetition in many sectors, and a reduction in the stimulus–response time open to organizations (hence experiments with how organizations use time). Pressure is placed on vertical information and decision flows.

4 *Power*: Power has shifted both in terms of locus and concentration. Power derived from possession of tangible assets has been superseded by power derived from the possession of knowledge and information. There is growing asymmetry of power between managerial agents in charge of large global firms and most other groups in society (consumers, employees and local communities). Power becomes a more complex matter, with multiple stakeholders who are not organized hierarchically.

To summarize the situation now faced by organizations, there are many challenges that are being created by the path that they have taken. They have become much more dependent on the fortunes and actions of others, they cannot be sure that they will perform better just by owning important assets, the speed at which they have to function effectively has accelerated, and power now resides in the location of knowledge. All these developments carry important messages for the employment relationship.

The political economic context for work

The editorial to a recent Special Issue of *Journal of Organizational Behavior* on Brave New Workplace: Organizational Behavior in the Electronic Age recently began by stating that:[28]

> . . . The very nature of the 'business model' which dominates organizational thinking is changing. Contracts rather than hierarchies are becoming essential co-ordination tools. Information systems and electronically linked workgroups are prevalent. New frames of reference and new stakeholders are emerging. And the social role of the corporation is undergoing important transformations as markets dominate communities.

It is now generally assumed by critical management theorists such as Beck[29] – if not also by the average citizen – that there is an increasing divide between capital, the welfare state and the free market. Political economists draw attention to two difficulties currently faced by a risk regime based on insecurity, uncertainty and a loss of boundaries. The first is motivational, experienced when economic and social expectations are not met and when members of society sense a lack of meaning and motivation in their employment life. The second concerns legitimation, where the legitimacy of key state and organizational institutions become threatened with disintegration and fragmentation as people neither trust them nor continue to behave in a normative manner. New work practices are therefore designed to create a flexible labour market that serves the purpose of shifting some of the risks of employment away from the state and the economy and onto individuals. Personal risk has now become diffused across a wide range of organizations and occupations. Smith identifies three important divides that have been created in the new economy:[30]

1 A movement towards flexibility in the workplace and flexible specialization within production systems, with control systems that either allow workers to learn new skills and retool for new more complex tasks, or which just introduce new structures of power and inequality.
2 A divide between 'good jobs' and 'bad jobs', i.e. either high information or technology intensity jobs, or jobs requiring low skill, giving low pay, and affording low training.
3 Differences between a stable workforce versus a new contingent workforce.

The new flexibilities

The effect that these new organizational forms will have on the employment relationship is still broadly unknown. The shift towards an information-based economics of production as opposed to a materials-based economics does appear to be redefining what is core employment and what is peripheral employment and core work increasingly consists of knowledge work and professional work that leads to the design of soft concepts and hard technologies. For individuals too there are a number of deep changes taking place within their employment relationship. We have argued in other work that a series of complex changes in the psychological contract at work are taking place.[31] Most of the popular business literature points to a series of deep qualitative shifts taking place in the nature of work. Although the issue of flexibility has been discussed now for nearly 20 years within the HRM literature, Sparrow argues that three issues lie at the heart of this debate:[32]

1 The link between changes in technology and how these affect the organization structure and process
2 The impact that the resultant structural changes and new organizational forms have on the integration, organization and distribution of roles and tasks
3 Changes in the content of jobs, the form in which they are designed, and the way in which they need to be coordinated by HRM systems.

Organizations have been seeking for quite a while to increase their versatility by tapping (and better matching) the skills, capabilities, adaptability and creativity of the workforce through a range of interventions such as total quality management, just-in-time, call centres, lean manufacturing, team work and empowerment. In combination these phenomena have already had significant implications for what is now meant when we talk of a 'job' and also for employees. Examining the impacts of changes in job design in the 1990s, Parker and Wall[33] pointed to five common developments in job content that occurred throughout the 1980s and 1990s. These were the increased relevance of *operational knowledge*, higher levels of *work interdependence*, a greater proportion of job responsibilities based around *direct production and service interfaces*, higher *cognitive-abstract qualifications* needed for proficient performance, and more emphasis on *social competencies*.

Yet, until relatively recently, certainly within the HRM literature, much of the debate about flexibility was still very narrowly focused. It tended to concentrate at the level of the job – the various tasks or work elements that were being bundled up into 'jobs' – and also on the process of negotiation about changes to these job conditions. This does not capture the quite profound changes taking place within the nature of jobs, work and the relationship that surrounds employment. Just consider what has already been happening to 'jobs'. Organizations have been repackaging significantly the work elements, tasks, duties and positions that are together bundled into definable 'jobs'. They have been redesigning the relationship between jobs and the organizational context into which these jobs are placed. In short, they have been simultaneously manipulating four things:[34]

1 The components that are bundled together into definable 'jobs' (through the tasks, operations, work elements and duties that are deemed still necessary for employees)
2 Redesigning the context into which jobs are placed and positioning new jobs into a broader organization design (through the family of jobs to which any one job is deemed to belong, the occupation of the job holder, the career stream to which jobs belong, and the work process of which it forms a part)
3 Changing the ways in which jobs relate to and interact with each other (through the roles assigned to particular jobs, the information and control systems applied to them, and the relative levels of power they possess)
4 Changing the ways in which HRM systems integrate the new bundles of jobs into the organization's strategic process (by reshaping the competence and commitment that must be possessed by employees).

Sparrow and Marchington[35] outlined seven flexibilities that were discussed in the HRM literature throughout the 1990s that summarize these job-level changes (see Box 1.2).

The seven flexibilities outlined in Box 1.2 should really be considered simply as consequences of there being a much deeper drive within organizations towards what may be termed 'strategic flexibility'. The rhetoric from the management gurus therefore has suggested that radical changes are taking

Box 1.2   The pursuit of seven simultaneous flexibilities in organizations

Sparrow and Marchington noted that organizations may chose to pursue one of seven flexibilities discussed in the literature. Historically they tended to pursue one form of flexibility for one job, a combination of flexibilities for another, but are increasingly attacking the whole organization across a series of fronts. Each type of flexibility also tends to be associated with a different 'battle' or struggle between interested parties (stakeholders) in the employment relationship:

1 *Numerical flexibility,* where the battle is around who owns (and therefore has some legal obligation towards) the employment relationship. Does the job need to be one within the internal labour market, or can it be sufficiently controlled through outsourcing, peripheral forms of employment, or the use of various associate relationships?

2 *Functional flexibility,* an organization's ability to deploy employees between activities and tasks to match changing workloads, production methods or technology. The battle is around the roles and competencies deemed appropriate for the job. When the new package of elements, tasks and duties are considered, does the job need to staffed by a multi-skilled individual, are there new core competences that must be delivered, or are there important cross-business process skills that must be acquired?

3 *Financial flexibility,* where the battle is around the reward–effort bargain to be struck with the job-holder. What is the best balance between the type and nature of reward and the delivery of performance? Would a more efficient wage–effort bargain be struck by the use of performance-related pay, gainsharing, or cafeteria benefits?

4 *Temporal flexibility,* where the battle is the need for continuous active representation on the job. What time patterns should the job be fitted into and will employees be able to switch themselves onto the highest levels of customer service and performance throughout these time patterns? What is the role, for instance, of flexitime, nil hours, or annual hours?

5 *Geographical flexibility,* where the battle is around the ideal location of the job and its constituent tasks. Does the job need to be carried out in specific locations, or is there latitude for homeworking, or even operating through virtual teams?

6 *Organizational flexibility,* where the battle is around the form and rationale of the total organization and its design, into which the job may be fitted. Does the organization operate as an ad-hocracy, a loose network of suppliers, purchasers, and providers, or a temporary alliance or joint venture?

7 *Cognitive flexibility*, where the battle is around both the mental frames of reference required effectively to perform in the job and the level of cognitive skills required. Does the job require people with a particular sort of psychological contract? What sorts of strategic and cognitive assumptions cannot be tolerated?

Source: Sparrow and Marchington.[35]

place within organizations and that the end of the 'job' is nigh, that there are fewer old-style jobs in existence, and that it has become increasingly hard to package work into discrete 'jobs'. Despite much of this rhetoric – which we shall explore through different 'lenses' throughout this book – the reality is that organizations are still currently structured around jobs. Yet, at the same time, it is undeniable that the flexibility they seek is far more profound than simply considering new time patterns of work, high-commitment work practices, and new forms of pay. Whilst all these issues have to be considered, increasingly this consideration is just as part of a total package of changes intended to deliver what the strategists refer to as *strategic flexibility*.[36]

HR practitioners, work and organizational psychologists, and social scientists in general, are trying to find an acceptable path through the many dilemmas that we know we shall face in dealing with the issues raised by this pursuit of strategic flexibility. Moreover, no one field seems to have all the answers. As we work our way through the changes, the fields of academic knowledge that will carry most weight will also change rapidly.[37] We are witnessing a dialogue and sharing of ideas between a number of disciplines:

- Work and organizational psychologists, who consider how best to partition work into manageable units, and the behavioural and employee mindset outcomes that one should expect from the nature of the employment relationship
- Organization design academics, who seek to understand how best to coordinate work across important vertical, horizontal, and external boundaries within and across organizations
- HRM specialists, who consider how best to create systems to both control and gain commitment from employees that will enable them and the organization jointly to implement the new systems.

New psychological contracts, new careers?

We shall see throughout this book that the consequences of changes in the employment relationship are viewed in quite different ways. For some writers many developments associated with the creation of flexibility are resulting in a worker underclass with low wages, few benefits, negligible job security, little investment in their capabilities and deteriorated chances of advancement.[38] We shall review the reality of these trends in Chapters 3 and 4 in particular. Associated with this view is discussion and awareness of the negative consequences of changes in the employment relationship, with concern expressed about problems to do with work–life balance, coping with a long work culture and impacts on stress, health and general well-being. These issues are considered in Chapter 9. However, the changing employment relationship has many faces and not all are negative. Much attention has also been given to the new opportunities that exist for individuals and the benefits that might flow from an unfettering of their careers and capabilities. The evidence that argues that we are faced with a greater individualization of work, the associated war for talent, the need for organizations to create far more focused and individualized 'deals' with their employees and the psychological factors that make such a world more or less attractive to individuals are considered in Chapters 6 and 7.

We begin the analysis, however, in Chapter 2 which considers the topic of psychological contracts at work. Why do we start our analysis of the employment relationship by looking at it through psychological lenses? Regardless of the ideological stance that one takes on our future, it is clear is that the impact of changes taking place in organizational form is extremely pervasive. One of the reasons for this is that the new organizational forms actually send very important signals about the level of trust that exists within the employment relationship. *Trust* – be it the lack of it or changes within it – has strong behavioural consequences. We need to understand the impact that changes in trust will have. In Chapter 10 we speculate about possible consequences that arise from recent trust shocks – such as the US corporate governance crisis – but we begin by linking changes in *trust* to the changing nature and shape of organizations.

Trust has always been seen as a pervasive feature of organizational design choices. For example, Bradach and Eccles[39] argue that the level of trust in employees is reflected in the way that a new organizational form is realized. In particular, the discretion afforded control and coordination systems, and the way that incentives are used to direct behaviour, tell us much about the extent to which we are trusted. Higher levels of trust are associated with fewer controls and fewer controls mean that there are lower 'transaction costs' incurred by the organization. When managers redesign the organization, they are making two important trust-related judgements, again either consciously or unconsciously:

1 Is there implicit employee 'task reliability', i.e. do employees have the capabilities and potential to exercise responsible self-direction and self-control?
2 Is there sufficient 'values congruence' with the purpose of the organization, i.e. is there a dominant written and spoken philosophy that will guide the ultimate way in which employees will act?

We consider the nature of trust from a psychological perspective in Chapter 5, but shall return to the topic throughout this book. This is because for psychologists there is often a conflict between the higher levels of trust that are both implicit in and a necessary ingredient of the operating logic of many of the new organizational forms (such as network organizations) and the levels of trust that are actually reflected in the attitudes and psychological contract of employees.

Given many of the changes in organizational design outlined above and the pursuit of flexibility, the traditional boundaries that used to demarcate the world of work (such as job, function, hierarchy) continue to be eroded. But as these boundaries dissipate, then organizations find that they are having to manage the psychological boundaries that still seem to govern the extent to which employees remain committed at work, engaged in the organization's strategic purpose, and capable of enjoying the rewards that work offers whilst balancing its demands on their life. Sparrow[40] argued that in the new employment relationship HR practitioners do not just have to manage the employment or job contract. They have to manage the consequence of the changes taking place in the minds of their employees – what have been called the psycho-social or 'soft-wired' boundaries that still determine employee behaviour.[41] There is a soft set of expectations held by employees that have to be managed and coordinated.

In early work on the psychological contract – a term which we define more formally in the context of recent research in the next chapter – the organizational perspective on the employment relationship was generally treated simply as the *context* for the creation of each individual psychological contract. In describing this context, researchers were able to compare and contrast the 'old' versus a 'new' psychological contract and then use discussion of the 'new' psychological contract to articulate some of the challenges at work. Baruch and Hind[42] reviewed literature on career management to show how a series of new concepts had been used to signal the realities of the new employment relationship. Handy brought the concept of *'employability'* into mainstream management thinking in the late 1980s.[43] It refers to the absence of long-term commitments from the organization, but commitment to provide training and development that enables the employee to develop a portable portfolio of skills and find alternative employment when the relationship ends.

A series of generic changes, summarized in Table 1.1, are often used to represent the shifting balance in the psychological contract that has resulted from the pursuit of 'employability'. Cavanaugh and Noe point out that there is no consensus on the components of the new psychological contract.[44] Nonetheless, the majority of commentators would agree that there has been a shift from relational aspects in the employment relationship to more transactional components. The old deal was stereotyped as one in which promotion could be expected, and when granted was based upon time-served and technical competence. As long as the company was in profit and you did your job then you had no cause to fear job loss. The organizational

Table 1.1 Past and emergent forms of psychological contract.

Characterstic	Past form	Emergent form
Focus	Security, continuity, loyalty	Exchange, future
Format	Structured, predictable, stable	Unstructured, flexible, open to (re)negotiation
Underlying basis	Tradition, fairness, social justice, socio-economic class	Market forces, saleable, abilities and skills, added value
Employer's responsibilities	Continuity, job security, training, career prospects	Equitable (as perceived) reward for added value
Employee's responsibilities	Loyalty, attendance, satisfactory performance, compliance with authority	Entrepreneurship, innovation, enacting changes to improve performance, excellent performance
Contractual relations	Formalized, mostly via trade union or collective representation	Individual's responsibility to barter for their services (internally or externally)
Career management	Organizational responsibility, in-spiralling careers planned and facilitated through personnel department input	Individual's responsibility, out-spiralling careers by personal reskilling and retraining

Composite from Hiltrop[47] and Anderson and Schalk.[48]

culture was paternalistic, and essentially encouraged an exchange of security for commitment. Responsibilities were always part of an instrumental exchange, but were progressively linked to the career hierarchy. Personal development was the company's responsibility. High trust in the old employment relationship was not widespread, but was deemed to be possible.

The new employment contract has been stereotyped in a different way. Change is seen to be continuous. There is less opportunity for vertical grade promotion and is against new criteria. Anyway, isn't promotion only something for those who deserve it? Tenure cannot be guaranteed. In a globalizing economy you are 'lucky to have a job'. More responsibilities are encouraged, balanced by increased accountabilities. Status is based on perceived competence and credibility. Personal development is the employees' responsibility – individuals have to keep themselves employable whilst the organization offers employability (the opportunity to develop marketable skills). High trust is still deemed desirable, but organizations accept that employees are less committed to them, but more committed to the project they work on, their profession and their fellow team members. Organizations therefore build attachment to proxies – such as the team – for whom employees will still perform. It is argued that managers' loyalty to their employer has declined[45] and that commitment to type of work and profession appears to be stronger now than commitment to organization.[46]

Globalization therefore, has induced both organizations and employees to take a different perspective on the psychological contract and the way the change agent manages these changes. In the light of the many changes taking place in the nature of work, a number of writers such as Sparrow and Cooper have argued that today, as the process of globalization continues and in the aftermath of downsizing, the increased levels of flexibility, more short-term contracts, greater reliance on virtual workers and pursuit of more boundary-less careers may be resulting in a new and very different psychological contract.[49] In line with this view, Hartley[50] and Tetrick and Barling[51] have argued that new theories and approaches are therefore needed in the field of organizational psychology.

Critical views of the psychological contract

The concept of the psychological contract has then helped to jump-start this process of reassessing both academic theory and the practical challenges facing the employment relationship. It has provided academics and practitioners with an umbrella concept to understand the changes taking place in the nature of work. It has brought a new vocabulary into their discussions – with talk about employee mindsets, implicit deals, disengaged behaviour and a host of other issues in modern organizational life about which people are concerned.

By the 1990s this management of 'hearts and minds' had become a central human resource management task.[52] Sparrow[53] notes that it has been used to bring together a series of organizational behaviour studies on related topics such as commitment, job satisfaction, socialization and the fit between the employee and employer and in terms of definition it has been used to encompass several psychological phenomena – such as perceptions, expectations, beliefs, promises and obligations – each of which actually implies different levels of psychological engagement. In the same way that ideas about culture, climate and competencies were used to help practitioners capture complex changes needed in their organization, the psychological contract has been used as a *frame of analysis* that helps to:

- Capture changes taking place at the individual, organizational and societal level
- Discriminate between organizational responses
- Serve as a basis for predicting individual behaviour.

Research on the psychological contract tends to concentrate on the implicit and open-ended agreement about what is given and what is received within the employment relationship. Discussion of the psychological contract there-fore is often closely associated with discussion about the nature of trust in organizations.[54] We discuss this in the next chapter. At this point, however, it is important to note that in capturing expectations of reciprocal behaviour in the employment contract, discussion of the psychological contract also covers a range of societal norms and interpersonal behaviour and is based on changing perceptions of the employer–employee balance of power. Indeed, this has been one of the main benefits of early work on the topic. It has diverted attention back to the employee side of the employment relationship in an era of change when the needs of the firm and economic markets took centre-stage. The sense of mutuality implicit in the psychological contract has proved a useful vehicle to capture the consequences of perceived imbalances of exchange in the new employment relationship.

It has begun to open the 'black box' of the employment relationship and helped to reveal some of the important psychological processes that serve to 'regulate', 'legitimate' and 'enact' the employment relationship. Guest ques-tions whether a contract in which all the terms are explicit, written down or expressed remains a psychological one. He also expresses the concern that in opening up this 'black box', as with other constructs such as flexibility, job satisfaction and commitment, discussion about the psychological contract can easily present an 'analytic nightmare'.[55] He feels that our understanding of the construct does not yet enable us to either build theory or to develop precise operationalizations. Despite such concerns, he too feels that the construct should still be retained because of its ability to capture complex organizational phenomena and to act as a focus for organizational policy. He notes three reasons why the psychological contract has become a viable construct for capturing changes in the employment relationship:

1 It reflects the process of individualization of the employment relationship that has been taking place, in which the market philosophy views the individual as an independent agent offering knowledge and skills through a series of transactions in the marketplace,
2 It focuses attention on the relative distribution of power and the cost of power inequalities in the new employment relationship,
3 It has the potential to integrate research on a number of important organizational concepts such as trust, fairness and social exchange, and to add additional explanatory value to the prediction of a series of con-sequences such as job satisfaction, organizational commitment, sense of security, motivation, organizational citizenship, absence and intention to quit.

Future psychological contract scenarios

It must be noted that we do not for sure yet understand the outcomes that will follow from the nine challenges that we have used to inform this book. Indeed, providing more insight into these challenges is the purpose of this book. The fact that there is room for debate was of course signalled in our first attempt to construct a framework to examine the challenges presented to organizational HRM systems of changes in the psychological contract at work. Sparrow and Cooper[56] reviewed a range of published work and noted four different assumptions – or scenarios – that were being presented by various writers. These four scenarios were not considered to represent alternative futures but rather reflected the different findings that emerged from work in this area. These different findings sometimes reflected the methodologies that were being used by researchers – and the levels of behaviour that their method-ologies were capable of exposing. To some extent the different pictures also reflected what was happening in different industrial sectors being studied and the reaction of employees traditionally employed in such sectors.

Figure 1.1 presents four quadrants that each describe and capture a different set of assumptions that are being made about the *adaptive responses* that are being exhibited by individuals as they adjust to the demands of the new employment contract. We argued then that the combination of varied individual responses, and the assumptions we make about the level of environmental complexity and change that is really taking place, inevitably generates a range of different scenarios and discussions about what is happening to the psychological contract.

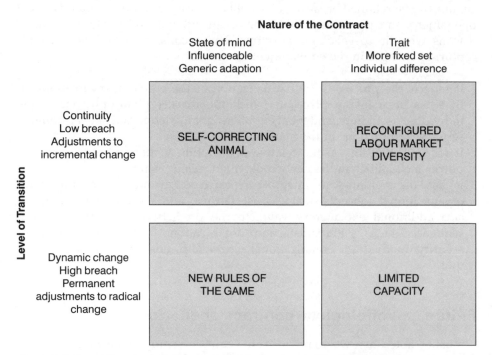

Figure 1.1 Four different adaptation processes to the new employment contract

There are two sets of bi-polar conclusions that can be drawn from existing research when considering the sort of adaptations that we are seeing to the new employment contract. The first axis reflects assumptions that are being made about the nature of the organizational environment and the scale of changes that are required in individual behaviour and adaptation. This axis really concerns the level of transition that we believe we are witnessing. This transition may be seen as low or high. Those who feel that the level of change in psychological contract is currently low will point to much continuity in the nature of the employment contract, argue that we are witnessing relatively low levels of breach of contract, or that research tends to overstate the amount of breach of contract. They argue that people have to make relatively modest or incremental adjustments to change. Those who feel that the level of transition – or change in the psychological contract – is high will tend to point to very dynamic changes taking place in the level of employment. They highlight some of the more subjective views that people might have about the level of insecurity, conduct research that suggests relatively high levels of breach of contract, and draw attention to some more permanent changes that might be taking place in employee behaviour.

The second axis in Figure 1.1 highlights our first attempt to draw some conclusions about the nature of the individual adaptive reaction to change. This dimension reflects the level of flexibility or malleability that is assumed will govern the individual adaptive response to the challenges facing the employment relationship. Again, two contrasting pictures have been painted by research. On the one hand, some researchers argue that the challenges facing individuals (and their psychological contract) depends very much on their attitudes and state of mind. This state of mind – and the scale of challenge presented – is flexible and open to influence. It tends to argue that most people are actually capable of adapting. In any event, don't people compensate for the challenges that they face, perhaps by the sort of activity that they engage in outside work (such as their leisure or non-work activities)? This position tends to present people as being a lot more flexible than we often give them credit for. On the other hand, some researchers question this flexibility. They do not present the challenges facing the psychological contract as a state of mind to which we can all adjust. Instead they tend to present individual reactions to changes in the employment contract more like a stable individual difference. The level of flexibility is considered to be relatively low and therefore some people can make the adaptations and some simply cannot, or will not. People have limits to how much change they can take. Therefore they tend to describe the psychological contract in much more inflexible ways and with more serious or dysfunctional consequences for a significant number of individuals. The four different scenarios are briefly outlined here:

1 The *self-correcting animal* scenario is based on assumptions about the generic capacity of individuals to adapt to the environment that they face. This generic ability of individuals to cope with the challenges faced in the employment relationship in turn makes them more manageable from an

HRM perspective – it is a case of changing their state of mind or attitude. In any event, the scale of changes that they face are not that different from what has gone before. We face incremental change and not radical change.

2 The *reconfigured diversity* scenario. This type of research generally assumes that the scale of change is not necessarily dramatic or radical, i.e. we face a more limited and measured scale of change. However, even though perhaps the majority of individuals are capable of adjusting to the new employment contract, there are significant individual differences in terms of individual reaction, there are some clear limits to some people's adaptability, and there will be wide variation in the responses seen. This scenario – while arguing that changes in the employment relationship may not be radical – still tends to focus on difficulties that will be faced by organizations. It argues that organizations will need to devise new and more effective ways of understanding the individual reactions to the new employment relationship and better ways of managing the greater variety in psychological contracts that will exist. These more diverse responses may also be driven along unfamiliar lines because the factors that are associated with different individual responses tend not to have been too important in the past.

3 The third scenario is labelled the *limited capacity* scenario. Research here also concerns the differential ability of people to adjust and adapt to their environment and some of the inflexibilities that will exist. However, it presents the changes being faced by individuals as being more rapid, radical and paradigm-breaking. Therefore the issue facing organizations is not just one of coping with greater diversity in response, but one of perhaps having to understand that the capacity of many individuals to adapting to this radical change will likely be more limited. Again, a series of important individual differences will account for the responses, there will be higher levels of failure to cope and more dysfunctional effects such as decreases in well-being and higher costs of stress, at least for a significant time to come. This fallability of significant numbers of individuals will make them much more unmanageable from the perspective of the organization.

4 Finally, we signalled what we called a *new rules of the game* scenario. Again, this type of research presents the environment as being unstable, changing quite radically and in directions that we haven't faced before. However, individual differences are less important in helping us understand the adaptive response, the issue is much more to do with different states of mind, and what differences do exist pattern in much broader and more generic ways – perhaps across different generations and the age or life-cohorts that they represent. People, then, are presented as being pretty flexible and adaptable to the challenges that they face. However, because the level of change in the employment relationship is high and more novel, then the adaptations that we will see may be characterized as new rules for 'playing the game' at work. In this scenario it is the organization that might have limited capacities, rather than individuals, in that many organizations will find it hard to cope with the new behaviours and the new rule-sets that will govern the adaptive response of all employees.

The reality is of course more complex than this. In the subsequent chapters we unravel the evidence that enables us to understand with more certainty what changes are taking place in the employment relationship and the challenges that these create.

References

1. D'Avini, R. (1994). *Hypercompetition: managing the dynamics of strategic maneuvering.* New York: Free Press.
2. Porter, M.E. (1996). What is strategy? *Harvard Business Review, 74 (6),* 61–78.
3. Zohar, A. and Morgan, G. (1998). Refining our understanding of hyper-competition and hyperturbulence. In A.Y. Ilinitch, A.Y. Lewin and R. D'Aveni (Eds.), *Managing in times of disorder: hypercompetitive organizational responses.* London: Sage.
4. Ilinitch, A.Y., Lewin, A.Y. and D'Avini, R.D. (1998). Introduction. In A.Y. Ilinitch, A.Y. Lewin and R. D'Avini (Eds.), *Managing in times of disorder: hypercompetitive organizational responses.* London: Sage, p. xxi.
5. Volberda, H.W. (1996). Towards the flexible form: How to remain vital in hypercompetitive environments. *Organization Science, 7,* 359–374; Volberda, H.W. (1998). *Building the flexible firm.* Oxford: Oxford University Press.
6. See, for example, Bartlett, C.A. and Ghoshal, S. (1993). Beyond the M-form: Toward a managerial theory of the firm. *Strategic Management Journal, 14 (Special Issue),* 23–46; Brown, S. and Eisenhardt, K.M. (1997). The art of continuous change: linking complexity theory and time-paced evolution in relentlessly shifting organizations. *Administrative Science Quarterly, 42,* 1–34; Floyd, S.W. and Woolridge, B. (2000). *Building strategy from the middle: reconceptualizing strategy process.* Thousand Oaks, CA: Sage; Ghoshal, S. and Bartlett, C.A. (1990). The multinational corporation as a differentiated interorganizational network. *Academy of Management Review, 15,* 603–625; and Nohria, N. and Ghoshal, S. (1997). *The differentiated network: organizing multinational corporations for value creation.* San Francisco, CA: Jossey-Bass.
7. See Pfeffer, J. (1992). *Managing with power,* Boston: Harvard Business School Press; and Creed, W.E.D. and Miles, R.E. (1996). Trust in organizations: a conceptual framework linking organizational forms, managerial philosophies and the opportunity costs of control. In R.M. Kramer and T.R. Tyler (Eds.), *Trust in organizations: frontiers of theory and research.* London: Sage.
8. Aldrich, H.E. (1999). *Organizations evolving.* Thousand Oaks, CA: Sage.
9. Rao, H., Morrill, C. and Zald, M.N. (2000). Power plays: How social movements and collective action create new organizational forms. In B.M. Staw and R.I. Sutton (Eds.), *Research in organizational behavior: an annual series of analytical essays and critical reviews. Volume 22.* New York: JAI Press.
10. Offsey, S. (1997). Knowledge management: linking people to knowledge for bottom line results. *Journal of Knowledge Management, 1 (2),* 113–122.

11. McKeen, J.D. (2001). Editorial. Special Issue on The Study of Knowledge-based Enterprises. *International Journal of Management Reviews, 3 (1)*, iii–iv.
12. Turuch, E. (2001). Knowledge management: auditing and reporting intellectual capital. *Journal of General Management, 26 (3)*, 26–40.
13. Child, J. and McGrath, R.G. (2001). Organizations unfettered: organizational form in an information-intensive economy. *Academy of Management Journal, 44 (6)*, 1135–1148.
14. See, for example, Boisot, M. (1995). *Information space: a framework for learning in organizations, institutions and culture*. London: Routledge; McGrath, R.G. (2001) Exploratory learning, adaptive capacity, and the role of managerial oversight. *Academy of Management Journal, 44*, 118–131.
15. Clegg, S.R. (1990). *Modern organization: Organization studies in the post-modern world*. London: Sage.
16. Hammer, M. and Champy, J. (1993). *Reengineering the corporation: a manifesto for business revolution*. New York: Harper Business.
17. See, for example, Chesbrough, H. and Teece, D. (1996). When is virtual virtuous? Organizing for innovation. *Harvard Business Review, 74 (1)*, 65–73; Davidow, W.H. and Malone, M.S. (1992). *The virtual corporation: structuring and revitalising the corporation for the 21st century*. New York: HarperCollins.
18. Devanna, M.A. and Tichy, N. (1990). Creating the competitive organization of the 21st century: the boundaryless corporation. *Human Resource Management, 29*, 455–471; Hirschhorn, L. and Gilmore, T. (1992). The new boundaries of the 'boundaryless' company. *Harvard Business Review, 70 (3)*, 104–115.
19. Castells, M. (1996). *The rise of the network society.* Cambridge, MA: Blackwell; Jones, C., Hesterly, W. & Borgatti, S. (1997). A general theory of network governance: Exchange conditions and social mechanisms. *Academy of Management Review, 22*, 911–945; Miles, R.E. and Snow, C.C. (1986). Causes of failure in network organizations. *California Management Review, 34 (4)*, 53–72; Nohria, N. and Eccles, R.G. (Eds.) (1992). *Networks and organizations*. Boston, MA: Harvard Business School.
20. Daft, R.L. and Lewin, A.Y. (1993). Where are the theories for the 'new' organizational forms? An editorial essay. *Organization Science, 4 (4)*, i–vi; Lei, D., Hitt, M.A. and Goldhar, J.D. (1996). Advanced manufacturing: organizational design and statistical flexibility. *Organization Studies, 17*, 501–523; Sanchez, R. (1995). Strategic flexibility in product competition. *Strategic Management Journal, 16*, 135–159; Sanchez, R. and Mahoney, J. (1996). Modularity flexibility, and knowledge management in product and organizational design. *Strategic Management Journal, 17*, 63–76.
21. Warnecke, H.J. (1993). *Revolution der Unternehmenskultur. Das Fraktale Unternehman*. Berlin: Springer; Wildermann, H. (1994). *Die Modulare Fabrik. Kundennahe Produktion durch Fertigungssegmentierung*, Munchen: TCW.
22. Ryf, B. (1993). *Die atomisierte Organisation: ein Konzept zur Ausschöpfung von Humanpotential*, Wiesbaden: Gabler.

23. Pfeffer, J. (1998). Seven practices of successful organizations. *California Management Review, 40 (2)*, 96–124.
24. Nonaka, I. (1991). The knowledge-creating company. *Harvard Business Review*, November-December, 96–104; Nonaka, I. (1994). A dynamic theory of organizational knowledge-creation. *Organization Science, 5 (1)*, 14–37; Nonaka, I. and Takeuchi, H. (1995). *The knowledge-creating company.* New York: Oxford University Press.
25. Tsoukas, H. (1996). The firm as a distributed knowledge system: a constructionist approach, *Strategic Management Journal, 17*, 11–25.
26. Schilling, M.A. and Steensma, H.K. (2001). The use of modular organizational forms: an industry-level analysis. *Academy of Management Journal, 44 (6)*, 1149–1167, p. 1149.
27. Child and McGrath, (2001). *Op. cit.* p. 1149
28. Gephart, R.P. Jr (2002). Introduction to the brave new workplace: organizational behavior in the electronic age. *Journal of Organizational Behavior, 23*, 327–344. p. 327.
29. See Beck, U. (1992). *Risk society: towards a new modernity.* Thousand Oaks, CA: Sage; Beck, U. (2000). *The brave new world of work.* Cambridge: Polity Press.
30. Smith, V. (2001). *Crossing the great divide: worker risk and opportunity in the new economy.* Ithaca, NY: ILR Press.
31. See, Sparrow, P.R. and Cooper, C.L. (1998). New organizational forms: the strategic relevance of future psychological contract scenarios. *Canadian Journal of Administrative Sciences, 15 (4)*, 356–371; Sparrow, P.R. (2000). The new employment contract: Psychological implications of future work. In R. Burke and C. Cooper (Eds.), *The organization in crisis: downsizing, restructuring, and privatization.* London: Basil Blackwell.
32. Sparrow, P.R. (1998). The pursuit of multiple and parallel organizational flexibilities: reconstituting jobs. *European Journal of Work and Organizational Psychology, 7 (1)*, 79–95.
33. See Parker, S.K. and Wall, T.D. (1996). Job design and modern manufacturing. In P. Warr (Ed.), *Psychology and work. 4th edition.* London: Penguin Books; Parker, S.H., Wall, T.D. and Cordery, J.L. (2001). Future work design research and practice: towards an elaborated model of work design. *Journal of Occupational and Organizational Psychology, 74*, 413–440.
34. Sparrow, P.R. (1998). New organizational forms, processes, jobs and psychological contract: resolving the HRM issues. In P.R. Sparrow and M. Marchington (Eds.), *Human resource management: the new agenda.* London: Financial Times/Pitman Publishing.
35. Sparrow, P.R. and Marchington, M. (Eds.) (1998). *Human resource management: the new agenda.* London: Financial Times/Pitman Publishing.
36. Hitt, M.A., Keats, B.W. and DeMarie, S.M. (1998). Navigating in the new competitive landscape: Building strategic flexibility and competitive advantage in the 21st century. *Academy of Management Executive, 12 (4)*, 22–42; Nadler, D. and Tushman, M. (1999). The organization of the future: strategic imperatives and core competencies for the 21st century. *Organizational Dynamics, 28 (1)*, 45–60.

37. Sparrow, P.R. (2000). New employee behaviours, work designs and forms of work organisation: what is in store for the future of work? *Journal of Managerial Psychology, 15 (3)*, 202–218.
38. See, for example, Kalleberg, A.L., Rasell, E., Cassirer, N., Reskin, B.F., Hudson, K., Webster, D., Appelbaum, E. and Spalter-Roth, R.M. (1997). *Nonstandard work, substandard jobs: flexible work arrangements in the US.* Washington, DC: Economic Policy Institute and Women's Research and Education Institute; Parker, R.E. (1994). *Flesh peddlars and warm bodies.* New Brunswick: Rutgers University Press; Rogers, J.K. (2002). *Temps: the many faces of the changing workplace.* Ithaca, NY: Cornell University Press.
39. Bradach, J.L. and Eccles, R.G. (1989). Price, authority, and trust: from ideal types to plural forms. *Annual Review of Sociology, 15*, 97–118.
40. Sparrow, (1998). *Op. cit.*
41. Hirschhorn, L. and Gilmore, T. (1992). The new boundaries in the 'boundaryless' company. *Harvard Business Review, 7 (3)*, 104–115.
42. Baruch, Y. and Hind, P. (1999). Perpetual motion in organizations: effective management and the impact of the new psychological contracts on 'survivor syndrome', *European Journal of Work and Organizational Psychology, 8 (2)*, 295–306.
43. Handy, C. (1989). *The age of unreason.* London: Hutchinson.
44. Cavanaugh, M.A. and Noe, R.A. (1999). Antecedents and consequences of relational components of the new psychological contract. *Journal of Organizational Behavior, 20 (3)*, 323–340.
45. Stroh, L.K., Brett, J.M. and Reilly, A.H. (1994). A decade of change: managers' attachment to their organizations and their jobs. *Human Resource Management, 33*, 531–548.
46. Ancona, D., Kochan, T., Scully, M., Van Maanen, J.V. and Westney, D.E. (1996). *The new organization.* Cincinnati, OH: South-Western College Publishing.
47. Hiltrop, J.M. (1995). The changing psychological contract. *European Management Journal, 13 (3)*, 286–294.
48. Anderson, N. and Schalk, R. (1998). The psychological contract in retrospect and prospect. *Journal of Organizational Behavior, 19*, 637–647.
49. Cooper, C.L. (1999). The changing psychological contract at work. *European Business Journal, 11 (3)*, 115–120; Sparrow, P.R. (1996). Transitions in the psychological contract: Some evidence from the banking sector. *Human Resource Management Journal, 6 (4)*, 75–92; Sparrow (2000). *Op. cit.*; Sparrow and Cooper, (1998). *Op. cit.*
50. Hartley, J. (1995). Challenge and change in employment relations: issues for psychology, trade unions and managers. In L.E. Tetrick and J. Barling (Eds.), *Changing employment relations: behavioral and social perspectives.* Washington, DC: American Psychological Association.
51. Tetrick, L.E. and Barling, J. (1995) (Eds.) *Changing employment relations: behavioral and social perspectives.* Washington, DC: American Psychological Association.

52. Guzzo, R.A. and Noonan, K.A. (1994) Human resource practices as communications and the psychological contract. *Human Resource Management*, *33*, 447–62; Rousseau, D.M. and Greller, M.M. (1994) Human resource practices: administrative contract makers. *Human Resource Management*, *33*, 385–401.
53. Sparrow, P.R. (2000) The new employment contract: Psychological implications of future work. In R. Burke and C. Cooper (Eds.) *The organization in crisis: downsizing, restructuring, and privatization.* London: Basil Blackwell.
54. Herriot, P, Hirsh, W. and Reilly, P. (1998) *Trust and transition: managing today's employment relationship.* Chichester: Wiley; Sparrow and Cooper (1998). *Op. cit.*
55. Guest, D. (1998) Is the psychological contract worth taking seriously? *Journal of Organizational Behaviour, 19* (Special Issue), 649–664.
56. Sparrow and Cooper (1998). *Op. cit.*

2

The Psychological Contract

In the introductory chapter we ended by mentioning that there has been a change in the 'psychological contract' at work. What exactly does this mean? In this chapter we will explain what is meant by the term 'psychological contract' and discuss how it is considered to regulate the employment relationship. We introduce some key mechanisms involved in this psychological contract and note some of the ways in which it is typically measured. We examine the overlap between the elements that are considered to form the basis of the psychological contract and the elements incorporated into the legal regulation of the employment relationship. We then present the essential elements of psychological contracting theory. This allows us to explain how psychological contracts are first formed and how they can be managed – or transformed. A number of elementary issues are introduced – such as the difference between there being a breach in this contract (or deal) or a more serious perceived violation. We end the chapter by examining the link between these perceptions and the emotional experience of them, arguing that the reactions that we as individuals will experience to changes in the employment relationship – and the challenges that these reactions will create for organizations – will vary depending on the intensity of our individual relationship with the organization.

Key mechanisms of the psychological contract

However, we first begin by explaining the concept of the psychological contract. The term was first introduced in the early 1960s, originally by Argyris, followed by Levinson and colleagues and finally Schein.[1] It was originally used to acknowledge the fact that employees have expectations and beliefs about a series of reciprocal and mutual obligations in the employee–organization relationship. The way the term has been used has itself evolved and there are some minor differences between writers. For example, for Schein all the elements of the contract are implicit as the contract is an unwritten set of expectations whilst for Levinson and colleagues some elements of the contract might be very clear and explicit but others may remain implicit and unspoken. For Schein the psychological contract has an obligatory element – functioning in much the same way as a legal contract – because the consequences of violations can be equally serious for both parties, such as a decline in performance or reduced involvement.

Most observers feel, however, that the obligatory nature of the psychological contract is more a consequence of there being a norm of reciprocity – the two parties are bound to one another: '. . . contributions will be reciprocated and that . . . the actions of one party are bound to those of another'.[2] When the employment relationship is seen in terms of an exchange relationship, these exchanges are seen either in economic or social terms. There is a 'social exchange' involved in the employment relationship, based on voluntary actions that are motivated by expected returns. Coyle-Shapiro and Kessler[3] argue that the idea that reciprocation is a key explanatory mechanism within the psychological contract itself drew upon parallel work by sociologists such as Gouldner and Blau on social exchange theory. Gouldner[4] argued that the norm of reciprocity created a universal demand that people should help and not injure those who helped them. This demand to reciprocate is contingent upon the receipt of benefits. For Blau,[5] social exchange theory entails unspecified obligations. The terms of this exchange are not specified in advance and are left to the discretion of those who make the exchange. However, fair treatment of employees by the organization initiates a social exchange. Favours or spontaneous gestures of goodwill by the organization (or its agents) engenders an obligation on behalf of the employee to reciprocate. There is then a diffuse obligation to reciprocate to the organization. The future return is based on an individual trusting that the other party will fairly discharge their obligations over the long term. Exchange partners will strive for balance in the relationship and will attempt to restore balance if an imbalance occurs.

There are three main points of agreement in the various analyses and discussions that have subsequently taken place.[6] Psychological contracts are:

1 *Subjective, unique and idiosyncratic*: they refer to individual expectations, perceptions and beliefs. Each party or individual selects, perceives and interprets these elements in their own way. They exist '. . . in the eye of the beholder'[7] or '. . . in the minds of the parties'.[8] They can be assessed by questioning one party in the employment relationship.
2 *Reciprocal*: they arise in the context of an employment relationship which always involves two parties.[9] Both parties in this exchange relationship – the employee and the organization – have their own psychological contract. The expectations expressed concern the individual's present employer and not just general expectations about work.

3 *Cognitive dimension*: This set of expectations and obligations represent a set of beliefs regarding the exchange relationship between the individual and the organization. These beliefs are based on *individual perceptions, i.e. what individuals feel are their obligations to their employer.* Psychological contracts are therefore very idiosyncratic in nature, varying from one individual to another and from one organization to another.

A popular definition is that provided by McLean Parkes and colleagues:[10]

> . . . The psychological contract between an employer and an employee is the idiosyncratic set of reciprocal expectations held by employees concerning their obligations (what they will do for their employer) and their entitlements (what they expect to receive in return).

Herriot puts it more simply:[11]

> . . . The perception of the two parties, employee and employer, of what their mutual obligations are towards each other.

Getting the measure of the psychological contract

It is important to appreciate that a series of important distinctions have been made in the psychological contract literature to help categorize different types of contract. Rousseau[12] argues that organizations have moved from a bureaucratic phase, with relational-based tendencies, to an 'adhocratic' phase, in which psychological contracts vary with the type of relationship between each individual and the employer. The first distinction to consider is that the contract can rest on a continuum ranging from *transactional* to *relational*.[13] A transactional contract is composed of specific, short-term, often monetary obligations based on the adage 'a fair day's work for a fair day's pay'. A relational contract, on the other hand, is composed of broad, open-ended, long-term obligations which are socio-emotional as well as monetary. Obligations might therefore concern such issues as training and development, flexibility, or personal support. When Rousseau wrote her seminal work in the late 1980s it was often the case that normative contracts were developed in organizations. In a normative contract the members of the organization agreed on terms in their individual contracts. People tended to interpret their commitments and obligations similarly. When a contract gets shared on the basis of such norms, then it tends to become stronger and also part of the organizational culture. However, when significant organizational change occurs, there is less likelihood that a normative contract will be developed. Millward and Brewerton[14] note that in the context of the significant levels of restructuring and much more widely scattered workforces of today – the increased reliance on teleworkers or people on short-term contracts for example – then even if a normative psychological contract already existed it could be damaged or changed.

The second important point to appreciate is that there are, of course, numerous contracts in existence at any one point in time. The perceptions that employees hold about the exchange and reciprocity in the employment relationship are considered to be based upon *a rich and multi-party web of interactions* that govern the relationship. Within the web of exchanges, there are two basic types of contract makers:

- Principals: individuals or organizations making the contract for themselves.
- Agents: individuals – such as managers, supervisors and co-workers – acting for another.

In practice an individual may be a principal in relation to their own psychological contract, but also an agent in the agreement between others. Researchers took the view that even though the organization (and its agents) may have its own understanding of the psychological contract – or the 'deal' that exists between the employee and the organization – and that this might be at odds with the view held by the individual, the psychological contract is best viewed as that part of the contract that is *held by the employees alone*. When this is done there does appear to be some communality in the content of these contracts. Herriot, Manning and Kidd[15] examined the perceived mutual obligations of 184 UK managers and 184 UK employees drawn from a range of industrial sectors. They used critical incidents to generate the perceived mutual obligations and found that eighteen constructs were sufficient to capture them. Organizations expected seven categories of obligation from employees:

- to work contracted hours;
- to do a quality piece of work;
- to deal honestly with clients;
- to be loyal and guard the organization's reputation;
- to treat property carefully;
- to dress and behave correctly;
- to be flexible and go beyond one's job description.

It is input, not output, that matters to the employer, whereas: '. . . for employees, the preference was for a basic transaction of pay and a secure job in return for time and effort'.[16] What does the employee expect of the employer? Eleven constructs were revealed:

- to provide adequate induction and training;
- to ensure fairness in selection, appraisal, promotion and redundancy procedures;
- to provide justice, fairness and consistency in the application of rules and disciplinary procedures;
- to provide equitable pay in relation to market values across the organization; to be fair in the allocation of benefits;

- to allow time off to meet family and personal needs;
- to consult and communicate on matters that affect them;
- to minimally interfere with employees in terms of *how* they do their job;
- to act in a personally supportive way to employees;
- to recognize or reward special contribution or long service;
- to provide a safe and congenial work environment;
- to provide what job security they can.

A similar set of items are typically used to assess the employer and employee side of the contract in survey work.[17] 'Employer obligation' items typically measured relate to long-term security, good career prospects, support with personal problems, information on important developments, involvement in decision making, up-to-date training and development, necessary training to do the job well, freedom to do the job well, policies and procedures that help to do the job well, support to learn new skills, pay increases to maintain a standard of living, fair pay in comparison to employees doing similar work in other organizations, fair pay for responsibilities in the job, and fringe benefits that are comparable to employees doing similar work in other organizations. Not much to ask for! The obligations that the employee owes to their employer include: working extra hours when necessary, volunteering to do tasks that are not part of the job, looking for better ways of doing the job, looking to improve the ways that things are done in their work area, being flexible in what is done as part of the job, being flexible in working hours, working unpaid hours to finish a task, looking for ways to save costs, and adapting to changes in the way the job is done. This understanding about the basic territory that the contract covers makes it easier for both parties to establish a 'fair exchange deal'. It is argued that employers need to attend to the delivery of the basic and transactional constituents of the psychological contract to establish (or restore) mutual trust and commitment. Indeed, legal regulation of the employment relationship is also based on some interesting assumptions about mutual contracts.

The employment contract: legal regulation of the relationship

We noted that the employment relationship is seen in terms of two exchanges – social and economic – and have introduced the nature of the first of these exchanges. The second type of exchange, which is economic, rests on a formal contract that stipulates exactly what is to be exchanged. This economic contract can be enforced through legal sanctions. Before analysing the theory of psychological contracting, it is worth noting the remarkable parallels between the territory established by Herriot and his colleagues and the way in which UK employment law treats implied terms[18] of the *employment contract*. The information contained in the following brief analysis of legal regulation of the employment contract is relevant to several issues discussed throughout this book. Most immediately it relates to the issue of breach of psychological contract. However, given some of the developments in the employment relationship that we are witnessing in relation to new technologies, new forms of work organization, and new more entrepreneurial forms of remuneration, it will be interesting to see how the 'law' catches up with reality, and how it will defend or not the implied terms of the employment contract.

The employment relationship in the UK is governed by a complex mix of individual and collective agreements, implicit and explicit understandings and rights and obligations enshrined in legal statutes. An individual is considered to be an employee when three conditions are met: if the employer is entitled to exercise control over what the individual does and how he or she does it; if the individual is integrated into the structure of the organization; and if there is a mutual obligation to supply and accept work.

In general, the state has remained absent from the employment relationship, but statute law impinges in three ways: by establishing a 'floor of rights' for the individual on issues such as unfair dismissal, redundancy, equal opportunities, maternity leave, health and safety at work; and confidentiality of computerized data; by determining the nature of structural support for collective bargaining; and by establishing restrictions on what may be deemed lawful industrial action. Much employee protection, however, exists in parallel with rights accumulated through the precedents of common law, established through judicial reviews over time. Numerous rules in both contract law and employment law relate to the contract of employment, whether it is an express contract (written or verbal) or implied (by law, custom and practice). Many terms can be implied on behalf of parties, deemed to apply in the absence of any express provision to the contrary. These implied terms were evolved through the courts before Parliament became involved in the employment relationship – indeed most of the following terms stem back to the nineteenth century. The implied terms that bind the employee to the employer are faithful service (also called a duty of trust and confidence), obedience and care. The duty of trust is a series of fidelity obligations of which failure to perform constitutes a breach of contract. It incorporates the obligation not to commit theft, defraud the employer, to cooperate with the employer and not to frustrate the common venture. Part of an employee's unwritten duties are to further the employer's objectives at all times. Faithful service covers fighting at work, drinking, swearing, lateness or absenteeism, accepting secret bribes and profits, misusing confidential information, and working in competition where the employer has confidential information to impart. Obedience means that at all times the employee must obey lawful and reasonable orders.

The employer is also bound to the employee under implied terms of the employment contract. These include: trust and confidence (also called respect); payment of wages; provision of work; indemnity; and reasonable care. The employer will be deemed to have breached respect if it fails to provide adequate support for the employee, undermines authority when found to be unable to cope with a role that the employer promoted the individual into, falsely accuses an employee of theft or incompetence in front of other employees, fails to listen to grievances, fails to provide an adequate working environment in terms of health and safety, or arbitrarily treats an employee less favourably than colleagues. If the employee is available for work then he or she is entitled to full payment even if no work is provided to do. Finally, given the issue of 'employability' mentioned earlier in the context of Handy's work, it is interesting to note that although the employee cannot complain if there is no work to do if the employer is still prepared to pay them, but where the work of the employee is commission-based or is based on the maintenance of high skill levels, then the employee must be provided with work so that they can maintain their skill levels.

Theory of psychological contracting: promises and mental models

In order to understand ways of managing the psychological contract – how best to maintain them or how best to revise them effectively – then we must examine the way in which psychological contracts are first formed. In an attempt to bring some clarity to the field, Rousseau – the researcher now most associated with the construct – defined the psychological contract as a set of beliefs and promises held by an individual employee about the terms of the exchange between the employee and his or her organization, or the agent of the organization.[19] As a psychological rather than a legal construct, it refers to beliefs about the deal as opposed to what is written down about it in the formal employment contract.[20] The formal contract clearly contributes to the psychological one in that legal terms and conditions affect the perceptions that an individual has about the organization's obligations. The term 'psychological' does not imply that the contract is all in the mind and never expressed. Far from it. It becomes explicit to varying degrees and the more explicitly expressed it becomes, the clearer the idea of what the other party believes is. The 'contract' between an individual and an organization represents a set of subjective beliefs about the exchange agreement between the individual, the employing firm and its agents.[21]

In this exchange, obligations are offered and considered to be implied promises. The psychological contract therefore captures at any one point in time what the perceived deal between two parties is.[22] Rousseau pointed out that there is a clear distinction between psychological contracts – which consist of the expectations held by the individual that *may or may not be shared by others* – and implied contracts – which consist of commonly understood and shared expectations. It is, however, more than just a set of expectations. This is because expectations can exist in the absence of a perceived promise. Only expectations that originate from a perceived implicit or explicit promise by the employer can be considered to be part of the psychological contract. Robinson[23] makes the distinction between expectations and obligations to reinforce this point (see Box 2.1).

Box 2.1   The language of the psychological contract

Expectations: Beliefs held by employees about what they will find in their job and organization, stemming from a variety of sources such as past experiences, social norms and observations.

Obligations: What employees believe they are entitled to or should receive, because they perceive that their employer conveyed promises to provide these things.[24] Reflections '. . . of future contributions to the exchange relationship that may or may not be fulfilled contingent upon the other party's behaviour'.[25]

Transactional contract: Specific short-term and monetizable obligations requiring limited involvement of both parties in the employment relationship.

Relational contract: A broad, open-ended and long-term obligation based on the exchange of not only monetizable elements such as pay for service, but also elements such as loyalty and support.[26]

Technically, a psychological contract is seen as a *within-person* phenomenon – something that should only be seen in relation to the history of each individual and the exchanges and expectations that they have experienced. It is no more than *a mental model constructed on the basis of perceived promises* – a model of the employment relationship, the promises that employment within this relationship conveys, and the level of agreement between the parties to the contract. This mental model of perceived mutual 'promises' is, however, relatively stable and durable over time. Psychologists call these stable mental models *schema*.

We have said that an individual builds up a model of the employment relationship based on their perception of promises that have been made. Rousseau points out that a *promise* is defined in the *Oxford English Dictionary* as a spoken or written assurance made to another, a commitment to oneself, or conditions that create expectations on the part of another.[27] Social psychologists argue that promises increase the psychological attractiveness of the transmitter and increase the odds that agreement will be reached because they indicate *an intent to provide the recipient with some benefit*. In the act of promising, it is not what the maker intends, but what the receiver believes that is important. For a promise to form part of a psychological contract, it has to be believed, accepted and relied upon. The creation of a contract '. . . hinges on the belief that an agreement exists'.[28] A credible promise only exists when there has been a communication that is interpreted as a public affirmation of a promise and trust that the other is acting in good faith. The trust and reliance that is created on the basis of this perception of a promise means that future monitoring and control become less important – hence the contract becomes an implicit and taken-for-granted 'deal' in the mind of the employee.

Rousseau and Greller argue that the employment relationship as we know it only exists *because of promises*. *Promises* are inherent in every aspect of human resource management, be it the signals sent by the recruiter in the selection interview, the informal incentives that a supervisor uses to motivate and incentivize workers, or the promises that the applicant makes in terms of their willingness to join and remain with an organization.[29] Neither the words nor the actions in themselves convey a promise, but when seen in a broader context (the facts of the situation that give it meaning) they signal that *a commitment has been made*. It is the connection between the context, the words and the actions that creates the real meaning (see Box 2.2). These promises regulate the

---

Box 2.2   Different types of promise in the employment relationship

Promises derived from spoken or unspoken words

Verbal statements that expressed facts are true (known as Warrantees, or Assertive speech); for example:

A cv or application form is assumed to verify that the applicant has the education, background and competence as asserted

Financial information about the health of the organization is used to facilitate higher levels of share ownership

Communications and verbal statements of future intent or explicit courses of action (known as commissive speech); for example:

A recruiter mentioning the experiences of recent hires construed as signalling the experiences that can be expected by the interviewee

Discussion of potential rewarding assignments in a performance appraisal in the context of the achievement of high levels of performance

Promises derived through action

Indirect and non-verbal contract makers; for example:

Observations and history of top management, co-workers

Interaction contract makers; for example:

Dealings with recruiters, managers, co-workers and mentors

Administrative/organizational practices contract makers: for example:

Signals sent by recruiting policies, training programmes, performance review and incentive systems.

---

exchange between the two parties to the employment relationship. They also can act as a form of self-regulation, because the individual will accept and set certain goals, or maintain a self-image as a promise-keeper in order to avoid the losses for other parties or the social pressure that might ensue from reneging on the 'deal'. In relation to the psychological contract at work, two types of promises are important (see Box 2.2):

1 Promises derived from spoken or unspoken words (commitments, voluntary agreements, pledges and warranties)
2 Promises derived from behaviours and repeated practices/interactions that are interpreted as actions.

Psychological contract theory then postulates that the psychological contract becomes in itself a 'mental model' that guides the actions of the individual. These individual mental models act as deep drivers of motivation, career behaviour, reward and commitment. The process of psychological contracting (i.e. the way in which contracts are made, managed and breached) is assumed to follow a generic sequence. Our limited cognitive and information processing capacity means that we form differential mental constructions of key information during the same interaction. The images and ideas (frames of reference) that we create by interpreting what a promise or commitment means are wholly individual, as are our perceptions of mutuality and what warrants a 'promise'. Contracts then are portrayed as an individual-level phenomenon: in every mind there is a different world.[30]

So how is an individual's psychological contract with the organization created? Past experiences are organized in our minds into a series of conceptually related elements. These conceptual elements – *schema* – guide the way that new information is perceived, interpreted and organized.[31] *Schemas* play an important role in interpreting the promises implicit in the employment relationship. They serve to organize this experience in meaningful ways, thereby making it possible for individuals to deal with ambiguity and for organizations to predict their behaviour. Schema formation is a very individualized process because although some elements of a schema are shared with other people who work in the same setting, most are idiosyncratic and tied to particular individual experiences. Beliefs regarding the employment relationship become interconnected in ways that give rise to broader units of meaning. Cognitive schema vary in their complexity (and the meaning that this conveys to the individual) along two dimensions (see Figure 2.1). The greater the number of beliefs of which they comprise, the more an individual can differentiate between elements (i.e. there is greater horizontal structure to the schema). The higher the levels of abstraction that characterize these beliefs and the greater the number of linkages between them (known as vertical structure of a schema), then the more components can be used to develop finer-grain interpretations.

The most fundamental level of complexity in the employment relationship psychological contract are the beliefs that the individual holds concerning

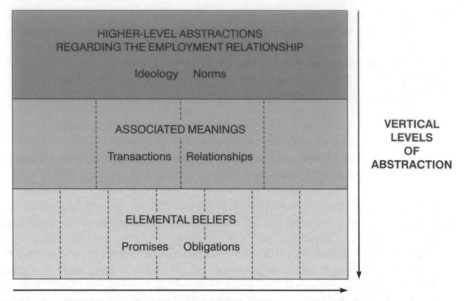

Figure 2.1 The psychological contract represented as a schema. (After Rousseau[40])

promises and discrete obligations. Individuals develop more complex meanings by combining these many perceived promises and obligations into a
smaller number of higher-level categories. The belief that the organization has
committed to a long-term internal career may be combined with the belief that
it has also committed to providing employability elsewhere if business
necessitates to suggest that the employment arrangement has become a
relationship and not a transaction. The associated meanings that are used to
categorize the fundamental promises and obligations may themselves be
combined into a smaller number of ideologies and norms. Beliefs about the
appropriate fulfilment of a relational agreement may form an assumed
occupational ideology (for example, 'this is how employers handle the
employment relationship for medical doctors or for MBA students'). An
employee will view their psychological contract with a new employer through
the lens of their pre-employment schema and the obligations that this creates.
Socialization within society, occupations and previous employment create
professional norms and ideologies.

   Figure 2.2 shows the factors that shape the creation of an individual's
psychological contract. As the employment relationship develops, individuals
fill in 'missing information' on the basis of the schema that they have
developed. A number of agents become important in this process and help the
individual correctly to interpret the signals sent by their employer. The mental
model therefore reflects a common understanding that binds the parties to a
course of action. Accurate schema facilitate appropriate reactions to key

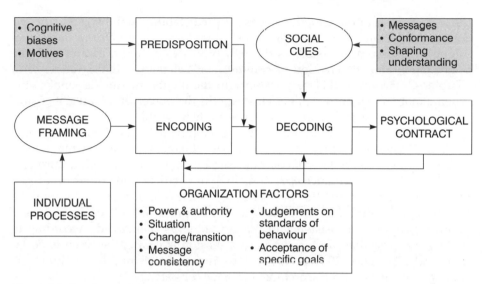

Figure 2.2 Creating an individual's psychological contract

organizational or job events. These automated reactions are called *scripts by cognitive* psychologists. The most pertinent information that leads towards the creation of accurate schema appears to come from:

- Information received from co-workers regarding job security[32]
- Supportive immediate managers.[33]

During this socialization process the individual's psychological contract is incomplete, but because individuals are motivated to discern patterns and to create meanings that will subsequently help them to predict future events and guide their own behaviour, they seek to fill in the missing information. Isolated facts are incorporated into their knowledge structures (schema). Socialization processes enable the individual to more finely tune their psychological contract and to understand what they need to provide in return. Clearly, then, individuals within the same firm also develop different psychological contracts in relation not just to important individual differences and pre-employment experiences, but also to the quality of their sources of information during the socialization phase.

Managing change in an individual's psychological contract

The schema that represents the employment relationship reaches a stage of completeness once the individual's experiences become consistent with the beliefs in their schema. The psychological contract serves several functions, but the most notable of these are the needs for predictability, stability, security and control. In Chapter 8 we consider some other ways in which the individual might meet these needs, such as through processes of identification with the organization and the creation of commitment behaviours (cross-reference in Chapter 4). However, this very stability in the mental model also makes the schema more resistant to change. This benefits the perceiver, because it creates a sense of order, structure and coherence to their world.

Rousseau[34] argues that although the development of beliefs in the schema satisfies these needs, this comes at a cost. Elements of a schema persist stubbornly even in the face of contradictory evidence through what Lord and Foti[35] called a 'perseverance effect'. As long as predicted outcomes occur in a manner consistent with the old schema, then the assumptions within the psychological contract go unchallenged. When predicted outcomes no longer occur, the cognitive consistency of the individual is challenged. According to Festinger's[36] *cognitive dissonance theory,* a tension is created between expectations and experience. Individuals seek to avoid this distress by avoiding the source of challenge and searching for new consistency by either changing behaviour or changing the cognition. In most work situations they do not have the power to change the behaviour of the perpetrator (the organization or its agent) and so the consequence is schema shift in line with the new situation. Individuals search for information and attempt to make sense of inconsistent acts in order to reduce their own emotional losses that would be associated with a loss of security, predictability and control over events.

Sudden conversions in the psychological contract are then few. Rather, the organization has to present individuals with unambiguous information that cannot be interpreted within the old schema if it seeks to rebalance the psychological contract. The problem is that most change processes the messages sent by the organization are far from unambiguous, but are instead very mixed. Given these continual cognitive adjustments, psychological contracts rarely remain static and can change without any formal efforts made on behalf of the organization. Rousseau refers to three different adjustment processes:[37]

1 *Drift:* occurs when beliefs about whether the terms of the psychological contract still being performed start to diverge, or when terms of the contract take on a new meaning, or new terms are acquired without the other party understanding this.
2 *Accommodation:* occurs when there are acknowledged changes in the terms of work, but the same schema remain. The terms of the contract are modified, clarified, substituted or expanded.
3 *Transformation:* occurs more occasionally but also reflects a more fundamental change in the relationship between parties creating a shift in meaning or interpretation of contract items. At this point the old psychological contract ends – perhaps by breach or violation – or simply because the employee or employer feels that the terms of the deal have been completed – and a new psychological contract is created.

When a major adjustment in the form of a transformation of the psychological contract is needed, it follows four stages: the reasons for change have to be perceived, understood and interpreted as legitimate (challenging); the old contract is unfrozen and efforts are made to reduce and offset losses (reframing): a new contract becomes solidified and replaces the old one (generation); and finally acceptance only occurs as the terms and nature of reciprocity in the new deal become tested enough to be relied upon (testing and reliance).

This cognitive view of the psychological contract conveys two important principles about managing change in an employee's mindset.[38] First, it is inferred that experts (individuals with complete psychological contracts) process discrepant information differently from novices. They can apply their schemas to new situations more effectively, thereby placing some constraint on the likelihood that they will resort immediately to their underlying beliefs when they have to respond to a situation. They can make a more sophisticated assessment of the situation. Conversely, however, they are less likely to be influenced by new information that is particularly meaningful and suggests that the whole schema needs to be changed. This means that if an organization seeks to change the psychological contract of an expert, then it needs to give priority to creating accurate information that will not simply lead to the maintenance of the old schema.

To get people to change their psychological contract, they have to be encouraged to process new information as if they were a newcomer, rather than as an established veteran. Creating a revision of the psychological contract can be achieved in extreme ways – for example, firing all employees and then rehiring them the next day. However, psychological contracting theory posits that a new psychological contract is best engendered by getting employees actively to frame the changes that take place during a transition process towards a new relationship. Organizations have to afford both input to and participation in the creation of the new 'terms' of the deal. Examples include getting employees actively to negotiate new job conditions after a merger, or having old hands interview employees for new positions whilst having to make the potential benefits and gains of the new positions clear. The contribution that role plays designed around such reframing exercises in the management of new psychological contract formation seems evident. It is argued too that the use of trusted change agents – those whose information immediately carries credibility with employees – can also promote the processing of discrepant information.[39] Rousseau draws attention to a number of practical things that organizations must do to assist transformation in the psychological contract (see Box 2.3).

Psychological contract violation

In the previous sections we have highlighted work that has focused on the 'cognitive' aspects of the psychological contract – the way in which it is formed

---

Box 2.3   Factors influencing psychological contract transformation

- Well-articulated externally validated reasons for the change
- Members involved in gathering information on factors contributing to the change
- Acknowledgement of the old contract
- Scrupulous efforts to assess and then offset the losses involved in the change
- Strong communication links during the transition to a new contract using planning task forces and cross-functional meetings
- Responding to the need for more information and structure during uncertain times with transition arrangements such as short-term projects and long-term change initiatives
- Aligning the many contract makers (people and structure) by integrating them into HR policies
- Promoting acceptance by evoking new contract-making events, orientations, new blood recruitment, participation in planning
- Soliciting input on how thoroughly the new contract is implemented, taking corrective action on potential breach early

Source: Rousseau and Tijoriwala.[39]

---

in the mind of the employee. However, the psychological contract is also very emotive in nature – academics argue that you often only know what the contract was when you breach it. Rousseau has pointed out recently that the majority of research on the psychological contract to date has examined the *aftermath of contract violation*.[40] This research not only shows that workers have different types of psychological contract and that they respond differently both to its violation and to planned processes of organizational change, but it always draws upon different research insights. Notably, it forces us to consider the nature and role of emotions in organizations and the consequences of potential emotional disturbances at work for several 'deep' psychological structures – such as an individual's fundamental attitude to justice and even their identity at work. Throughout this book we shall explore the challenges being created by the current employment relationship. At this stage, however, we introduce the topic of breach of psychological contract.

Given the changing conditions in the employment relationship most research has understandably investigated the reactions that employees have to unfilled promises and the way in which these lead to a 'breach' of the psychological contract. Breach of contract is one of the most important constructs in psychological contract theory because it is considered to be the main way in which the psychological contract affects both the employment relationship and employee behaviour. Contract breach research generally shows that intense emotional experiences tend to follow contract violation.

Early writings on the psychological contract often used the terms 'breach' and 'violation' interchangeably. Indeed, many studies have not truly measured the real psychological response. For example, Turnley and Feldman[41] distinguish four types of response: 'no violation, the organization has fulfilled all promises'; 'the organization never made any commitments in the first place'; 'work might not be what I expected it to be, but this is just part of doing business, not a contract violation'; and finally 'my contract has been seriously violated'. Even in high-change sectors such as banking and state agencies they found whilst 25 per cent of employees felt they had received less than they had been promised, only 25 per cent felt their contracts had been violated. Researchers rarely distinguish between breach of contract – commonplace but inconsequential – and violation – more emotive with more serious psychological consequences.

Subsequently, however, breach and violation have come to be seen as representing different levels of severity or consequence:

- *Breach:* Occasions when the organization breaks its promise. The perception that one's organization has failed to fulfil one or more of its obligations or promises comprising one's psychological contract[42]
- *Violation*: Strong affective responses to more extreme breaches of contract, such as feelings of injustice, betrayal and deeper psychological distress whereby the victim experiences anger, resentment, a sense of wrongful harm.[43]

Much of the current discussion therefore presents breach of contract as primarily a cognitive response, with elements of an individual's schema being challenged, whilst violation of contract is presented as an emotional and affective state, in which cognitive challenge is supplemented by a more visceral response. Violation as opposed to breach is also assumed to act as a more powerful catalyst for the creation of a new psychological contract. Robinson and Morrison[44] conducted research on perceived *breach* of the psychological contract (where the breach is perceived by the employee and has been considered to be committed by the employer). Their research, and that conducted with Rousseau,[45] suggests that when breach of contract is perceived, *violation naturally occurs*. Even the more moderate 'breach' of psychological contract has been shown to be associated with a number of negative outcomes, such as lower levels of job satisfaction and organizational commitment and higher levels of withdrawal behaviours.[46] Breach of contract does not automatically lead to violation of contract of course. In a more recent study Robinson and Morrison found a correlation of 0.7 between breach and the more serious violation of contract.[47] In their modelling of the process of contract violation, Morrison and Robinson made the distinction between breach and violation more explicit.[48] Perceived breach of contract occurs when the individual makes a cognitive assessment that their organization has failed

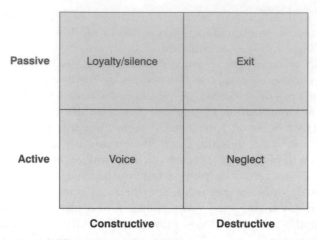

Figure 2.3 The nature of different contract responses

to meet one or more of the obligations within the psychological contract. It is a combination of 'disappointment emotions'. The more serious outcome – a violation of contract – is an emotional affective state that follows from the belief that one's organization has failed adequately to maintain the psychological contract.

Violation of contract is therefore an emotional experience that arises from a cognitive interpretive process. The feelings go beyond disappointment into feelings of betrayal that have a destructive effect on the employment relationship. It can result in a number of responses that often come about during any organizational change. Hirschman[49] used social exchange theory to argue that different employees appear to react similarly to contract violations or fulfilment. This theory postulates that when fulfilled, employees are assumed to reduce their indebtedness by reciprocating with more effort directed at the source of the benefits.

Turnley and Feldman[50] identified four responses in relation to violation of contract. As shown in Figure 2.3, these differ across two dimensions of being active or passive and constructive and destructive:

1 *Exit:* Voluntary termination of the relationship, e.g. attempts to remedy the psychological contract have failed, or other potential jobs are available.
2 *Voice*: Actions taken to remedy violation, such as reducing losses or restoring trust through talking, threats and changes to behaviour. Exit may follow soon after a voice channel is deemed to have failed.
3 *Loyalty/silence:* Non-response, serving to perpetuate the existing relationship. Willingness to endure or accept unfavourable circumstances because no voice channels are open or there is no alternative employment. Might reflect pessimism (no alternative) or loyalty/hope (waiting for conditions to improve).

4 *Neglect*: Complex response. Might reflect passive negligence or active destruction. Likely when there is a history of conflict, mistrust and violation, no voice channels, or the majority of other employees demonstrate neglect and destruction.

Clearly, organizations attempt to use active and constructive responses to violation where the violation is recognized, unless there is a political ambition of one party that requires the destruction of the other's psychological contract.

Morrison and Robinson[51] developed a model to explain the dynamics underlying violation. A simplified version of this model is shown in Figure 2.4. Their model argues that *reneging* and *incongruence* are the two main factors which first alert either party to the possibility that the psychological contract may be damaged. Reneging on the contract is seen as a consequence of the organization being either unable or unwilling to meet its promises. Incongruence in the psychological contract results from high levels of ambiguity and complexity in the employment relationship, poor levels of communication and consequently divergent schemata between individuals. Two factors also contribute to the perception that the organization has not met its promises: salience and vigilance. *Salience* refers to the importance placed on the perceived breach and *vigilance* refers to the amount of time or effort put into determining whether the breach is important enough to worry about. The higher the perceived costs of broken promises, the less trust there is in the relationship, and the higher the level of uncertainty, then the greater the level of vigilance. Once the individual decides that unmet promises are apparent then they assess whether the breach is significant enough to worry about in the light of how far they have kept to their side of the contract. Consequently a *comparison* is made between the two. Finally, the individual attempts to make sense of what has happened and act on it by responding via violation. This *interpretation process* as we have noted above is often emotional in nature. The level of intensity of these emotions and the ensuing perceived level of violation depends on the way in which attributions and judgments about fairness are made by the individual. A delicate balance that has to be achieved by organizations attempting to repair a breach in psychological contract:

> . . . We caution organizations against misrepresenting purposeful reneging by trying to convince the employee that it was due to either uncontrollable factors or incongruence. Although in our model we suggest that this behaviour may minimize violation, it is highly risky and may backfire if employees fail to accept the explanation and consider it as one more act of deception. This perception will further undermine, and perhaps even destroy, the trust that is critical to the maintenance of the psychological contract.[52]

It is difficult to be sure how often breach of psychological contract – let alone violation – occurs in the natural course of organizational events (Figure 2.4). It

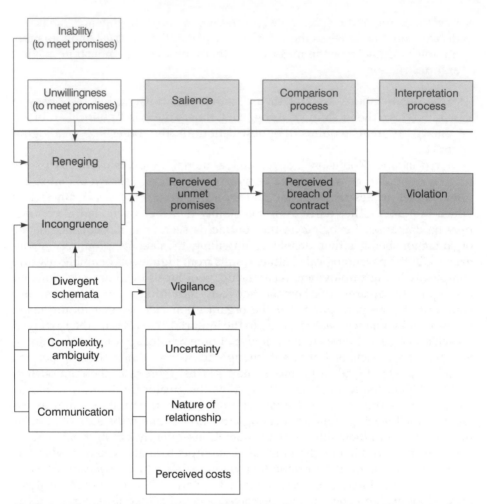

Figure 2.4 The development of violation in psychological contracts. (Adapted from Morrison and Robinson[53])

is even more difficult to be sure if there is a higher incidence of breach or violation in the context of the significant changes taking place in the employment relationship at the moment, although of course when put into historical context research on psychological contract breach tended to be conducted as a means of demonstrating that the employment relationship was entering a parlous state. Robinson and Rousseau's[54] study of breach of contract for recent MBA graduates found that 55 per cent believed that some aspect of their psychological contract had been breached during their first two years in the job (so 45 per cent had experienced no breach over two years). When comparing recent MBA graduates, expatriates and employees working in downsized or restructured organizations, Turnley and Feldman[55] found that those in working in downsized or restructured organizations were both more likely to perceive breach of contract and to use exit, voice and neglect as their violation responses. They were also less loyal to the organization when talking to outsiders. Coyle-Shapiro and Kessler[56] surveyed 703 managers and 6953 employees in a British public sector local authority. They found that there were high levels of perceived breach of contract: 89 per cent of employees felt that their employer had fallen short of valued transactional obligations and 81 per cent felt that their organization had fallen short of valued relational obligations.

A lot of research on the psychological contract has used constructs such as organizational commitment, job satisfaction, organizational citizenship behaviour and intention to exit as a proxy measure of the state of the contract at any one time or over time (we examine some of these constructs in more detail in Chapter 8). Guest argues that the problems associated with the empirical measurement of these constructs, in addition to the fact that career structures and levels of security have changed so significantly, make many statements about levels of violation in the psychological somewhat of an exaggeration.[57] He also makes the point that there are so many agents within the organization who form part of the web of relationships by which an individual judges a perceived broken promise, someone somewhere might be perceived to have violated your contract. This does not automatically mean that there is any serious consequence.

There is now some debate over the relative stability of the psychological contract and therefore the frequency with which a breach might occur. The answer tends to depend on the research method used to examine it. Most research into breach of psychological contract has, however, used questionnaires to measure perceived failures of the organization to fulfil its obligations. Researchers are trying to develop a better understanding of the circumstances that lead up to the more serious violation of contract in order to limit the more destructive impacts on the employment relationship.[58] A recent study (see Box 2.4) used daily diaries to examine the responses that employees had to both psychological contract breach and exceeded promises.[59]

We outlined the nature of promises within the psychological contract earlier in the chapter. The intensity of reactions to perceived broken promises depends on the way in which the individual interprets the initial breach. Conway and Briner use psychological contracting theory to argue that *four* properties of a perceived promise at work have a significant bearing on the subsequent intensity of the employee's response:

1 *The explicitness versus implicitness of the promise.* The more explicit the promise, the greater the reaction that might be expected from employees, for employees can more easily judge whether or not an injustice was involved in any violation.[62]
2 *Attributions regarding the intentions of the other party.* Employees will experience more intense emotional reactions to broken (or exceeded) promises when the other party is considered to be personally responsible. If

Box 2.4   Emotional responses to psychological contract breach and exceeded promises

Conway and Briner used quantitative and qualitative techniques to examine breach of contract at a micro level.[60] They view breach of psychological contract as a series of 'events' (both positive and negative) that happen in work or in relation to work and argue that the true consequence of breach is best examined immediately after occurrence, rather than through the use of retrospective survey questions. In line with Schein's[61] view, the psychological contract is viewed as a constant process of renegotiation that can be broken or exceeded on a daily basis. To examine this, they measured the outcomes of daily mood and emotions associated with the occurrence of breach events over a 10-day period in a sample of 45 employees. Their findings suggested that both broken and exceeded promises occur regularly at work – on a daily basis – and in relation to many aspects of work. Line managers were the main agents for breaking or exceeding promises: 69 per cent of participants reported at least one broken promise over the period of diary analysis and 62 per cent reported at least one exceeded promise. The importance of the promise contributes significantly to the intensity of the emotional reactions that follow and also to daily mood. The emotions reported immediately after breach were negative and of two sorts (factors):

● 'feeling hurt' (feelings of shock, disappointment and frustration, such as embarrassment, surprise, hurt and fear), and
● 'feelings of betrayal' (fairly extreme emotions and visceral emotions of anger, resentment, bitterness, hate and outrage).

Broken promises were more likely to be associated with feelings of betrayal rather than just hurt. Because the research also examined the response to promises that were met and exceeded, the positive emotional side to the psychological contract was also revealed. Again there were two factors, with exceeded promises associated more with feelings of self-worth:

● 'self-worth' (feelings of pride, excitement, respect and being valued) and
● 'cared-for' (feelings of being cared for, indebted, secure, affection and admiration).

Daily mood changes associated with broken promises were of a significant order and larger than those generally reported in relation to daily stressors at work. Psychological contract breach was considered to be one of the most distressing of events in terms of its impact on daily mood.

Source: Conway and Briner.[59]

failure to deliver is considered to be under the control of the perpetrator, violation as opposed to breach is the more likely consequence.[63]

3 *The unexpectedness and infrequency of the event.* Employees experience more emotional responses to broken or exceeded promises when the event has happened infrequently in the past and appears to be in contrast to a previous history of met obligations. Unexpected events arose higher levels of anxiety and unprecedented events greater levels of shock.[64]

4 *The importance of the goal and relationship with the other party.* This is directly correlated with the intensity of emotional reactions towards it,[65] with promises of greater importance to the relationship likely to result in stronger emotional reactions when breached.[66]

References

1. Argyris, C. (1960). *Understanding organizational behavior.* Homewood, IL: Dorsey; Levinson, H. (1962). *Organizational diagnosis.* Cambridge, MA: Harvard University Press; Levinson, H., Price, C., Munden, K., Mandl, H. and Solley, C. (1962). *Men, management and mental health.* Cambridge, MA: Harvard University Press; Schein, E.H. (1965). *Organizational psychology.* Englewood Cliffs, NJ: Prentice Hall.

2. Rousseau, D.M. (1989). Psychological and implied contracts in organizations. *Employee Rights and Responsibilities Journal, 2*, 121–139, p. 123.

3. Coyle-Shapiro, J.A. M. and Kcoolor, I. (2002). Exploring reciprocity through the lens of the psychological contract: Employee and employer perspectives. *European Journal of Work and Organizational Psychology, 11 (1)*, 69–86.

4. Gouldner, A.W. (1960). The norm of reciprocity. *American Sociological Review, 25*, 161–178.

5. Blau, P. (1964). *Exchange and power in social life.* New York: Wiley.

6. Sels, L., Janssens, M., Van den Brande, I. and Overlaet, B. (2002). Assessing the nature of psychological contracts: conceptualisation and measurement. *Research Report Department of Applied Economics*, Katholieke Universiteit Leuven.

7. Rousseau, D.M. (1990). New hire perceptions of their own and their employer's obligations: a study of psychological contracts. *Journal of Organizational Behavior, 11*, 389–400, p. 391.

8. Herriot, P. and Pemberton, C. (1995). *New deals: the revolution in managerial careers.* Chichester: Wiley, p. 17.

9. Herriot, P., Manning, W.E.G. and Kidd, J.M. (1997). The content of the psychological contract. *British Journal of Management, 8*, 151–162; McLean Parks, J., Kidder, D.L. and Gallagher, D.G. (1998). Fitting square pegs into round holes: mapping the domain of contingent work arrangements onto the psychological contract. *Journal of Organizational Behavior, 19*, 697–730.

10. McLean Parks *et al.* (1998). *Ibid*, p. 697.

11. Herriot, P. (2001). *The employment relationship: a psychological perspective.* Hove: Routledge.
12. Rousseau, D.M. (1995). *Psychological contracts in organizations: understanding written and unwritten agreements.* Newbury Park, CA: Sage.
13. Morrison, E.W. and Robinson, S.L. (1997). When employees feel betrayed: a model of how psychological violation develops. *Academy of Management Review, 22 (1)*, 226–257
14. Millward, L.J. and Brewerton, P.M. (1999). Contractors and their psychological contracts. *British Journal of Management, 10,* 253–274.
15. Herriot, P., Manning, W.E.G. and Kidd, J.M. (1997). The content of the psychological contract. *British Journal of Management, 8 (2),* 151–162.
16. *Ibid.,* p. 160.
17. These items are operationalized by Coyle-Shapiro and Kessler (2002) *op. cit.,* and derived from items used by Rousseau in her research.
18. Snape, R. (1999). Legal regulation of employment. In G. Hollinshead, P. Nicholls and S. Tailby (Eds.), *Employee relations.* London: Financial Times/ Pitman Publishing.
19. Rousseau, (1989). *Op. cit.*
20. Herriot, P. (1998). The role of the HR function in building a new proposition for staff. In P.R. Sparrow and M. Marchington (Eds.), *Human resource management: the new agenda.* London: Financial Times/Pitman Publishing.
21. Rousseau (1995). *Op. cit.*
22. Herriot (1998). *Op. cit.*
23. Robinson, S.L. (1996). Trust and breach of the psychological contract. *Administrative Science Quarterly, 41,* 574–599.
24. *Ibid.*
25. Coyle-Shapiro and Kessler (2002). *Op. cit.,* p. 72.
26. Rousseau, D.M. and McLean Parks, J. (1993). The contracts of individuals and organizations. In L.L. Cummings and B.M. Staw (Eds.), *Research in organizational behavior, Volume 15.* Greenwich, CT: JAI Press, 1–47.
27. Rubin, J.Z. and Brown, R. (1975). *The social psychology of bargaining and negotiation.* New York: Academic Press.
28. Rousseau (1995). *Op. cit.,* p. 20
29. Rousseau, D.M. and Greller, M. (1994). Human resource practices: administrative contract makers. *Human Resource Management, 33,* 385–401.
30. Sparrow, P.R. (1996). Careers and the psychological contract: understanding the European context. *The European Journal of Work and Organizational Psychology, 5 (4),* 479–500.
31. Stein, D.J. (1992). Schemas in the cognitive and clinical sciences. *Journal of Psychotherapy Integration, 2,* 45–63.
32. See Feldman, D.C. (1976). A contingency theory of socialization. *Administrative Science Quarterly, 21,* 433–452; Thomas, H.D. and Anderson, N. (1998). Changes in newcomers' psychological contracts during organizational socialization: a study of recruits entering the British Army. *Journal of Organizational Behavior, 19,* 745–767.

33. Gundry, L. and Rousseau, D.M. (1994). Communicating culture to newcomers. *Human Relations, 47*, 1068–1088.
34. Rousseau, D.M. (1996). Changing the deal while keeping the people. *Academy of Management Executive, 10*, 50–61.
35. Lord, R.G. and Foti, R.J. (1986). Schema theories, information processing and organizational behavior. In H. Sims and D. Gioia (Eds.), *The thinking organization*. London: Jossey-Bass, pp. 2–45.
36. Festinger, L. (1957). *A theory of cognitive dissonance*. Stanford, CA: Stanford University.
37. See respectively Rousseau (1995), *op. cit.*, pp. 144, 154 and 161 for definitions of these adjustment processes.
38. Rousseau (2001). *Op. cit.*
39. Rousseau, D.M. and Tijoriwala, S.A. (1999). What makes a good reason to change? Motivated reasoning and social accounts in organizational change. *Journal of Applied Psychology, 84*, 514–528.
40. Rousseau, D.M. (2001). Schema, promise and mutuality: the building blocks of the psychological contract. *Journal of Occupational and Organizational Psychology, 74*, 511–541
41. Turnley, W.H. and Feldman, D.C. (1998). Psychological contract violations during corporate restructuring, *Human Resource Management, 37 (1)*, 71–83.
42. See, for example: Robinson, S.L. and Rousseau, D.M. (1994). Violating the psychological contract: not the exception but the norm. *Journal of Organizational Behavior, 15*, 245–259.
43. Rousseau (1989). *Op. cit.*
44. Robinson, S.L. (1996). Trust and breach of the psychological contract. *Administrative Science Quarterly, 41*, 574–599; Morrison, E.W. & Robinson, S.L (1997). When employees feel betrayed: a model of how contract violation develops. *Academy of Management Review, 22*, 226–257.
45. Robinson, S.L. and Rousseau, D.M. (1994). Violating the psychological contract: not the exception but the norm, *Journal of Organizational Behavior, 15*, 245–59
46. Coyle-Shapiro, J. and Kessler, I. (2000). Consequences of the psychological contract for the employment relationship: a large scale survey. *Journal of Management Studies, 37*, 903–930; Turnley, W.H. and Feldman, D.C. (1999). The impact of psychological contract violations on exit, voice, loyalty and neglect. *Human Relations, 52*, 895–922; Turnley, W.H. and Feldman, D.C. (2000). Re-examining the effects of psychological contract violations: unmet expectations and job dissatisfaction as mediators. *Journal of Organizational Behavior, 21*, 25–42; Robinson and Rousseau (1994). *Op. cit.*
47. Robinson, S.L. and Morrison, E.W. (2000). The development of psychological contract breach and violation: a longitudinal study. *Journal of Organizational Behavior, 21*, 525–546.
48. Morrison and Robinson (1997). *Op. cit.*
49. Hirschman, A.O. (1970). *Exit, voice and loyalty: responses to decline in firms, organizations and states*. Cambridge, MA: Harvard University Press.

50. Turnley, W.H. and Feldman, D.C. (1998). Psychological contract violations during corporate restructuring. *Human Resource Management, 37 (1)*, 71–83.
51. Morrison and Robinson (1997). *Op. cit.*
52. *Ibid.*, p. 252.
53. *Ibid.*
54. Robinson and Rousseau (1994). *Op. cit.*
55. Turnley, W.H. and Feldman, D.C. (1999). The impact of psychological contract violations on exit, voice, loyalty and neglect. *Human Relations, 52 (7)*, 895–920
56. Coyle-Shapiro, J. and Kessler, I. (in press). Consequences of the psychological contract for the employment relationship: a large scale survey. *Journal of Management*.
57. Guest (1998). *Op. cit.*
58. Turnley, W.H. and Feldman, D.C. (2000). Re-examining the effects of psychological contract violations: unmet expectations and job dissatisfaction as mediators. *Journal of Organizational Behavior, 21*, 25–42.
59. Conway, N. and Briner, R.B. (2002). A daily diary study of affective responses to psychological contract breach and exceeded promises. *Journal of Organizational Behavior, 23*, 287–302.
60. *Ibid.*
61. Schein, E. (1980). *Organizational psychology. 3rd Edition.* New Jersey: Prentice Hall.
62. Turnley, W.H. and Feldman, D.C. (1999). A discrepancy model of psychological contract violations. *Human Resource Management Review, 9*, 367–386.
63. Ortony, A., Core, G. and Collins, A. (1988) *The cognitive structure of emotions.* Cambridge: Cambridge University Press.
64. Morrison and Robinson (1997). *Op. cit.*
65. Weiss, H.M. and Cropanzano, R. (1996). Affective events theory: a theoretical discussion of the structure, causes and consequences of affective experiences at work. *Research in Organizational Behavior, 18*, 1–74.
66. Turnley, W.H. and Feldman, D.C. (1999). The impact of psychological contract violations on exit, voice, loyalty and neglect. *Human Relations, 52*, 895–922.

3

The Changing Structure
of Employment

Introduction

In the previous chapter, we considered some of the debate around a changing psychological contract, perceived breach of contract and the potential deterioration of trust levels within the employment relationship. In the next two chapters we question whether such a shift should be taken for granted and examine the evidence of there being a fundamental change in the employment relationship or not – where possible on a longitudinal basis. Why is this important? In the opening chapter we headlined much of the popular literature on the future of work and pointed towards some of the new career competencies that this literature assumes are emerging. It would be easy – but also a mistake – to equate this future with the 'end of jobs'. To recap, end-of-jobs theories point to the following scenario:[1]

- *Long-term jobs with a single employer are a thing of the past* – job stability will not return
- *The labour market will offer mainly short-term and unstable jobs*, which will be split into either high- or low-quality work in terms of wages, skills and working conditions
- Individuals will experience *more frequent changes between jobs*, and spells of inactivity
- This will require *constant readjustment, lifelong education and learning* and a set of behavioural competencies that prepare the individual for change
- The *attitudes most appropriate for this employment relationship are entrepreneurial*, because individuals will need to manage their careers efficiently to maintain their own 'employability' (a 'status' that allows people to change jobs within or between organizations more easily)

- Social protection of the employment relationship, traditionally based on continuous employment, will not be sufficient to protect a much larger segment of people in *contingent employment relationships*
- New social security systems will be designed therefore requiring the individual to *take much greater responsibility and to share the risk* (either through actual risk sharing or more expensive risk-avoidance payments) than before.

Will the general trends in employment destroy all of the various employment relationships that exist? While it would be foolhardy to reject the opening analysis as speculation or prescription, this chapter will show that the long-term employment relationship has proved to be a good deal more resilient than the opening scenario suggests. We draw together evidence that places some boundaries around the end-of-jobs scenarios.

There is a second thesis that cuts across recent analyses of changes in the labour market. Following on from these job conditions, Heery and Salmon[2] have drawn attention to what is called the 'insecurity thesis'. This is a broad social theory that attempts to connect the above developments in the world of work with changes in an individual's and society's life beyond. They note that governments, policy makers, trades unions and management organizations have all expressed concern at the levels of risk and instability that have, by many accounts, become defining features of contemporary life. This thesis represents a criticism of changes in the labour market and argues that:

- Economic risk is being transferred increasingly from employers to employees through shortened tenure and contingent employment and remuneration
- Therefore both continued employment and the level of remuneration have become less predictable and contingent on factors that lie beyond the employee's control[3]
- Developments in labour markets have raised the costs of job loss, increasing the risks and severity of periods of job separation[4]
- Deregulation of the labour market and the weakening or removal of institutions designed to protect employees has compounded levels of insecurity.[5] Recent legislative precedents in the UK protecting the rights of part-time workers should be seen in the context that in 1975 94 per cent of full-timers and 77 per cent of part-timers were covered by protective legislation compared to only 74 and 57 per cent respectively by 1995.[6]
- Insecurity is damaging to long-term economic performance
- The employment relationship becomes founded on opportunism, mistrust and low commitment
- The emergence of an insecure workforce imposes severe cost both on individuals and society.

A variety of factors have made it important to establish the true nature of changes in the employment relationship. In this chapter we shall develop a more circumspect picture of both the end-of-jobs and insecurity theses, principally by drawing upon the following longitudinal and international sources of evidence:

1 work by labour economists on *previous flexible employment relationships*
2 work by labour economists on the *types* of jobs currently in existence, through a review of non-traditional jobs and the reasons for their growth

In the next chapter we shall develop this understanding by considering work by employment strategists looking at the stability of jobs, through an analysis of job or employment tenure, and work by HRM academics on historical levels of job satisfaction.

Have we been here before? Historical changes in the employment relationship

In discussing the changing employment relationship we have to be aware of the issue of historical relativity.[7] There have been periods of intense change in the employment contract before, with low levels of trust. Cappelli argues that we are seeing the demise of a post-war blip in employment: '. . . we think of the system of long-term employment relationships and related practices that is now being overthrown as having always been in place, but in fact it is a relatively recent in place not much longer than a generation'.[8] Indeed, despite his concerns about the new employment contract, Cappelli reminds us that the 'traditional' employment contract in the USA was a contractor system (see Box 3.1). Many of the practices and trends that we outline in this chapter were widespread in US industry 100 years ago. Only the need to coordinate more complex organizations and safeguard the supply of large integrated operations (reinforced by wartime controls) brought the workforce inside organizations (called the system of internalized employee management) and led to the development of longer-term relationships.

Changes in structure of firms from small single-unit operations to multi-unit enterprises made it more efficient for a while to internalize business transactions, and employ a cadre of professional middle managers scientifically to manage production. In Ford, a pioneer of Taylorism, the turnover rate among employees was 370 per cent and daily absence rates were 10 per cent. Employee concerns were considered to be important and best handled by taking responsibility for recruitment and pay away from foreman by having a centralized employment department and pay based on seniority and objectives. Turnover fell to 54 per cent. Policies to promote from within, job-classification systems and promotion ladders based on similarity of skill soon followed. By the 1920s leading companies had introduced many of the personnel practices that are common among progressive employers today. Wartime labour shortages cemented many of the new practices in place and millions of jobs which had previously been held on a day-to-day basis were

---

Box 3.1   The arrangements we left behind

Cappelli reminds us that in the 1800s a typical firm was a single-unit operation, paired down to 'core competencies', which was the current advice being given at the time. They were headed by executives who were either partners or major stockholders (venture capitalists). Organizational structures were flat and there were no middle managers between these executives and the workforce and the authority to produce goods was pushed down to the foremen and workers. 'Putting out' systems meant that the majority of work was pushed out to suppliers and contractors, often to workers at home. It was only the expense of more productive manufacturing equipment that brought production work in-house. Such arrangements, however, persisted in several sectors with, for example, miners separately contracting pay rates for each rockface well into the twentieth century. Until the 1890s steel workers were paid like contractors on a rate per ton of steel produced which varied with the market price of steel. Skilled workers hired their own less skilled helpers and paid them out of their own pocket. 'Inside contracting systems' meant that even in complex manufacturing facilities contractors took entire responsibility for an aspect of the production process while working on the owner's premises, receiving payments for work produced but having complete autonomy over how production occurred. Separate accounts were held for each worker detailing scrap and wastage rates, tools, units of product in process and materials used.

Source: Cappelli,[8] p. 50.

---

converted into lasting connections. The system of internalized employment relationships was put into place by most large organizations after the Second World War based on four broad principles: work was organized around principles of scientific management with low-skill entry tasks and internal labour markets to provide skill formation; for practical purposes managers had a job for life subject to minimally acceptable performance and the business survival of the organization; shareholders and employees took the risk with respect to business outcomes; and systematic rules and a personnel bureaucracy provided important criteria for employment relationship decisions. Yet, within a decade from the 1980s:

> we saw this entire system coming unbundled across virtually every dimension of the employer/employee relationship. Companies . . . win praise for returning to the system of internal contracting, unbundling their vertically integrated systems and employment relationships. Fortune calls for the outright abolition of the human resources function and the administrative practices that go with it, just as others in the business press had done more than sixty years earlier.[9]

While Cappelli does not endorse historical practices as being automatically more beneficial to either employers or employees, the underlying point is that there is nothing sacred or even stable about a particular employment relationship and people are more resilient than many insecurity proponents suggest and their behaviours likely more adaptable. We also have to separate out the extent to which changes in the employment relationship are a matter of demand (imposition on employees) and supply (more a matter of choice) and accept that 'the back and forth movement between market and internalized employment relationships may well go on in the future as well'.[10]

Demand factors behind the changing structure of employment

What is meant by the 'new' employment contract? Organizational sociologists, such as Budros, call it the 'new capitalism'. They argue that this emerged from 1980 onwards. It is characterized by stiff international competition, state deregulation of industry, institutional ownership of firms, rapid technological change, smaller firm size, structural simplicity and flexibility.[11] Human capital theory argues that labour market outcomes such as levels of employment and wages are driven mainly by the employer's perceptions of an individual's long-term marginal productivity. Primary (internal) labour markets with full-time employment provides both stability to the employee and a means for the employer to capture the productivity of the employee and to recoup training and hiring expenses. Efficient firms, in theory, should have high human capital workers, defined career paths and a relatively long employment relationship. Both Japan and large Western corporations seemed to follow this model until the 1980s. Given the move away from the more stable and long-tenured industrial labour markets of the 1970s and 1980s it would be easy to assume that the main forces for change have been demand-led. As technical change, global exposure to competition, changes in levels of domestic protection, microeconomic reform of monopolies and the need to produce higher rates of return for shareholders associated with this new capitalism took hold, the initial response was to control labour costs through downsizing rather than through a shift towards non-traditional employment. In the 1981–2 recession, 73 per cent of US blue-collar workers with three or more years' service lost their jobs. A decade later in 1991–2 this rate had fallen to 5.2 per cent. In stark contrast, displacement rates for white-collar employees had risen consistently since 1981–2.

There was an initial wave of downsizing in white-collar employment which was used to reduce the absolute number of employed. However, subsequent white-collar adjustment has been used to rearrange the core competencies of the firm.[12] A subsequent statistical association now exists between employment growth rates and the propensity to hire non-standard employees in the USA, the UK, Australia, Canada, Israel, the Netherlands, Sweden and Taiwan.[13]

In the following sections we consider whether there has really been a notable shift in the *types* of job available. Following on from Capelli's analysis of the labour market as it has developed since the nineteenth century, Mangan,[14] another labour market economist, has examined the spread of what are strangely still referred to as non-traditional forms of employment on an international scale:

> . . . There now exists a host of alternative working arrangements ranging from the familiar categories of part-time, temporary, casual, contract and seasonal workers to more recent developments such as leased or franchised workers, out-workers, teleworkers, freelancers and portfolio workers. Those in alternative employment relations are now in such numbers that they can no longer be regarded as peripheral to the main labour market.[15]

These employees have variously been described as the 'just-in-time workforce',[16] 'peripheral',[17] 'disposable'[18] or 'contingent workforce'. Each word is in itself highly value-laden and, as we shall see, tends to mask a series of complex reasons that explain why the employment relationship may appear to be developing this way. Indeed, Carnoy and colleagues[19] remind us that the term 'contingent labour' originated at a 1985 Conference Board in New York and was used to cover conditional and transitory employment relationships that were initiated by a need for labour because a firm had increased its demand for a particular service. The term was then used to cover any arrangement differed from full-time, permanent, wage and salary employment (see Box 3.2).

Mangan[22] highlights five *demand factors* to explain this shift driven by theoretical arguments about the flexible firm, shortened planning horizons, lower social costs of employment, technical change and employer screening strategies. Marler and colleagues[23] add explanations from resource-dependency theory and transaction economics to these drives. Briefly, the demand arguments are as follows:

1 *Flexible firm theory*: Labour force skills have dated more quickly than in previous generations as new economic powers emerged in South-east Asia and as technical change has shortened the life cycle of products and services. Long-term and specifically trained employees became negative cost factors rather than a continuing source of returns on investment. Both Piore and Sable[24] and then Atkinson and Meager[25] developed the concept of flexible firm strategy to explain how Western firms coped with these pressures. This theory argues that firms have consciously subdivided their workforce into core and non-core (peripheral) groups in order to achieve greater flexibility in hiring and firing, the numbers of hours worked, job demarcation and worker remuneration. Flattened managerial structures, team working and process innovation have also become associated with the drive for flexibility. While generally plausible, there is little consistent empirical support that

Box 3.2   Contingent labour: What is in a word?

There are three theories of contingency. The job stability (tenure) theory concentrates on how long a worker has held a particular job regardless of the contractual conditions or wages of the job. The secondary labour market theory concentrates on deterioration in wages and stability characteristics. The employer–employee separation (non-standard contract) theory includes temporary workers, part-time workers, self-employed workers and workers employed in business services. It was only in the 1990s that the term 'contingent labour' took on a negative connotation. The narrowest definition of contingent employment based on ideas of job instability came from Polivka and Nardone,[20] who see it as involving both a lack of expectation of continued employment and unpredictability and variability in the hours worked. This definition would exclude part-time work and business service or self-employed workers. Tilly[21] uses a secondary job definition, including part-time jobs in contingent work if the character of work associated with them deserves such a label, i.e. requires low levels of skill, training and responsibility; offers low pay and few benefits; involves high rates of turnover; and tends to be entry-level, dead-end jobs. Most categories of contingent labour are then inherently controversial, especially if the underlying definition implies that contingency is associated with asymmetric benefits between employer and employee. Such definitions force us to try to understand if such asymmetric benefits are a matter of desire or involuntary participation. Non-standard contracts tend to make employees more vulnerable to economic fluctuations, but not all non-standard jobs are low paid or marked by poor working conditions. Some non-standard contracts simultaneously provide employees with increased risk but also new opportunities and improved working conditions, especially if they have the right skills and employment networks. Much attention therefore has been devoted to trying to unravel the balance between demand and supply for this form of work.

Source: Carnoy *et al.*[19]

demonstrates any general plans across industries to sub-divide workforces in this way.[26]

2 *Shortened planning horizons and internationalization of market forces.* Cappelli[27] argues that the planning horizons of firms have simply shortened to periods much less than the span of an individual career. Firms therefore think of employees more in terms of the completion of specific tasks and projects rather than in terms of maintaining consistent flows of products and services. New management practices must stress labour force flexibility and reinforce market forces within the firm. For Cappelli, the 'traditional' relationship was ended by a variety of management practices that brought

both the external product market and the labour market inside the organization. These included competitive pressures to cut time to market and an acceleration in the obsolescence of fixed investments in capital (including human capital). Information technology replaced the coordination and monitoring tasks of middle managers and enabled a large range of business functions to be outsourced. Financial arrangements made it possible to advance the interests of shareholders far ahead of other traditional stakeholders, increasing the squeeze of fixed costs. Finally, management techniques such as profit centres, external benchmarking and core competencies exposed every business process and employee to market pressures. Market principles have therefore quickly replaced the old behavioural rules of reciprocity, equity, loyalty, attachment and long-term commitment. Cappelli notes that managers who believe that they can draw up a new employment contract that will deliver high performance based on lowered expectations and heightened individual responsibility for 'employability' have some nasty shocks in store. There is a contradiction. The nature of most managerial work does not lend itself to market-based relationships and free agency legal contracts. It operates on the basis of open-ended relationships and adjusting obligations as the situation changes. The need to develop unique skills within the organization, and a degree of mutual commitment and trust, are inevitable, he argues, yet there is pressure on organizations to shed obsolete skills and poach marketable skills from others. The new contract is an 'uneasy dance' because '. . . while both parties know that the relationship is unlikely to last forever, neither knows exactly when it will end, while either side can end it unilaterally when it so desires'.[28] There are new sets of winners and losers. In the 1980s and 1990s the employers were clear winners, but the return of tight labour markets in the USA has created new bargaining power advantages for some employees. The 'revenge effects' of employee behaviour are also creating hidden cost calculations in the delivery of effective organizational performance.

3 *Lower social costs of employment*: A number of writers have drawn attention to the costs of employment imposed by governments through payroll taxes and provision for social costs, such as pension, absenteeism and vacation entitlement. The level of legislation control or the potential threat of litigation are associated with this factor. There is, for example, a correlation between the average length of job tenure of employees and the OECD's Employment Protection Legislation (EPL) strictness ranking, such that the less strict the legislation, the shorter the average tenure of job holders.[29] It is also evident that there are lower on-costs of employment and lower benefit provision for contingent workers. Levels of health insurance and pension arrangements for US workers vary markedly by type of work arrangement: 83 per cent of traditional full-time employees have health insurance compared to 67 per cent of contingent workers (workers who do not have an explicit or implicit contract for long-term employment) and 46 per cent of temp agency employees. The figures for employer provided pension coverage for the same groups are 48 per cent, 16 per cent and 4 per cent

respectively.[30] This problem is repeated in many other countries, including Australia, where many non-standard workers do not receive sick or holiday pay and are not covered by employer-sponsored health cover.

4 *Technical change*: Changes in technology are a frequently cited demand factor given that they provide both an incentive to locate work off-site and the means of facilitating this. Technical changes have blurred more centralized administration across large geographical distances. The pace of such technical change is accelerating. For example, it took 38 years before 30 per cent of the US working-age population had access to the telephone, 17 years for television to reach this diffusion level, but only 7 years for regular Internet usage to diffuse.[31] The main impact of accelerating technical diffusion rates has been an escalation in the cycle of job growth, destruction and creation. For example, a recently trained IT specialist reaches peak earnings within six years of graduation, after which time they need to retrain or face skills obsolescence.[32] The US Department of Labor estimates that nearly half of all US workers will be in industries that produce or intensively use information technology by 2006.

5 *Screening strategies based on the level of resource dependency and cost of transactions*: Lepak and Snell[33] use resource-based theory to argue that organizations adopt staffing strategies that are consistent with their particular human resource needs. They draw upon the ideas of Barney and Wright and his colleagues to stipulate that organizations enhance their value by determining which human resource capabilities should remain within the firm and which should be acquired in the market.[34] Organizations will only develop in-house the knowledge, skills and abilities that contribute to its unique capabilities. Those that do not will be acquired on demand in the external labour market. High commitment is less important from such employees. The economic transaction cost perspective of Williamson follows a similar logic.[35] Transactions that are not unique nor specific to a particular asset can be easily imitated in the marketplace. A more costly internal labour market associated with full-time employment is not justified for such transactions. Capabilities that are too specialized, used too infrequently or easily imitated are better acquired in the external labour market on a temporary basis.

These emerging staffing strategies result in a dramatic increase in the demand for both high- and low-skill temporary workers, creating a more favourable environment for the temporary help industry and economies of scale, lowering their costs and increasing their profits. A range of studies suggest that employers do operate staffing strategies that increase the demand for contingent employees. They now regularly use non-traditional work arrangements as a precursor to offering more permanent employment.[36] The motivation to do this of course varies. In a country like Spain it might be to avoid potentially punitive employment protection legislatives, while in the USA the large number of lawsuits brought by dismissed employees provides an incentive for firms to screen employees before making a commitment. The screening aspect might not always be central to the HR strategy, but can develop as such. For example, the initial employment decision to employ a temp agency worker might have nothing to do with screening, but evidence suggests that permanent employment follows a period of non-standard employment quite regularly. A survey by the Institute for Employment Studies in the UK found that 68 per cent of firms that employed temporary staff went on to appoint at least one of these temporary employees to a permanent position.[37] In some instances the whole employment strategy of the firm might be based around the creation of a peripheral but highly characteristic workforce. For example, in the UK, students have become a permanent part of the temporary labour force. The number of 16–24-year-olds with a part-time job while studying rose from 319 000 to 893 000 from 1984 to 1998. Some 4.4. million students undertake some form of paid work during their studies. Indeed, students account for some 60 per cent of employees in Pizza Hut, 40 per cent at Kwik Save and 35 per cent at Waitrose.[38]

The slow demise of long-term attachments

Labour market economists view changes in the employment relationship through demand and supply factors, and many of these patterns have been experienced before. It is undoubtedly true that by taking a historical perspective on the employment relationship, as Capelli[39] has, it is clear that the post-war definition of 'traditional' employment based on long-term attachments, skills development internal to the firm, and a psychological contract based on mutual obligations has only really held good for little more than a generation. Moreover, the arguments used today to support contracting and outsourcing in the pursuit of organizational flexibility and a need for reduced costs are probably little different from those used in the nineteenth century to support the old 'putting out systems' described by Capelli.

Although it is now very difficult to know where traditional employment ends and non-traditional employment begins,[40] Mangan argues that the present fundamental transition taking place in the employment relationship '. . . is much more than an inevitable correction away from an unsuitable golden age'.[41] We are not going to see either the disappearance of traditional employment or a return to past systems of employment. Labour markets are going through a renewed period of flux that is driven by not just technological and economic factors, but a new social context. Mangan distinguishes the present flux from some of the historical throw-backs that it inevitably reflects as follows.

1 *Labour market diversity*: The employment systems of the 1920s serviced a predominantly low-skill male and immobile (by today's standards) work-force. Traditional employment satisfied both organizational demand and societal supply factors. It satisfied the organizational demand for more internalized control over the skills of labour to match sophisticated

production systems. On the supply side labour unions had developed considerable power. The traditional employment system provided firms with a reliable workforce that was willing to acquire new firm-specific skills alongside an institutional setting that allowed for collective negotiation of benefits for union members. How can these systems successfully adapt to a labour market that is characterized by the large-scale participation of women, large numbers of skilled and mobile workers, a globalized production system, and an economic system designed around mass consumption?

2 *Supply-driven factors*. These have become much more important. Significant sections of the population now seek non-standard employment in preference to more traditional forms.[42]

3 *Simultaneous existence of work-rich and work-poor*: At the same time that newspaper headlines highlight heightened levels of job insecurity and downsizing, they also talk of overwork and the long work hours culture. There is a significant structural dichotomy between workers in areas of short supply being required to work more hours in return for job security, and workers in increasingly precarious and involuntary situations.[43] This is generally explained by a shift in the nature of the core–peripheral model of organizations. The core now appears to be becoming much smaller than the peripheral sections, with enhanced job security for the highly skilled professionals and technocrats at the centre (with permanent full-time or permanent part-time jobs). This job security for some becomes enhanced by the flexibility of a much larger group of casual and contracted workers on the periphery. This autonomy divide is evidenced, for example, in data from the US Civilian Population Survey which shows that on a like-for-like industry basis managers have much greater autonomy over their work time than their administrative support staff.[44] There is some support for evidence of a shrinking core. The Institute of Management/Manpower Survey of Long Term Employment Strategies in the UK found that by 1996 79 per cent of employers considered that they would have a 'core' of 90 per cent of employees, but when they looked at their manpower strategies for the next four years only 47 per cent considered that they would maintain a 'core' of 90 per cent of their workforce. The proportion who considered that their 'core' would represent 75 per cent of the workforce increased from 17 per cent to 45 per cent.[45] Excepting such anecdotal snapshots, there is little evidence that this is a deliberate organizational strategy aimed at demarcating jobs.

4 Flexible competence substituting for short life-cycle jobs: changes in industrial organization mean that specific jobs and tasks have a shorter life-span, and as a consequence rather than by design, those who are able to adapt and who have the behavioural and cognitive competencies associated with flexibility, find themselves, rather than their roles, taking on the characteristics of permanent or core employees. Those without such competency face the prospect of downgraded or outsourced roles. As we shall see, it is a matter of both desire as well as capability.

The situation facing employees then is neither as pessimistic as that portrayed in Bridges' *The end of jobs* nor as optimistic as Arthur's *The boundaryless career*. The reality will be far more mixed and complex. Organizations too will face conflicting experiences, and they will likely oscillate between strategies that pursue a high-flexibility future, and periods of adjustment and recoil, as they experience undesirable waves of economic costs associated with the downside of flexible employment, such as productivity losses associated with declines in morale, skills shortages and turnover rates and the disproportionate labour market power and expectations of those with such power. The economics of employment have changed such that most firms will require at least *some* level of non-traditional employment. The US Department of Labor described the situation at the end of the 1990s as follows: '... the age of just in time production giving rise to the just in time worker.'[46]

The growth of non-traditional employment

It is notoriously difficult to build an international picture of developments in non-traditional work arrangements. The definitions used for many arrangements are not compatible, the qualifying rules for even agreed categories of work are frequently different, the security of tenure, status and rewards of work classifications differ markedly, as does the labour market legislation. Official data-gathering techniques are often irregular and rely on self-perception. Although the incidence and specific form of non-traditional employment is very country-specific, it is important to look across these national 'snapshots'. It is only when this is done that it becomes clear that:

- There is much synergy between these different forms of work
- Non-traditional working arrangements are replacing traditional arrangements across the world being driven by a common set of demand and supply factors

By identifying core workers and treating the residual as non-standard, it seems that the proportion of employees in non-core work ranges from 21.4 per cent in Germany, 24.9 per cent in the UK and Japan, 26.1 per cent in the USA, 27.3 per cent in Sweden, 33 per cent in Australia and up to a massive 59.9 per cent in Spain (where the institutional arrangements offer strong inducements for firms to avoid hiring traditional employees).[47]

In Japan non-standard workers represent about 25 per cent of all employees and a further 20 per cent of the workforce and are classified as non-regulars. This includes people working part-time (classified as such not on the bases of time worked but employer perceptions of the relative importance of the job), with side jobs, temporary (contracts of less than one year), day labour and dispatched workers. *Arubaito* is the literal translation of side-job worker and refers to irregular short-term jobs in Japan normally taken by students, females or moonlighters. There are differences in motivation within this group (which represents around 6 per cent of paid employment), with students viewing the work as transitory and a means of financing education, but many of the married women preferring *arubaito* status over the *nenko* wage system and lifetime employment because it allows more time for family activity.[48]

In the USA the relative proportion of part-time work has remained constant since 1983. From 1983 to 1999 the employment share of all non-regulars in Japan nearly trebled from 11 per cent to roughly 30 per cent of all paid employed.[49] Non-regular work is being used not just to increase workplace flexibility, but to dismantle and reform the *nenko* lifetime employment system. Temporary workers in Japan are fixed-term contract workers with contracts of less than one year. They negotiate directly with the employer rather than through labour hire agencies which were banned from 1947 to 1985 because they were associated with exploitation. The sector grew rapidly in the 1990s, as did the number of *sukko* (workers transferred to a subsidiary of the company for a temporary stay). However, another labour market phenomenon has grown. These are multiple job holders classified as full-time because their total work at all jobs exceeds 35 hours or more. The US Department of Labor estimated that there were 6.5 million such workers in 1995, or 5 per cent of the workforce. Sixty-nine per cent of these multiple job holders were full-time workers with one or more part-time secondary jobs and 14 per cent had multiple part-time jobs.[50] By 1997 60 per cent of all US multiple job-holders worked from home for at least one of their jobs (Table 3.1).[51]

Except in the USA, the proportion of part-time employment has been rising. The UK saw the proportion of the workforce working part-time rise from 16.1 per cent to 22.2 per cent from 1979 to 1997.[52] Similarly in Australia the proportion of part-time employees (permanent, self-employed and casual) rose from 9.3 per cent to 24.5 per cent from 1971 to 1998.[53] The general rule is that part-time employment has been increasing most slowly in countries that started from a low base, especially in Southern Europe, has grown most rapidly in France and Belgium and has levelled off in the USA.

It is generally argued that the US economy completed the transition to greater reliance on contingent work in the 1980s and in fact since then (until at least the collapse of the e-commerce bubble, stock market and then corporate governance scandals) has been operating to a vigorous, growing and tight labour market. This appears to have stopped much of the peripheralization of employment, on the surface at least. Between 1979 and 1989 the *Fortune 500* companies shed one quarter of their workforce.[54] By 1989 from 25 to 30 per cent of the workforce were already categorized as contingent,[55] almost half of new job creation in the 1980s had been part-time or temporary,[56] and around 40 per cent of part-time jobs creation was 'involuntary', i.e. jobs held by individuals who would rather work full-time.[57] Of the 5 million US workers paid at or below minimum wage in 1987, 44 per cent were women working part-time.[58] More recent data suggest that the level of involuntary occupancy of peripheral work roles may have increased. Citing a US Department of Labor Statistics[59] survey of workers engaged in contingent and alternative work structures,

Table 3.1 Incidence of comparable forms of non-traditional employment

Country	% of workforce part-time <30 hours a week (1997)	Temporary jobs female employment	Involuntary part-time workers as % of economically active population (1993)	Proportion of women in part-time employment (1996)
Netherlands	24.7	14	5.6	73.8
Australia	22.9		6.9	73.4
Switzerland	22.7	–	–	82.8
Iceland	22.3	–	–	78.9
Norway	20.9	–	–	79.3
UK	19.9	8	3.2	81.3
Canada	18.2	–	5.5	69.1
Sweden	17.2	14	6.2	79.5
Belgium	16.5	7	3.8	87.4
Ireland	15.3	13	3.3	73.3
Denmark	14.5	13	4.6	72.2
France	14.1	14	4.8	81.7
Germany	13.4	11	1.5	87.4
Poland	13.3	–	–	57.2
USA	12.8	–	5.0	67.9
Italy	11.1	9	2.3	69.4
Austria	10.3	7	–	84.2
Greece	8.0	11	7.1	–
Finland	7.4	19	2.9	64.3
Portugal	6.8	11	1.8	67.2
Spain	6.2	38	1.0	74.5
Czech Republic	4.7	–	–	–
Hungary	2.6	–	–	72.3
Japan	–	–	1.9	68.0

Source: Mangan[14].
Other Sources: Le Maitre, G., Marianna, D. and Van-Bastelar, A (1997). International comparisons of part-time employment. *OECD Economic Studies*, *29*, 139–52; International Labour Organization (1997). ILO highlights global challenge to employment. *ILO News*, 3 November.

Murphy and Jackson[60] note that almost two-thirds of respondents worked in such roles involuntarily and would prefer a more traditional full-time employment contract.

Episodes of temporary employment

Temporary employment has also become quite extensive, averaging around 10 per cent of paid employment across the European Union, but more prevalent among women (see Table 3.1). Employees of temporary hire agencies make a significant contribution to economies. Between 1983 and 1992 temporary employment in the USA rose by 250 per cent – ten times faster than overall employment growth[61] and 20 per cent of new jobs created between 1991 and 1993 were temporary.[62] Around 45 per cent of temporary staff are clerical, 34 per cent industrial and 18 per cent professional. The number of temporary help service companies in the USA grew from 3133 to 10 611 between 1975 and 1987.[63] In fact, Manpower Inc., the temp agency, has become the largest employer in the USA and its chief competitor, Kelly Services, is the second-largest employer. While the US experience would not be classed as an explosion, it has contributed to the view expressed by Ostermen that standard employment conditions are on the wane.[64]

It must be stated at the outset that temporary work cannot be summed up as all 'good' or 'bad': as Rogers points out, 'temporary employment has many faces'.[65] She notes that the meaning of temporary work arrangements depends on class, gender and race as well as the specific labour market conditions associated with different occupations. A number of individual factors also make a difference to the meaning of temporary work, as outlined in Chapter 8. Analysis of temporary employees therefore tends to distinguish two broad groups depending on their skills and preferences:[66]

1 Traditional temporary workers: considered to have limited skills, a desire to find standard work within bureaucratic organizations,[67] e.g. clerks, receptionists
2 Boundaryless temporary workers: individuals whose current career consists of quasi-contractual commitments and temporary projects as a matter of choice,[68] e.g. accountants, lawyers, engineers and medical professionals.

The demand for temporary work is not homogeneous and temporary workers with both low and high skills are becoming attractive to organizations. Opinion is also divided as to whether the more transactional nature of contingent employment relationships is good or bad in terms of organizational performance. Tsui and colleagues[69] have argued that the impact may be detrimental, but others such as Matusik, Hill, Lepak and Snell[70] argue that

---

Box 3.3   Temporary work in the UK

From 1984 to 1990 temporary work represented a fairly stable 5 per cent of employment, but it has since grown, reaching 7.7 per cent by 1999, by which date temporary jobs represented at least one-third of all new hiring.[71] At least one in five temporary employees are professionals or high-skill tradespeople (representing 10 per cent of all professional employees).[72] Around half of all temporary employees are on fixed-term contracts, 15 per cent work for temping agencies, and 18 per cent are involved in casual work. Fixed-term contracts are most prevalent in the public sector (administration, education and health). The UK, however, makes relatively less use of temporary work than most other EU countries.

contingent employees can create valuable new knowledge at relatively low economic cost that increases the effectiveness of organizations.

Between 1985 and 1998 the share of temporary employment increased significantly in a number of countries,[73] including Spain (15.6 per cent up to 32.9 per cent), Finland (10.5 per cent up to 17.7 per cent), the Netherlands (7.5 per cent up to 12.7 per cent), France (4.7 per cent up to 13.9 per cent) and Portugal (14.4 per cent up to 17.3 per cent). It remains relatively low and stable still in countries such as Austria, Belgium, Ireland, Italy and the UK (but see Box 3.3 for recent developments). There has also been a broad tendency towards significant deregulation of temporary work. In Belgium, Denmark, Germany, Italy, the Netherlands and Spain fixed-term contracts and contracts with temporary employment agencies can now be used in a much wider range of situations than at the beginning of the 1990s.

Moreover, labour economists point out that for the total stock of temporary employment to increase, then there is likely to be an even bigger shift in the flows in and out of employment. Evidence here is more anecdotal, sadly. However, even by the late 1980s when the annual stock of temporary workers in France was 4 per cent, 70 per cent of all workers hired by firms with more than 50 employees were initially given a temporary contract. By 1987–8, 38.5 per cent of all job terminations in France and 30 per cent in Germany were because of the expiry of a temporary contract.[74] More recent figures continue to show values for in-flows and out-flows to employment.[75] Even the very circumspect analysis of labour market stability conducted by employment strategists for the International Labour Organization concluded that by 2000 '. . . being employed on a fixed-term contract at some point in the course of a career is therefore rather the rule than the exception, hence, perhaps the image of a very volatile labour market'.[76] In a similar vein, Mangan's analysis concludes that '. . . the relative contribution of non-standard employment will (in future) remain relatively stable, although the relative contribution of the different components of non-standard employment will change. The relative importance of part-time work may decline with corresponding increases in temp agency employees at one end of the spectrum and self-employed contractors at the other.'[77]

Is the growth of temporary and part-time employment a demand or supply factor?

In the USA government data show that over 60 per cent of temporary workers want a permanent work arrangement,[78] suggesting that demand-side factors are very important in explaining the shift in employment. Nonetheless, despite such evidence, the success of such a strategy on behalf of employers must in part depend on finding 'receptive pockets of labour supply' such as women with family responsibilities.[79] A sizeable minority of employees do appear to prefer temporary status. Employees vary in their preference for this type of employment and the opportunities for skill accumulation and wage growth that it offers.

Becker has used *Human capital theory* to explain the behaviour of non-traditional employees.[80] This suggests that individuals will not invest in skill development unless the value of the returns on their investment are greater than the value of the costs. This investment is made in the expectation of higher salary returns over an extended period of time, suggesting that longer-term employment is a preferred option. Temporary work should only be attractive to less skilled employees. The evidence indeed shows that the majority of temporary workers are younger and less educated than traditional employees and are therefore less likely to have as much experience and formal training.[81] However, this situation rests on two assumptions that may be questioned:

1 That decisions of employees are primarily influenced by financial outcomes. This is a false assumption. A number of studies have shown that many contract workers place as much if not more value on other factors such as autonomy.[82] Also, many people taking up temporary work are not the primary breadwinners in the family and again are less motivated by purely economic outcomes.
2 That temporary employment prevents high-skill employees from recouping their investments in their human capital. The outlook is changing in several sectors such that some agencies can provide such a volume of temporary assignments that the risks of insecurity are significantly diminished. Individuals with specialized skills can be more assured of a string of opportunities and can now enhance their value in the marketplace by holding multiple jobs in multiple firms.[83]

Recent work suggests that we are indeed seeing the emergence of a new type of temporary worker, called the boundaryless contingent employee. In response to the trend of establishing 'core' and 'peripheral' employees and the emphasis of 'employability' over a longer-term employment relationship, '. . . a subset of higher skilled workers is voluntary entering into alternative employment relationships as temporary employees and using temporary employment agencies to facilitate this transition'[84] Marler and colleagues analysed the US labour force to identify what proportion of temporary employees fell into this more proactive group. They found that from 60 to 71 per cent of contingent employees were neutral to or disagreed with the statement that they preferred temporary work. However, 20 per cent of temporary employees were boundaryless, showing a positive set of attributes in terms of preference, skill level and experience (see Box 3.4 for details). The performance implications for such employees would be expected to be quite different. Far from being less involved they may be more so.

Given that some organizations use temporary work as a means of screening job applicants, traditional temporary employees may have an incentive to work hard. Boundaryless temporary employees also might do so. For example, high-technology temporaries are aware that better performance can lead to

---

Box 3.4   Boundaryless and traditional temporary employees

Marler and colleagues[88] examined various organizational behaviours of both traditional contingent employees and boundaryless contingent employees. They surveyed 614 employees from the US Bureau of Labor Statistics' Current Population Survey Contingent Work Supplement, which is a scientifically selected sample of US households. They also examined data from a regional sample of 276 temporary employees in the north-east USA. A large range of variables were measured, including skill accumulation, education, preference for temporary work, number of job alternatives, wage and pay satisfaction, client commitment, and task and contextual performance. Cluster analysis revealed two distinct types of temporary employee. Type 1 (traditional contingent employee) did not prefer temporary work, had lower levels of education, were in blue- or pink-collar jobs. Type 2 (boundaryless contingent employee) were mainly in white-collar jobs and were more likely to prefer their arrangements and appreciate the flexibility. Boundaryless employees had skills that were in higher demand and were part of dual-earner families. They earned significantly more than their traditional counterparts and preference for temporary work worked on a continuum and was dependent on a number of factors that framed how they viewed their chances. Women were more constrained than men by the competing demands of family and reported work–life balance as a reason for their preference for temporary work, whereas men tended to cite a desire for pursuing other interests as their reason for preference.

Source: Marler *et al.*[88]

---

more referrals and repeat business. They may also be in more enriched jobs.[85] In fact, there is little consistent evidence concerning the performance of temporary employees. Again, the situation likely depends on the way in which they are used. In a study of independent contractor engineers, higher extra-role performance (also called organizational citizenship behaviours or OCBs) was found[86] whereas OCBs were found to be lower than core employees among a sample of temporary loan officers and nurses.[87]

As would be expected, several studies have found a positive correlation between voluntariness and overall satisfaction for temporary workers.[89] The recent study by Marler and colleagues found, for example, that the relationship varies across type of temporary employee. The correlation between work satisfaction and task performance was higher for the traditional temporary employees (involuntary work preference) than for the boundaryless temporary employees. Performance of traditional (involuntary) temporary employees is more sensitive to how they feel about their assignment and their attitudes. For boundaryless temporary employees, high performance is not the incentive. It is the traditional temporary employees who are under more pressure to perform while transitioning to a more permanent job. Traditional contingent employees were also more likely to be cooperative with the broader project team, and to show more positive organization citizenship behaviours than their boundaryless colleagues. The challenge for organizations presented by this new (albeit minority) type of boundaryless contingent worker is clear: '[they] may want to consider adopting practices that will encourage more cooperative behaviours among boundaryless temporary workers engaged for project-based work.'[90]

References

1. Auer, P. and Cazes, S. (2000). The resilience of the long-term employment relationship: Evidence from the industrialised countries. *International Labour Review, 139 (4)*, 379–408.
2. Heery, E. and Salmon, J. (2000). The insecurity thesis. In E. Heery and J. Salmon (Eds.), *The insecure workforce*. London: Routledge.
3. Heery, E. (1996). Risk, representation and the new pay. Personnel Review, 25 (6), 54–65.
4. Gregg, P., Knight, G. and Wadsworth, J. (2000). Heaven knows I'm miserable now: job insecurity in the British labour market. In Heery and Salmon (Eds.), *op. cit.*
5. Robinson, P. (2000). Insecurity and the flexible workforce: measuring the ill-defined. In Heery and Salmon (Eds.), *Ibid.*
6. Gallie, D., White, M., Cheng, Y. and Tomlinson, M. (1998). *Restructuring the employment relationship.* Oxford: Oxford University Press.
7. Sparrow, P.R. (2000). The new employment contract. In R. Burke and C.L. Cooper (Eds.), *The organization in crisis.* London: Basil Blackwell.
8. Cappelli, P. (1999). *The new deal at work.* Boston, MA: Harvard University Press, p. 50.
9. *Ibid.*, pp. 67–68.
10. *Ibid.*, pp. 62.
11. Budros, A. (1997). The new capitalism and organizational rationality: the adoption of downsizing programs, 1979–1994. *Social Forces, 76 (1),* 229–250.
12. Cappelli (1999). *Op. cit.*
13. Fallick, B.C. (1999). Part-time work and industry growth. *Monthly Labor Review.* March, 22–29.
14. Mangan, J. (2000). *Workers without traditional employment: an international study of non-standard work.* Cheltenham: Edward Elgar.
15. *Ibid.*, p. 1.
16. Plewes, T.J. (1988). Understanding the data on part-time and temporary employment. In K. Christensen M. Murphee (Eds.), *Flexible workstyles: a look at contingent labour.* Washington, DC: Department of Labor, Women's Bureau.

17. Morse, D. (1969). *The peripheral worker*. New York: Columbia University Press.
18. Pollack, M.A. and Bernstein, A. (1985). Part-time workers: rising numbers, rising discard. *Business Week*, 1 April, 62–63.
19. Carnoy, M., Castells, M. and Benner, C. (1997). Labour markets and employment practices in the age of flexibility: a case study of Silicon Valley. *International Labour Review, 136 (1)*, 27–48.
20. Polivka, A.E. and Nardone, T. (1989). On the definition of 'contingent work'. *Monthly Labor Review, 112 (12)*, 9–16.
21. Tilly, C. (1996). *Half a job: bad and good part-time jobs in a changing labour market*. Philadelphia, PA: Temple University Press.
22. Mangan, (2000). *Op. cit.*
23. Marler, J.H., Barringer, M.W. and Milkovich, G.T. (2002). Boundaryless and traditional contingent employees: worlds apart. *Journal of Organizational Behavior, 23*, 425–453.
24. Piore, M. and Sable, C. (1985). *Second industrial divide*. New York: Basic Books.
25. Atkinson, J. and Meager, N. (1986). Is flexibility just a flash in the pan? *Personnel Management, 18*, 26–29.
26. Critiques of flexible firm theory were made by Pollert, A. (1991). (Ed). *Farewell to flexible*. Oxford: Basil Blackwell, and Hunter, L., McGregor, A., MacInnes, J. and Sproull, A. (1993). The flexible firm: strategy and segmentation. *British Journal of Industrial Relations, 31*, 383–407.
27. Cappelli (1999). *Op. cit.*
28. *Ibid.*, p. 3.
29. Auer, P. and Cazes (2000). *Op. cit.*
30. See Cohany, S.R. (1998). Workers in alternative employment arrangements: a second look: *Monthly Labor Review, 121 (11)*, 3–17; Hipple, S. (1998). Contingent work. *Monthly Labor Review, 121 (11)*, 22–35.
31. Atkinson, J. and Court, T. (1998). Temps catch up with permanent workers. *Industrial Relations Services Employment Review*, No. 680. London: IRS.
32. US Department of Labor (1999). *Futurework: trends and challenges for work in the 21st century*. Washington DC: US Dept of Labor.
33. Lepak, D. and Snell, S. (1999). The human resource architecture: toward a theory of human capital allocation and development. *Academy of Management Review, 24*, 31–48.
34. See Barney, J. (1991). Firm resources and sustained competitive advantage. *Journal of Management, 17*, 99–120; Wright, P.M., McMahan, G.C. and McWilliams, A. (1994). Human resources and sustained competitive advantage: a resource-based perspective. *International Journal of Human Resource Management, 5*, 301–326.
35. Williamson, O. (1990). Transaction-cost economics: the governance of contractual relations. In O. Williamson (Ed.) *Industrial Organization, Volume 9*. Aldershot: Edward Elgar.
36. Blau, F.D., Ferber, M.A. and Winkler, A.E. (1998). *The economics of women, men and work, 3rd edition*. Upper Saddle River, NJ: Prentice Hall.

37. Atkinson, J., Rick, J., Morris, S. and Williams, M. (1996). Temporary work and the labour market. *The Institute of Employment Studies Report No. 31*, 1–32. Brighton: IES.
38. Whitehead, M. (1999). Students get a taste of working life, *People Management*, 28 January, 14.
39. Capelli (1999). *Op. cit.*
40. Felstead, A. and Jewson, N. (1999). Flexible labour and non-standard employment: an agenda of issues, in A. Felstead and N. Jewson (Eds.), *Global trends in flexible labour*. London: Macmillan Press.
41. Mangan (2000). *Op. cit.* p. 3.
42. Simpson, M., Dawkins, J. and Maddern, G. (1997). Casual employment in Australia: incidence and determinants. *Australian Economic Papers, 36 (2)*: 194–204.
43. Picot, G. and Lin, Z (1997). Are Canadians more likely to lose their jobs in the 1990s? *Statistics Canada, Analytical Studies Branch, Research Paper Series*, No. 96, Ontario, August, 1–28.
44. US Department of Labor (1999). Workers on flexible and shift schedules in 1998, *Labor Force Statistics from the Current Population Survey*. Washington, DC: US Department of Labor.
45. Institute of Management/Manpower plc (1996). *4th Survey of long term employment strategies*. London: Institute of Management and Manpower plc.
46. US Department of Labor (1999). *Futurework: trends and challenges for work in the 21st century*. May, Washington DC: US Department of Labor, p. 7.
47. Mangan, (2000). *Op. cit.*
48. Houseman, S. and Osawa, M. (1995). Part-time and temporary employment in Japan, *Monthly Labor Review*, October, *118 (10)*, 10–18.
49. Data from the Somucho Tokeikyoku Employment Status Survey (1999) estimated from the Special Labour Force Survey, www.stat.go.jp/155.htm
50. US Department of Labor (1998). Employee tenure summary. *Labor Force Statistics from the Current Population Survey*. Washington. DC: US Department of London.
51. US Department of Labor (1998). *Issues in labor statistics*. Summary 98–5, Bureau of Labor Statistics, May.
52. Data from *Labour Force Survey*, Spring 1998.
53. Venden Heuvel, A. and Wooden, M. (2000). Diversity in employment arrangements. In J. Mangan (ed.) *Understanding unemployment: a national and state perspective*. Queensland Treasury.
54. New Ways to Work (1992). *New policies for part-time and contingent workers*. San Francisco, CA: New Ways to Work.
55. See Belous, R.S. (1989). *The contingent economy: The growth of the temporary, part-time and subcontracted workforce*. Washington, DC: National Planning Association; Polivka, A.E. and Nardone, T. (1989). On the definition of 'contingent' work, *Monthly Labor Review*, December, 9–16.
56. Tilly, C. (1990). Reasons for the continuing growth of part-time employment. *Monthly Labor Review*, March, 10–18.

57. Appelbaum, E. (1992). Structural change and the growth of part-time and temporary employment. In V.L. du Rivege (Ed.) *New policies for the part-time and contingent workforce*. Armonk, NY: Sharpe.

58. Levitan, S.A. and Conway, E. (1992). Part-timers: living on half rations. In B.D. Warme, K. Lundy and L.A. Lundy (Eds.), *Working part-time: risks and opportunities*. New York: Praeger.

59. US Department of Labor (1995). Contingent and alternative employment arrangements. *Bureau of Labor Statistics Report No. 900*. Washington, DC: US Department of Labor.

60. Murphy, P.E. and Jackson, S.E. (1999). Managing work role performance: challenges for twenty first century organizations and their employees. In D.R. Ilgen and E.D. Pulakos (Eds.), *The changing nature of performance: implications for staffing motivation and development*. San Francisco: Jossey-Bass.

61. Mangan (2000). *Op. cit.*, p. 24.

62. Von Hippel, C., Mangum, S.L., Greenberger, D.B., Heneman, R.L. and Skoglind, J.D. (1997). Temporary employment: can organizations and employees both win? *Academy of Management Executive, 11*, 93–103.

63. Carnoy, M., Castells, M. and Benner, C. (1997) Labour markets and employment practices in the age of flexibility: a case study of Silicon Valley. *International Labour Review, 136*, 27–48.

64. Osterman, P. (2001). Flexibility and commitment in the US labor market. *Employment Paper Services*. Geneva: International Labour Organization.

65. Rogers, J.K. (2000). *Temps: the many faces of the changing workplace*. Ithaca, NY: ILR Press.

66. Marler, J.H., Barringer, M.W. and Milkovich, G.T. (2002). Boundaryless and traditional contingent employees: worlds apart. *Journal of Organizational Behavior, 23*, 425–453.

67. See, for example: Kalleberg, A.L., Reskin, B.F. and Hudson, K. (2000). Bad jobs in America: standard and non-standard employment relations and job quality in the United States. *American Sociological Review, 65*, 256–278; Segal, L.M. (1996) Flexible employment: composition and trends. *Journal of Labor Research, 17*, 525–542.

68. See, for example, Arthur, M.B. and Rousseau, D.M. (1995). (Eds.), *The boundaryless career as a new employment principle*. New York: Oxford University Press.

69. Tsui, A., Pearce, J., Porter, L.W. and Hite, J. (1995). Choice of employee–organization relationship: influence of external and internal organization factors. *Research in Personnel and Human Resources Management, 13*, 117–151.

70. See Lepak, D. and Snell, S. (1999). The human resource architecture: toward a theory of human capital allocation and development. *Academy of Management Review, 24*, 31–48; Matusik, S.F. and Hill, C.W.L. (1998). The utilization of contingent work, knowledge creation, and competitive advantage. *Academy of Management Review, 23*, 680–697.

71. Employment Policy Institute (1999). Employment Audit, Summer 1999.

72. Sly, F. and Stilwell, D. (1997). Temporary workers in Great Britain. *Labour Market Trends*. London: Office for National Statistics.

73. Auer and Cazes (2000). *Op. cit.*
74. Auer, P. and Büchtemann, C.F. (1990). La dérégulation du droit du travail: le cas de la libéralisation du recours aux contrats de travail à durée déterminée. L'expérience de l'Allemagne fédérale et de la France. In P. Auer, M. Maruani and E. Reyneid (Eds.), *Chroniques internationales du marché du travail et des politiques d'emploi 1986–1989*. Paris: La Documentation Française.
75. Galtier, B. and Gautié, J. (2001). Employment protection and LMP: trade-offs and complementarities – the case of France. *Employment Paper Series*, Geneva: ILO.
76. Auer and Cazes (2000). *Op. cit.*, p. 396.
77. Mangan (2000) *Op. cit.*, p. 184.
78. Cohany, S.R. (1996). Workers in alternative employment arrangements. *Monthly Labor Review*, October, 31–45.
79. Thurman, J. and Trah, J. (1990). Part-time work in the international perspective. *International Labour Review, 24*, 23–40.
80. Becker, G.S. (1992). *Human capital, 3rd edition*. Chicago: University of Chicago Press.
81. Cohany (1996). *Op. cit.*
82. See, for example: Bartol, K.M. and Locke, E.A. (2000). Incentives and motivation: In S.L. Rynes & B. Gerhart (Eds.), *Compensation in organizations*. San Francisco: Jossey-Bass.; Kunda, G., Barley, S.R. and Evans, J. (2002). Why do contractors contract? The experience of highly-skilled professionals in a contingent labour market. *Industrial and Labor Relations Review, 55 (2)*, 234.
83. See, for example, Sullivan, S.E. (1999). The changing nature of careers. *Journal of Management, 25*, 457–484; Tolbert, P.S. (1996). Occupations, organizations and boundaryless careers. In M. Arthur and D.M. Rousseau (Eds.), *Boundaryless careers*. New York: Oxford University Press.
84. Marler, J.H., Barringer, M.W. and Milkovich, G. (2002). Boundaryless and traditional contingent employees: worlds apart. *Journal of Organizational Behaviour, 23*, 425–453, p. 446.
85. Kunda *et al.* (2002). Cited in Marler *et al.* (2002). *Op. cit.*
86. Pearce, J. (1993). Toward an organizational behaviour of contract laborers: their psychological involvement and effects on employee co-workers. *Academy of Management Journal, 36*, 1082–1096.
87. Van Dyne, L and Ang. S. (1998). Organizational citizenship behaviour of contingent workers in Singapore. *Academy of Management Journal, 41*, 692–703.
88. Marler *et al.* (2002). *Op. cit.*
89. See, for example: Marler, J.H., Barringer, M.W. and Milkovich, G. (2002). Boundaryless and traditional contingent employees: worlds apart. *Journal of Organizational Behaviour, 23*, 425–453; Van Dyne and Ang (1998). *Op. cit.*; Feldman *et al.* (1998). *Op. cit.*; Ellingson *et al.* (1998). *Op. cit.*
90. Marler *et al.* (2002). *Op. cit.*

4

Job Stability and Employee Outcomes

Introduction

In the previous chapter we considered work by labour economists on previous flexible employment relationships and on the *types* of jobs currently in existence, through a review of non-traditional jobs and the reasons for their growth. We continue our exploration of the end-of-jobs and job insecurity theses in this chapter by looking at work by employment strategists that considers the stability of jobs, through analyses of job or employment tenure and separation rates, and work by HRM academics on historical levels of job satisfaction.

Job stability

The employment relationship is, however, remarkably resilient in many ways. One of the ways in which this is examined is through data on employment tenure. Average tenure in jobs and the distribution of jobs in terms of this tenure in the USA, European Union and Japan has formed the subject of a recent examination by Auer and Cazes.[1] They argue that such data can help give a broad overview of job stability across countries over time. First, there is marked variation in the average tenure that people have in jobs across countries. In 1998 average job tenure was 10.5 years, though as can be seen in Table 4.1, the country with the shortest tenure is the USA, closely followed by the UK, Denmark and the Netherlands. Longer-tenure employment relationships exist in Greece, Italy and Sweden, closely followed by Belgium, Japan and Portugal. These differences have remained fairly stable over time as have average levels of job tenure.

Table 4.1 Distribution of employment tenure (per cent) by time, education and employment protection legislation strictness

Country	Employment tenure under 1 year (per cent)		Employment tenure 10 years and over (per cent)		Average tenure by education (years) 1998			EPL strictness rating: 0=low, 4=high
	1991	1998	1991	1998	Low	Medium	High	
Belgium	–	12.0	–	46.5	13.3	11.1	10.6	2.10
Denmark	–	22.0	–	33.5	7.6	8.7	9.0	1.20
Finland	11.9	19.9	34.2	42.5	13.4	9.7	9.7	1.95
France	15.7	14.3	41.4	45.0	12.4	11.2	10.0	3.00
Germany	12.8*	14.3	41.2	38.3	–	–	–	2.50
Greece	–	9.6	–	51.2	17.1	9.3	10.8	3.40
Ireland	–	18.3	–	37.7	–	–	–	0.90
Italy	–	9.9	–	49.2	12.8	11.0	12.4	3.40
Japan	9.8	8.3	42.9	43.2	16.3	15.2	11.1	2.40
Netherlands	24.0	14.9	26.2	36.5	–	–	–	2.05
Portugal	–	15.0	–	43.0	10.8	8.1	10.7	3.70
Spain	23.9	28.4	39.7	39.8	1036	8.6	9.7	3.10
Sweden	–	13.4	–	47.8	14.8	11.3	10.9	2.25
UK	18.6	19.9	28.9	32.3	–	–	–	0.50
USA	28.8	27.8	26.6	25.8	7.2	5.3	7.3	–

* Data refer to 1990 instead of 1991
After Auer and Cazes.[1]

Contrary to the widespread assumption of a radical labour market shift towards less stability, there has not been any universal trend to shorter-tenure jobs across the industrialized economies in terms of median tenure of jobs. In the UK average male employment tenure has fallen slightly while average female employment tenure has risen slightly. A similar pattern is found in the USA. In Japan, France and Spain there have been small increases in both male and female job tenure. Cappelli's[2] analysis of published data on voluntary and involuntary job leavers in the USA presents the following picture. In terms of attachment to an employer, then the overall length of time that the average employee stays with a given employer, while remaining quite constant until the mid-1990s, has more recently begun to erode. The percentage of the US workforce with long-tenure jobs (of ten years or more) declined slightly from the late 1970s to 1993, then fell sharply, and is now at its lowest level in twenty years of comparable data.

The evidence for growing insecurity in the USA is actually still fragile, and job tenure is widely acknowledged as a weak measure of insecurity, but the view that there has been significant economic restructuring at the expense of the workforce is generally supported by the evidence.[3] In the UK there are signs of a modest decline in aggregate job tenure over the past 20 years. Nearly three-quarters of the workforce have experienced greater job instability in the

---

Box 4.1   An increasing concern over the costs of staff turnover?

The evidence that shifts in employment tenure reflects supply-side behaviour by employees has led to concern over the costs of higher staff turnover among employers. Certainly these costs have been increasing in the UK. The Chartered Institute of Personnel and Development's 2001 Labour Turnover Survey (capturing movements in 2000 which was a tight labour market) reported an annual turnover of 25 per cent – the highest figure since the survey began in 1995.[6] The average cost of replacing staff was £3933 and for managerial and professional staff was £8317 – up 28 per cent on the previous year. One in four companies surveyed were introducing work–life balance policies to attract and retain employees. Such data, however, hide significant differences for specific employment groups, such as women being less likely to leave jobs voluntarily because of marriage or childbirth and older and less-educated males being more likely to have reduced tenure.

Source: Roberts.[6]

---

past 10 years, the greatest rise being among men for whom median job tenure has fallen by 12 per cent in a decade, and job tenure is also declining for childless women.[4] As the following analysis will show, however, the view that employees should forget any idea of career-long employment with a big company '. . . is exaggerated and premature even in regard to the flexible employment system of the United States . . . [There is a large] gap in interpretation between the media, management consultants and labour-market research'.[5] However, as we shall see in the next chapter, there is also a large gap in interpretation between labour market researchers and those who show more subtle aspects of job instability such as vulnerability and changes in the quality of the employment relationship.

However, although average organizational tenure is falling slightly in some important instances, if we ask how frequently employees have changed occupations rather than employers, then the opposite has happened.[7] If anything, workers seem to be staying in the same occupation longer, paralleling the increase in occupational as opposed to organizational loyalty noted by Stroh and colleagues.[8] As internal labour markets erode, then external labour market skill identities have become more evident.

Average employee tenure data can hide subtle changes, however, in that tenure in some classes of jobs or for certain types of employee may have increased while in others it might have decreased. They also create fears for organizations about the costs of staff turnover (see Box 4.1). Employees, for example, change jobs more frequently while they are young, so the age structure of a country can influence these figures. An ageing workforce can mask an underlying shift to more insecure jobs. When the effect of age is controlled for, in 8 out of 14 European countries there is actually a reduction in average employee tenure.[9] In the USA, for example, despite the ageing of the workforce, the average male median job tenure fell from 4.0 years in 1992 to 3.8 years in 1998. Econometric analysis shows that the tenure of young workers has declined in all countries considered except in Portugal. Younger workers are considered to be confronting a labour-market entry problem, queuing for more permanent jobs, but only having to do so temporarily (even though their stay on the outside is being prolonged).

Employment tenure operates counter-cyclically such that it decreases when employment growth is strong and increases when job creation slackens. In tight labour markets – when employment growth is strong and there are more job changes taking place – more workers may leave their jobs but fewer are dismissed, while in loose markets the opposite happens. This counter-cyclical behaviour of average employment tenure figures suggests that labour markets are driven more by the supply side (expectations of workers) rather than the demand side (expectations of firms) factors. Moreover, in the majority of countries employees with higher educational attainment have lower employment tenure than do workers with less education.[10] The decline in employment tenure up to the late 1990s may then just reflect economic growth and educational advancement over this period rather than a structural shift towards job instability.

The problem with the above data is that they are based on average employment tenure as it is accumulated today. Other measures of the stability of the employment relationship consider the probability that an individual will still be with their employer in the future (a calculated retention rate), i.e. how long will their employment relationship ultimately last? Even if accumulated tenure is stable, eventual tenure could shorten the probability of keeping a job significantly. Analyses of these 'disaggregated retention rates' by the OECD also show stability from the 1980s to the early 1990s.[11] There are some important exceptions, however. In the USA retention rates have declined significantly among young workers, and notably for those with lower education and from non-white ethnic groups.[12]

A final area of data on job stability examines *separation rates* (the rate at which individuals leave or are dismissed by their employer). These can be broken down into moves from employment to employment and employment to non-employment (which are further broken down to employment to unemployment and employment to inactivity moves). The incidence of employment to unemployment moves generally declined over the 1990s as employment growth was experienced in most countries. Involuntary separations became more marked for older and longer-tenured employees in the USA.[13] The flow of people out from employment to inactivity usually follows economic cycles, but in the UK, Ireland and Spain there has been a steady flow of around 4 per cent (3 per cent in Ireland) per year regardless of fluctuations in economic activity. In the UK rates of outflow from employment to inactivity are higher than outflows to unemployment. International differences in this last outflow tend to reflect institutional arrangements and measures of unemployment and invalidity.

Short-term instability is also assessed by looking at the failure rates of 'new job matches'. This is calculated for the interval between one and two years of tenure based on OECD data.[14] What percentage of workers with less than one year's tenure will fail to stay longer than two years within the same firm? The answer in 1998 for Spain, for example, was 63.1 per cent. In the USA the figure was 65.9 per cent in 1995. For most countries the figure is between 30 and 40 per cent. In Britain failure rates were 40.5 per cent in the mid-1980s falling slightly to 36.8 per cent by 1998.

Of interest too are generational cohort differences in job stability. Pollock's[15] analysis of the British Household Panel Survey – a national census which examines various socio-economic issues – provides an insight into labour market stability. Looking across generational cohorts, the percentage who have experienced only one employment status was only 28 per cent for the 1920s cohort, rising to 37 per cent for the 1930s cohort and peaking at 71 per cent for the 1940s cohort. It fell away again to 53 per cent for the 1950s cohort and 34 per cent for the 1960s cohort. Clearly, the 'traditional' employment contract was a historical blip, as noted by Cappelli.

However, it should be noted that while the evidence shows that the level of job change is not as drastic as some commentators suggest:

1 Within the job there is evidence of an acceleration of work role change, which can be just as destabilizing (see Chapter 6 and the discussion of work role transition theory)
2 Between generations there is evidence of an increase in the number of job positions held by young cohorts (see Chapter 10 and evidence from social surveys).

Therefore, we end this chapter by briefly considering work from sectors of the economy that might provide some more insight into the nature of the changing employment relationship and by noting some of the risks associated with this.

Changes in commitment?

At the same time that these changes in the type of jobs and stability of job tenure were happening, there were – at least potentially – significant changes in the experience of work for employees. Gallie, Felstead and Green[16] have produced a useful analysis of the link between employer policies and organizational commitment in Britain. They point out that the late 1980s and early 1990s were characterized by the advocacy of a new management philosophy (well, a philosophy that began in the USA in the late 1970s but was still being debated in the UK until recently) that involved a shift from control to commitment. There has been much debate about the particular policies – or bundles of policies – that together represent the existence of a high-commitment management philosophy. However, Gallie and colleagues focus on three key aspects of the employment relationship:

1 *Enrichment of jobs and enhanced employee discretion through skill development*: Following the logic of job design theory,[17] organizations offer more intrinsically more satisfying work and the potential for career advancement and also devolve responsibility for more task decisions. This task discretion is considered necessary to cope with the demands of sophisticated technologies and high quality, but also has the effect of enhancing the skills development of employees, generating greater satisfaction with the work task and lead to closer identification with the employer.
2 *Work control through a more distant relationship*: Traditional work control through directive supervision and machine pacing is replaced by a 'longer-distance' system[18] whereby line managers exert control by becoming more involved in personnel management matters (such as appraisals of performance and career development reviews).
3 *Mechanisms of employee involvement*: Following the logic of participative management[19], organizations develop procedures for involving employees in a wider set of decisions. This either involves providing regular channels of information feedback, or allowing employees greater opportunity to express views and solve problems through the use of quality circles or wider consultative meetings.

Gallie and colleagues, drawing principally upon the work of Wood[20], sum up the subsequent testing of whether there has been any evidence of such changes on a significant scale as follows:

> '. . . While there has been some scepticism in the literature about whether employers have coherent strategies on labour management issues, the evidence does show a tendency for many of the presumed commitment practices to be found together in the way that might be anticipated if there were some sort of strategic orientation'.[21]

A fundamentally important question to answer is whether or not there has been any impact on commitment as a result of changes at the work practice level. Has there been any increased identification of employees with their employers? This is a difficult question to answer because individuals have different perceptions of common changes. This formed the subject of Chapter 2, but more formal HRM research by Burchell, Rubery and colleagues[22] has also shown that individuals differ in their perceptions of the skill level of their job, the availability of career opportunities and the quality of relations between the organization and its employees. Practices generally differ markedly within an organization across different sectors, units or indeed teams. To assume that perceptions of the gap between the rhetoric of organizational practice and the reality as experienced by employees are based on an objective assessment assumes that there is remarkable transparency of practice.

It is also clear that there are differences across particular sectors and segments of the workforce. In the UK heightened perceptions of job insecurity are apparent among: higher-paid occupations (now only slightly less likely to express dissatisfaction with job insecurity than those in other occupations); fixed-term contract, casual and agency employees; freelancing workers in sectors such as publishing and television; the banking sector; central government services (as a result of market testing and competitive tendering processes); and privatized utilities.[23]

One way of sensing whether there may have been any significant change overall is to compare the results of similar surveys over time. The problem is that even longitudinal data seems to present a conflicting picture of changes in job satisfaction.[24] Longitudinal data provided by the OECD indicates that during the economic recovery from 1992 to 1996 the percentage of British workers worried about the future of their organization fell from 52 per cent to 47 per cent, but the percentage reporting satisfaction with their job security also fell from 52 per cent to 43 per cent.[25] Between 1985 and 1995 British workers registered the sharpest decline of confidence in employment security in Europe. Data from the British Social Attitudes Survey also show that while perceptions of insecurity vary in line with the level of unemployment, there has been an underlying upward trend since the early 1980s and these concerns are associated with lower levels of commitment in general and commitment to the current employer.[26] The pessimistic view is also exemplified by research funded by the Economic and Social Research Council Future of Work programme (we explore findings from this programme more fully in Chapter 9). Longitudinal comparison of data from a 1992 and a 2001 survey designed by the Policy Studies Institute and a team from the London School of Economics suggests that British workers are becoming more dissatisfied with long working hours and growing work pressures, and this is having serious repercussions on their motivation at work. A national survey of 2500 employees found that only 20 per cent of male employees who took part in the 2001 survey were either 'completely satisfied' or 'very satisfied' with their working hours. This compared with 35 per cent who took part in a similar survey in 1992. The attitudes of female employees are rapidly converging with men. In 1992, 51 per cent were satisfied, but this plummeted to 29 per cent in the more recent survey. Workers of all ages, in private and public sectors, were affected. The researchers concluded that the most dissatisfied workers were those who were highly qualified or formed the 'elite' part of the workforce. People claimed to be working long hours to earn extra money (30 per cent) and to improve their chances of promotion (14 per cent). However, most people working long hours said they had little choice: 58 per cent said it was simply required by the job while 14 per cent said they could lose their job if they refused.

In contrast, work carried out by Guest and colleagues[27] for the Chartered Institute of Personnel and Development (CIPD) in the UK found that job satisfaction for those working in the private sector in the UK actually rose marginally from 6.87 to 7.20 (out of 10) from 1998 to 2001. Indeed, these surveys suggest that the negative impacts on the psychological contract have been relatively constrained to a small proportion of the workforce. For example, in terms of job insecurity the 1997 data showed that only 14 per cent of UK employees felt fairly or very insecure in their present job and only 24 per cent fairly or very worried by this. Sixty-nine per cent had left their last job through personal choice, 58 per cent had only worked for one organization in the past five years and 56 per cent expected to stay with their current employer for the next five years. Employees on atypical contracts, including temporary and fixed-term contracts, were no more likely to report feelings of insecurity. Insecurity was more a concern, not surprisingly, for older and longer-service employees. It was not a generic labour market phenomenon. Guest concludes:

> ... much of the management of job security lies in the hands of management ... [they should] build confidence about future expecta-tions of employment security, should build and maintain a positive psychological contract, should promote progressive human resource policies and practices, including guarantees of no compulsory redun-dancies and should create a climate of high employee involvement.[28]

These findings have been generally interpreted by the HRM community as providing evidence that there has likely been a positive impact of a series of 'high-commitment work practices' and that these have mediated many of the adverse changes in the nature of employment.[29]

Gallie and colleagues[30] have tried to unravel what might be happening here by comparing the findings of the Employment in Britain Survey conducted in 1992[31] and the Skills Survey conducted in 1997,[32] based on samples of 3469 and 2224 employees respectively. Both surveys contained comparable measures of organizational commitment and perceptions of a range of management practices (we explore the different forms of organizational commitment further in Chapter 8). They measured commitment in terms of the level of identification that employees had with the organization and the acceptance of organizational goals. The questions tapped the willingness to work harder to help the organization, take any job offered within the organization and turn down outside employment, feelings of loyalty and pride, and congruence of values. There was some variation between 1992 and 1997 in these items but overall the findings showed remarkable consistency. In both years a majority of employees expressed a generally positive view of their organization on four out of six items. Only a minority, however, showed strong commitment. Commitment had fallen slightly for men over the years and remained the same for women, but at a higher level than for men. It was at a relatively low level for younger employees.

> ... When commitment was linked to potential costs in terms of the quality of the job or loss of potentially higher pay with another employer, only about a quarter of employees emerge as committed to any degree, and only about 5 per cent were strongly committed. It is

clear, then, that while there is little evidence that British employees are hostile to their organizations, there is little sign of strong positive commitment.[33]

Given that commitment has not risen, is this to do with any increase or decrease in the nature of work practices and the levels of job enrichment, control and involvement associated with these practices? The data showed that the apparent stability in commitment levels over time actually reflected a complex pattern of underlying change.

First, in terms of *job enrichment* there had been a general rise in skill levels between 1992 and 1997. The length of training required for jobs and the time needed for people to feel that they could do their job well have risen. More than 60 per cent of employees considered that the skill requirements of work had increased and only 9 per cent that their jobs had been deskilled. These changes in skill levels were driven by the need for employers to make use of new technologies. Upward change in skill level was an important predictor of commitment level. However, increasing skill level in jobs had not been associated with increased task discretion. Contrary to what might be expected on the basis of high-commitment theory, the trend from 1992 to 1997 was for there to be a reduction in the scope for decision making by employees, particularly for decisions that affected the quality of work. Employees in intermediate, semi-routine and routine jobs had experienced the greatest decline in the ability to exercise their own judgement. Not surprisingly, higher task discretion was associated with higher commitment. Therefore, the stable levels in employee commitment in fact hide positive changes in skill level of job but negative changes in the level of discretion afforded to employees.

In terms of *control of work performance* there was evidence of an overall tightening of control. Changes in controls arising from machine pace, clients and supervisors were relatively small. However, there was increased control in the form of pressure from fellow workers (likely due to an expansion of the role of work teams as a consequence of decentralization and delayering) and through an individualization of payment systems. Where there was more control through 'longer-distance' high-commitment work practices there were increases in commitment, but where there was more control through pay incentives there were decreases.

Finally, what was the impact of changes in forms of *participation and employee involvement*? The existence of meetings for diffusing information or for dialogue between management and employees was positively associated with greater commitment, while trade union membership was associated with lower commitment (this of course likely reflects a defence mechanism for employee in poor-quality work relationships). In general there have been modest increases in positive forms of participation, exerting an upward influence on commitment.

The final analysis showed that '. . . declining task discretion has played the major role in preventing a substantial rise in organizational commitment . . . changing forms of control make a further negative contribution'.[34] Management views appear to be in a state of flux on the relative advantages and disadvantages of giving greater decision-making responsibility to employees in order for them to use their skills as opposed to using tighter surveillance and control to increase a sense of predictability in this uncertain world. In the opening chapter we noted the pressures placed upon organizations caused by the speed of change impacting them. The pursuit of downsizing and the intensification of work effort has not created the best conditions for implementing high commitment work practices in a coherent and sensible way. As Gallie and colleagues conclude:

> . . . Organizational pressures may then have combined with techno-
> logical opportunity to swing the balance from empowerment to control,
> irrespective of the costs in terms of the commitment of employees to
> their organizations.[35]

A future model?

The risk, then, is that new technologies continue to create the conditions in which positive gains in the employment relationship are masked by ill-considered HR strategies. We have concentrated in this chapter by reviewing what appears to have happened to date, but what does the immediate future perhaps hold in store? When researchers attempt to understand some future patterns in terms of flexible employment they tend to have focused on developments in the employment relationship in Silicon Valley. Silicon Valley is considered to be a trend setter both for the USA and also for the world for two main reasons:

1 It is a new industrial region formed in the latter half of the last century that has gone through a number of industrial adaptations and business reorganizations associated with the information age. Its work patterns are therefore particularly visible.
2 It is an established centre of innovation and production in global high-technology industries for both the manufacturing and the service sectors. These industries are characterized by the advanced use of their own products in the delivery of their own management processes before such innovations are spread elsewhere.

Indeed, Bridges's[36] discussion of employability in which employees have to enhance their knowledge, skills and experience, thereby developing a portfolio of competencies in order to remain attractive in the marketplace, drew many examples from Silicon Valley. Guest[37] points out of course that Britain is not Silicon Valley. Silicon Valley is just one vision of the world and its practices are not yet widely shared nor practised. We need to be careful not to extrapolate behaviours from here to other contexts. However, Guest notes the beginnings of some parallel developments in the behaviour of UK employees:

. . . Young workers focused on their employability in the labour market, and as a result were quite prepared to move between organizations and at the same time report high levels of security. In contrast, some older workers appeared to define security more traditionally in terms of job security and although they had not experienced job loss, insecurity derived from the possible threat of the loss of a long-held job in a specific organization. By implication, those who think and act in terms of employability may feel less insecure. Of course, in a national employment culture that gives primacy to younger workers, this may be much easier for them than for those who, chronologically or psychologically, feel older.[38]

Carnoy and colleagues, on the other hand, argue, that with all due consideration given to the adaptations that are necessary in specific institutional environments, Silicon Valley is nonetheless of interest because it represents '. . . the laboratory of a new technological paradigm that is spreading worldwide'[39] (see Box 4.2). We examine the reality of developments

---

Box 4.2   Flexible employment in Silicon Valley

Temporary help services (THS) are the most visible form of flexible employment. In the USA employment in THS agencies has grown by 48 per cent since 1989 and employment in THS has tripled, while overall employment has grown by around 20 per cent. However, at any one point in time THS employment accounts for only 1 per cent of total US employment. In Santa Clara County, however, THS employment is roughly three times the national average, having grown from 1.6 per cent to 3.4 per cent of the county's total employment. From 1984 to 1995 THS employment in the county grew by 127 per cent compared to 7.5 per cent in total employment. Thirteen per cent of these jobs were in technical and related occupations – three times the rate elsewhere in the USA – and 6 per cent were in professional specialist services. In terms of part-time employment, the California Employment Department estimated that the number of part-time employees grew from 1 639 000 to 2 494 000 from 1975 to 1993 with little change in the proportion of part-time to full-time employees. Depending on definitions, the upper boundary suggests that 40 per cent of total employment in Santa Clara County is flexible, falling to 27 per cent with a more conservative definition. Flexible employment is growing at from 2.5 to 5 times the rate of overall employment, accounting for more than one half of all growth in employment in the last ten years. Janitors rank eighth in terms of employment growth by occupational category with more new positions than computer programmers and systems analysts.

Source: Carnoy *et al.*[39]

in Silicon Valley not to suggest that the concepts of employability will automatically sweep the world, but to demonstrate the complex behaviours and widely differing employment outcomes that exist when an employability mindset is pursued.

Building on the earlier comments that for some individuals non-standard contracts represent a form of flexibility and entrepreneurship that is desirable, attention has been given to the ways in which individual workers market their 'human capital portfolio' among various 'buyers' and balance the competing risks and returns of doing this. In markets where skills become obsolete quickly, such an employment relationship lowers the risk for workers because it takes the skill formation process out of the hands of the employer. They examined the experiences of flexible employees – individuals hired through temporary employment agencies, directly by firms on a temporary, contract or project basis, and part-time employees – by examining regional data and interviewing actors in leading employment and electronics agencies to understand their human resource strategy.

The THS agencies consider that virtually any skill can be, and is, provided on a temporary basis. They are entering into long-term contracts with major organizations, signalling their view that the use of temporary workers has become a permanent strategy for organizations. They use partnership programmes to place dedicated managers on-site to manage sourced employees. These partnership programmes account for around 20 per cent of THS business now. THS agencies have also developed 'secondary sourcing' arrangements where they enter into long-term contracts with smaller, more specialized agencies that can be called on to meet the demands of complex contracts. The labour market strategies of employing organizations reflected this shift. The principal concern was the undesirably high rate of turnover in high-skilled positions, and organizations were designing flexible compensation and training schemes in order to make these employees less flexible. However, the price of lowering turnover among creative employees was considered to be too high, and so more attention was paid to recruitment. Intangible benefits resulted from this flow of labour, notably in terms of extensive communication between organizations due to individuals moving, more rapid diffusion of innovations through the local economy, and bright career paths for the more highly skilled.[40] A strategy of 'blow and go fast' and a culture of 'temporariness' was an inevitable consequence of the inability to match the demands of the more high-value employees, but also reinforced the trend towards sub-contracting non-core activities such as cafeteria services, building maintenance, security, construction and so forth. A number of lessons about labour flexibility have been drawn from the experience of Silicon Valley.

1 Benefits of flexible labour do not automatically all accrue to organizations. For a proportion of the workforce there are some significant financial and social capital gains.
2 The success of individuals in flexible labour markets depends to a certain extent on their skill levels, but even more on their networks of relationships

and contacts outside their place of work. Reputation and connections spread through a network of firms increases employability. This, strangely, seems to be as true of high-skill employees as it is of janitors, who are organized primarily through social ties with immigrant Latino communities.[41]

In a similar analysis of some of the more extreme US experiences, *The Economist* concentrated on the situation in California in 2000[42] and changes in career behaviour. They described what they called 'The Palo Alto Career' (see Box 4.3). Since this time the collapse of the stock market has likely introduced a little more reality into the situation. This analysis considers that we will see individuals who can market a 'personal brand' and another class of 'no-brand' individuals.

However, this individual brand reputation strategy alluded to in Box 4.3 was not something that all employees experienced. For the 'no-brand' employee – in reality the majority – the risks were high. The biggest changes in work patterns in California in fact were experienced at the top – but also at the bottom – of the income scale. For example, the poorest 20 per cent of Silicon Valley households actually saw their real income fall by 8 per cent between 1991 and 1997 while income for the richest 20 per cent in the Valley grew by 19 per cent. Even by 2000 many employees faced the risk of low pay and a fistful

---

Box 4.3   The Palo Alto Career?

By 2000 the median job tenure for Californian workers was only three years. Nearly half of the Californian workforce had been with their employer for less than 2 years. Only 20 per cent had more than 10 years' tenure compared to the national average in the US of 33 per cent. However, one sixth of the adult population reported either losing their job or moving because they were about to lose their job within the last 3 years. The temporary employment sector had added as many jobs as the software and electronics sectors combined. However, Internet-based recruitment was having an effect on the volume of 'job trading' in California. The turnover rate was 20 per cent a year – with many employees moving to 'see how much I am really worth'. An example of how the labour market was operating was Icarian, a just-in-time jobs agency that sold employees to computer manufacturers, drug and finance businesses. They would summons freelance engineers at $90–200 an hour, technical writers at $75–150 an hour, marketing directors at $200–500 an hour and chief executives at $300–800 an hour. The prices reflected a starting position before equity stakes were negotiated. Talent agents were able to offer a package for their 'stars' and individuals were marketed on the basis of a strong 'brand value'.

Source: The Economist.[42]

of worthless stock options. Indeed, the computer industry and telecoms industry were even by that stage the third and fourth largest downsizers in the USA.

Or a risk of economic apartheid?

In conclusion, we return to the *societal dimension* of the trends outlined in the previous two chapters. We can see increasing evidence of social exclusion in terms for example of the job stability data for less-educated and less-privileged job groups. It is also argued that social exclusion exists on a global scale, but we are also faced with a paradox. Economic regeneration – and lest we allow discussion of the negative aspects of the new employment relationship to allow us to forget this, we should note that there is much of this taking place – is coming hand in hand with economic apartheid. For example, in the USA in 1998 385 000 manufacturing jobs disappeared, but more than 3 million new jobs were created. Key growth occupations include software programmers, management consultants, amusement park workers, mortgage lenders and temporary employees. By 1999 US unemployment had fallen to its lowest level (below 4 per cent) since the 1960s.[43] Participation rates were growing (the US workforce grew by 1 per cent in real terms in 1998) and wage levels are rising by about 3 per cent a year. But all was not well, as events a couple of years later were to reveal.

As we have seen, there has been considerable growth in part-time work and some of this has been involuntary. Freeman[44] conducted an economic analysis of the dangers of what he terms an apartheid employment contract. This shows that the problem facing the USA is not one of creating jobs but one of making work pay. He argues that comments about rising inequality, stagnant real wages, a declining middle class, high levels of child poverty, insecure workers, a waning union movement, homeless people in every city, bursting jails and prisons, and a fraying social safety net are not the products of soapbox radicalism or neo-Marxian philosophy. They simply reflect characteristics of life in the USA as we move into the twenty-first century. From 1910 to 1973 the average employee enjoyed substantial gains in real earnings (wage increases of 2 per cent per year leading to a doubling of generational income every 35 years) and leisure time. But from 1979 to the mid-1990s median earnings of male employees dropped by 13 per cent. Moreover, inequalities grew in this period. If the $2 trillion increase in GDP from 1980 to 1994 had been divided equally, each US family would have gained $2000. Instead, median family income was stagnant. The proportion of aggregate income for the top 5 per cent rose from 15.3 per cent to 19.1 per cent from 1980 to 1993, while the proportion going to 80 per cent of families fell. Nearly a decade of gains in GDP and in employment were accompanied by falling incomes for the bottom half of US families. The decline of trade unionism in the USA from 30 per cent to 11 per cent of the private sector accounts for about one fifth of the rise of inequality of earnings. Incarcerating a criminal costs roughly as much per year as sending someone to Harvard and in California more money is spent on the prison budget than on higher education. There are notable international differences in the purchasing power of the lowest paid. US workers in the bottom 10 per cent earn less real pay than in other countries – low-paid German workers earn 2.2 times more and low-paid Norwegians 1.8 times more. About one third of US workers are paid less (in purchasing power units) than comparable workers overseas. Freeman asks whether the continuance of what has become a low-cost structure and contingent workforce employment strategy will lead to a readjustment of expectations. In the next chapter we consider the evidence on trust, insecurity and transition at work.

References

1. Auer, P. and Cazes, S. (2000). The resilience of the long-term employment relationship: evidence from the industrialised countries. *International Labour Review, 139 (4)*, 379–408
2. Cappelli, P. (1999). *The new deal at work*. Boston, MA: Harvard Univesity Press.
3. Heery, E. and Salmon, J. (2000). The insecurity thesis. In E. Heery and J. Salmon (Eds.), *The insecure workforce*. London: Routledge.
4. Gallie, D., White, M., Cheng, Y. and Tomlinson, M. (1998). *Restructuring the employment relationship*. Oxford: Oxford University Press.
5. Auer and Cazes (2000). *Op. cit.*
6. Roberts, Z. (2001). UK businesses sustain their highest labour turnover costs. *People Management, 7 (20)*, p. 11.
7. Capelli (1999). *Op. cit.*
8. Stroh, L.K., Brett, J.M. and Reilly, A.H. (1994). A decade of change: managers' attachment to their organizations and their jobs, *Human Resource Management, 33*, 531–548.
9. Auer, P., Cazes, S. and Spiezia, V. (2001). *Stable or unstable jobs: interpreting the evidence in industrialized countries*. Employment Paper Series. Geneva: International Labour Organization.
10. Burgess, S. and Rees, H. (1998). A disaggregate analysis of the evolution of job tenure in Britain, 1975–1993. *British Journal of Industrial Relations, 36 (4)*, 629–655.
11. OECD (1997). *Employment outlook*. Paris: OECD.
12. Diebold, F.X., Neumark, D. and Polsky, D. (1997). Job stability in the US. *Journal of Labor Economics, 15 (2)*, 206–235.
13. Auer and Cazes (2000). *Op. cit.*
14. Gregg, P. and Wadsworth, J. (1995). A short history of labour turnover, job tenure, and job security, 1975–93. *Oxford Review of Economic Policy, 11 (1)*, 73–90.
15. Pollock, G. (1997). Uncertain futures: young people in and out of employment since 1940. *Work, Employment and Society, 11 (4)*, 615–638.

16. Gallie, D., Felstead, A. and Green, F. (2001). Employer policies and organizational commitment in Britain 1992–97. *Journal of Management Studies, 38 (8)*, 1081–1101.
17. Lawler, E. (1986). *High involvement management*. San Francisco: Jossey-Bass.; Lawler, E., Mohrman, S.A. and Ledford, G.E. (1995). *Creating high performance organizations*. San Francisco: Jossey-Bass.
18. Storey, J. (1983). *Managerial prerogative and the question of control*. London: Routledge and Kegan Paul.
19. Blumberg, P. (1968). *Industrial democracy: the sociology of participation*. London: Constable.
20. Wood, S. (1999). Getting the measure of the transformed high-performance organization. *British Journal of Industrial Relations, 37 (3)*, 391–417; Wood, S. and Albanese, M.T. (1995). Can we speak of a high commitment management on the shop floor? *Journal of Management Studies, 32 (2)*, 215–47; Wood, S. and De Menezes, L. (1998). High commitment management in the UK: evidence from the Workplace Industrial Relations Survey and Employers' Manpower and Skills Practices Survey. *Human Relations, 51*, 485–515.
21. Gallie *et al.* (2001). *Op. cit.*
22. Burchell, B. and Rubery, J. (1994). Internal labour markets from managers' and employees' perspectives. In J. Rubery and F. Wilkinson (Eds.). *Employer strategy and the labour market*. Oxford: Oxford University Press; Burchell, B., Elliott, J. and Rubery, J. (1994). Perceptions of the labour market: an investigation of differences by geneder and by working-time. In Rubery and Wilkinson (Eds.) *Op. cit.*
23. Heery and Salmon (2000). *Op. cit.*
24. Philpott, J. (2002) Can't get no satisfaction. *People Management, 8 (11)*, 20.
25. OECD (1997). *Employment outlook*. Paris: OECD.
26. Bryson, A. and McKay, S. (1997). What about the workers? In R. Jowell, J. Curtice, A. Park, L. Brook, K. Thomson and C. Bryson (Eds.), *British social attitudes: the 14th report*. Aldershot: Ashgate.
27. See Guest, D. (1999). Human resource management – the worker's verdict. *Human Resource Management Journal, 9 (3)*, 5–25; Guest, D. and Conway, N. (1998). *Employee motivation and the psychological contract*. London: Institute of Personnel and Development; Guest, D. and Conway, N. (1999). *Fairness at work and the psychological contract*. London: Institute of Personnel and development; Guest, D., Conway, N., Briner, R. and Dickmann, M. (1996). *The state of the psychological contract in employment*. London: Institute of Personnel and Development.
28. Guest, D. (2000). Management and the insecure workforce: the search for a new psychological contract. In E. Heery and J. Salmon (Eds.), *The insecure workforce*. London: Routledge, p. 144.
29. Gallie, *et al.* (2001). *Op. cit.*
30. *Ibid.*
31. Gallie, D., White, M., Cheng, Y. and Tomlinson, M. (1998). *Restructuring the employment relationship*. Oxford: Clarendon Press.

32. Ashton, D., Davies, B., Felstead, A. and Green, F. (1999). *Work skills in Britain*. Oxford: Centre for Skills, Knowledge and Organizational Performance.
33. Gallie *et al.* (2001). *Op. cit.* p. 1086.
34. *Ibid.* p. 1095.
35. *Ibid.* p. 1097.
36. Bridges, W. (1995). *Job shift: how to prosper in a workplace without jobs*. Reading, MA: Addison-Wesley.
37. Guest, (2000). *Op. cit.*
38. *Ibid.* p. 147.
39. Carnoy, M., Castells, M. and Benner, C. (1997). Labour markets and employment practices in the age of flexibility: a case study of Silicon Valley. *International Labour Review, 136 (1)*, 27–48, p. 28.
40. Saxenian, A. (1994). *Regional advantage: culture and competition in Silicon Valley and Route 128*. Cambridge, MA: Harvard University Press.
41. Granovetter, M.S. (1995). *Getting a job: a study of contacts and careers*. Chicago: University of Chicago Press.
42. *The Economist* (2000). The future of work: career evolution. *The Economist, 354*, No. 8155, 29 January, 113–115.
43. *Wall Street Journal* (1999). The outlook: the blessings of low unemployment. *Wall Street Journal, 233 (55)*, A1.
44. Freeman, R.B. (1996). Toward an apartheid economy? *Harvard Business Review*, September-October, 114–121.

5

Quality of the Employment Relationship: Trust and Job Insecurity

Quality of the employment relationship: social climate factors

In Chapter 2 we concentrated on the nature of the psychological contract and in the previous two chapters we have explored the end-of-jobs and job insecurity theses in more detail. We now turn to the topic of insecurity from a psychological perspective, and highlight our views on perceptions of trust and justice, the experience of downsizing, and the nature of job insecurity. It has long been recognized that positive attitudes of employees and contributions from them that go beyond their prescribed and contractually enforceable roles is a source of competitive advantage, but given the recent changes in the employment relationship renewed attention has been paid to the challenge of understanding and explaining the motivational basis of such positive attitudes and behaviour.[1] In Chapter 2 we drew attention to the role of social exchange in the employment relationship and pointed out that this is based on a longer-term trust-based one, predicated on the perception of fair treatment. In order for there to be a social exchange, the employee has to be able to trust others to discharge their obligations. In this chapter we examine a range of factors that act as important precursors to there being a healthy psychological contract at work, what we call social climate factors, as well as a series of significant outcomes that result from it – what we describe as organizational–individual linkages and concentrate on some of the social climate factors. In Chapter 8 we will consider the role played by a series of important individual–organizational linkages.

A number of factors set the *social climate* of the organization. This determines whether any significant exchange relationship and subsequent linkage between the individual and the organization is likely to be developed or maintained.[2] The 'social exchange relationship at work' has mainly been examined in relation to four factors that mediate the quality of the exchange:

1 The content of, and perceived breach in various forms of justice (see, for example, the work of Cropanzano;[3] Greenberg;[4] and Sheppard[5])

2 The support received from the organization, using the construct of Perceived Oanizational Support (POS).[6] This describes the quality of the employee–organization relationship. It is defined as a general perception by the employee of the extent to which the organization values their general contribution and cares about their well-being.

3 The support received from the supervisory relationship, using the construct of Leader–Member Exchange (LMX). This describes the quality of a relationship between a supervisor and an employee.[7]

4 The level of *trust* that exists in the relationship and the changing nature of trust (see, for example, the work of Konovsky and Whitener,[8] Bradach and Eccles;[9] Clark and Payne;[10] and Miles and Creed[11]). *Trust* in this context can be defined as '. . . the willingness of a party to be vulnerable to the actions of another party based on the expectation that the other party will perform a certain action important to the trustor irrespective of the ability to monitor or control the other party'.[12]

We focus in this chapter mainly on the role of justice perceptions and trust. However, in this opening section we briefly mention 'perceived organizational support'. One way of asking whether the research on the psychological contract presented in Chapter 2 actually affords us with a useful way of examining the employment relation is to ask if it helps to explain more behaviour and important organizational outcomes than can be done by using other existing constructs. Does the psychological contract account for useful *additional variance* in outcome behaviours when it is measured side by side with them? Coyle-Shapiro and Kessler argue that it does indeed have additional value over other constructs.[13] This is because the psychological contract is not just concerned with some of the individual constructs considered in this chapter, such as satisfaction, trust, justice and commitment. It of course involves an assessment of the 'fairness' of how a person is treated as well as the amount of trust that is involved in the relationship but it is a more holistic assessment of the 'deal' than this. Therefore, while organizational commitment might be construed as an 'input' to organizational performance provided by an employee, Millward and Brewerton argue that the psychological contract can be used to analyse the whole framework of perceived 'exchangeable' terms across the relational to transactional continuum.[14] Many academics therefore feel that the concept of the contract may be used to predict both employee and employer behaviour, and may also help in explaining the causal processes involved in contract development and violation. Recent research has therefore attempted to break the psychological contract down into a range of related elements, and has then examined the relationship between each element.

Coyle-Shapiro and Kessler[15] pointed out that we should make a distinction between perceived organizational support and the fulfilment of obligations in the psychological contract. Separating out the fulfilment of obligations within the psychological contract, from the perception of organizational support, is an important distinction to make in terms of the new employment relationship. An organization may not be able to offer jobs for life and may engage in more transactional relationships, but may still be capable of showing (or may be perceived as being able to show) high levels of personal support to the employee. They examined the consequences of both on 'organizational citizenship behaviours' and 'commitment', and asked whether perceived organizational support mediated the impact that the fulfilment of obligations and promises has on important psychological outcomes. Psychological contract fulfilment did indeed account for unique and additional variance in explaining levels of commitment and organizational citizenship behaviour, showing that it is a useful construct.

So, perhaps not unexpectedly, having helped to reveal some of the important psychological processes that regulate, legitimate and enact the employment relationship, researchers now find themselves wanting to do three things:

1 To continue to open up the black box that resides within the construct of the psychological contract and to understand in particular the ways in which it influences several other 'deep' structures such as *emotions* and *identity at work*. What are the real consequences of shifts in the psychological contract at work?
2 To explore the issue of *mutual ethicality* and *integrity of one's own actions* within the new employment relationship (do unto others as others do unto you, or perhaps not). What are the new bounds of employee behaviour in a more individualized employment relationship?
3 To consider not just the employee side of the psychological contract, but to understand this in the context of what is happening to the employer side of the relationship. How does an individual's own psychological contract and identity seem to influence the way that they construct and evaluate *the employer's perspective of the contract*, and vice versa?

As researchers have turned their attention to how you try to manage the psychological contract, it has raised some important questions. Coyle-Shapiro has asked whether we should we conceptualize the psychological contract as a dyad between the employee and their manager, or as a global construct between managers in general (as employer representatives) and representatives of the organization. How does a manager's own individual psychological contract influence what they see and interpret as the employer's obligations to employees?

The role of organizational justice

Some of the current business trends – explored in the two previous chapters – suggest that perceptions of injustice might become more common within today's employment relationship and that of the future. Kickul and colleagues[16] summarize the situation as follows:

> . . . Budgetary constraints are forcing organizations to expect, or in many cases higher, output from a smaller workforce. These expectations necessitate longer working hours for employees. Longer working hours are likely to produce perceptions of injustice since many employees are placing a premium on achieving more balance between work and family life. Increased competitive pressures and rising health care costs have also forced employers to rely more on the contingent workforce [and a] reluctance to pay employee benefits may also create feelings of perceived injustice.

Moreover, many HR textbooks start from the assumption that:

> . . . workers have the right to be upset and angry. They have been bought and sold and have seen their friends and relations fired and laid off in large numbers. There is little bond between employers and employee anymore.[17]

A lot of attention has therefore been given to the relationship between employee perceptions of fair or unfair treatment and subsequent work behaviour and performance, associated, in particular with the work of Folger, McFarlin, Sweeney, Konovsky, Cropanzano and Greenberg.[18] This has been conducted under the label *organizational justice theory* and focuses on the perception that the individual or a group has of the fairness of treatment that they have received from the organization and the behavioural reactions that follow from these perceptions. Justice is seen as having three main dimensions (see Box 5.1).

We ended Chapter 2 by discussing some of the behavioural and emotional reactions that follow from a breach of psychological contract. Considerable attention has been given to understanding which management actions can help to moderate these negative reactions. One of the areas of investigation has been to see if the judgement that employees come to in their mind about how fairly people were treated by the organization makes any difference to their eventual behaviour. This is called their *cognitive assessment*. Where the individual perceives that there were unfair procedures and treatment (i.e. low levels of procedural and interactional justice) then more intense feelings of anger and resentment result. Morrison and Robinson[23] predict that feelings of violation and the associated negative employee attitudes will be influenced by judgements about the outcome (perceived breach), the procedures implemented (procedural justice), and the quality of interpersonal

---

Box 5.1   Three dimensions of organizational justice

Most researchers now concentrate on three different types of justice within organizations which all relate to perceptions of social exchange:[19]

Distributive: The degree to which the employee perceives the distribution of praise, rewards, workloads or other organizational demands and rewards among members to be fair, i.e. the perceived fairness of the outcomes that the employee receives. Draws upon Adams' equity theory[20] of social exchange which proposes that people compare the ratio of their own inputs and outcomes according to the match between the inputs and outcomes of each party.

Procedural: The degree to which the application of organizational rules and procedures is perceived by the employee to be fair and consistent, i.e. perceived fairness of the means used to achieve the above outcomes. Concerns structures and systems. Leventhal[21] proposed that fair procedures are characterized by: consistency of implementation; impartiality; basing decisions on accurate information; mechanisms to correct inappropriate decisions; voice opportunities that allow employees to have their input into decisions or have their concerns represented; and compatibility with current ethical and moral standards.

Interactional: The degree to which an employee can openly communicate with his or her manager and trust him or her, i.e. the quality of interpersonal treatment received at the hands of decision makers. Bies and Moag[22] distinguished the nature of formal organizational procedures from the way in which they are enacted. Involves concerns about inter-personal treatment. This form of justice includes two elements: whether the individual feels that the reasons underlying a resource allocation were clearly and adequately explained to them; and whether those responsible for implementing a decision treated them with dignity and respect.

---

treatment received from the organization and its agents (interactional justice).

An important challenge for researchers is to find out which type of injustices have the greatest impact on the psychological contract. Paterson and colleagues[24] have pointed out that one of the problems with research in this area is that the perception of justice and the relative importance of each of the types shown in Box 5.1 depends very much on the context. Their study of Australian employees either undergoing the introduction of an enterprise-based collective bargaining process or a drastic downsizing of a public sector organization suggested, however, that there is evidence that more reliable and stable measures of justice perceptions can be developed.

A recent review by Brockner and Wiesenfeld[25] suggests that the strongest reactions to unfairness occur when the outcomes – rewards and resources – are unfair, i.e. distributive justice, followed by unfair procedures and unfair treatment. Breach of psychological contract is considered to be a form of distributive injustice in that promises made were broken and therefore not allocated fairly. The individual did not receive the outcome they expected.[26] A *self-interest model* is used to explain why procedural forms of injustice are among the worst received (distributive injustices are the worst). This theory[27] suggests that as individuals we seek to gain control of the decision-making process so we can maximize the material outcomes that we receive in the exchange relationship. We engage in the rules and procedures established by the group based on the belief that they will ensure equitable behaviour and assist us in achieving personal gain. More recently researchers have begun to unravel what inevitably is a much more complex situation by looking at the impact that each form of justice – distributional, procedural and interactional – has on the psychological contract.

One of the original conceptualizations of organizational justice described it as a cognitive dimension of job satisfaction. Job satisfaction is considered to result not just from affective reactions but also from an evaluation and calculation of the organization's fair dealings in the employment relationship and their efforts to maintain it in good working order.[28] This cognitive assessment is influenced by a number of factors. Lamertz[29] has demonstrated how impression management tactics by managers, where they attempt to cultivate impressions of fairness in the eye of the beholder, serve a role in influencing employees' perceptions of organizational justice. It has long been accepted that interpersonal treatment and the context for this treatment create a social basis in which judgements of fairness are rooted.[30] Employees today seek fairness not just in with respect to the outcomes they receive from the employment relationship, but also in terms of the way they are treated by the organization, its system and its agents. They validate these perceptions against reality and make social comparisons. Their judgements of fairness are influenced by the way that the organization treats its members and they then use this assessment as an automatic rule of thumb, or decision rule (heuristic), by which they evaluate the quality of the whole employment relationship.[31] In an environment of uncertainty, they seek information about procedures to confirm the trustworthiness and neutrality of organizational decision makers. For example, when a decision about downsizing is made it is argued that the perception of procedural justice is important and moderates the level of psychological contract breach, but Lamertz[32] points out that in reality few employees have access to objective information about why a decision to downsize was made. The judgement as to how much or how little justice behaviours have to be displayed for actions to be considered fair varies across organizational cultures and depends on how socialized the employees are and what they learned in that socialization process. Lamertz's study of 115 telephone operators and network designers in a downsizing telecommunications organization showed that social cues from the organization become important in activating a process of sense-making among employees. As they attempt to understand the meaning of organizational events, employees interpret this meaning by considering the impact on people who are socially close to themselves, people who they hold in esteem, and people who are members of valued social groups. Justice perceptions were strong predictors of satisfaction with the managerial maintenance of the employment relationship. Also, the larger the number of physical (social network) contacts between management and personnel, the higher the social identification and the greater the perception of interactional justice. By creating a bridge between higher-status social groups and employees organizations can increase perceptions of justice, even when implementing difficult and negative changes.

The nature of trust

Positive perceptions of fairness are also clearly more likely to occur when supported by other factors. One of the most commonly investigated is the level of trust that exists in the relationship.[33] This research tends, however, to have overly concentrated on the level of trust in the supervisor as opposed to other actors within the organization, or indeed trust in the organization itself.[34] From a psychological perspective, McAllister[35] argues that there are two ways in which trust is evident:

1 a rational calculation that the other party will carry out their obligations reflecting assessments about their reliability, dependability and competence (called cognitive trust); and
2 an emotional attachment that stems from a sense of mutual care and concern between individuals and parties (called affect-based trust).

It is argued that the former rational cognitive type of trust is more associated with economic exchanges in the employment relationship, while the latter emotional attachments are more associated with social exchanges in the relationship. Although once an exchange relationship exists between the individual and the organization the individual is already in a sense committed, have made certain investments that link them to the other party (we discuss the nature of commitment later in Chapter 8), before we decide whether the other party will reciprocate we make an assessment of their trustworthiness. Trust therefore precedes commitment, and is an essential precursor to the exchanges that take place within the employment relationship. This said, continued exchanges in themselves also reinforce and build trust.

Human resource practices and levels of procedural and distributive justice have been shown to be linked to subsequent assessments of trustworthiness of the organization.[36] Indeed, when studies examine the relationship between the various social climate factors that we have discussed here – justice perceptions, perceived organizational support and trust – and important outcomes such intention to leave the organization, job satisfaction or commitment – then a range of significant relationships exist. It is difficult to be sure about the causal path for most studies have been cross-sectional. However, it appears that perceptions of organizational justice generate higher levels of trust in the organization or in its managers. In their study of 179 Indian employees in a public sector organization, Aryee and colleagues[37] also found that trust in the organization is in turn associated with higher levels of job satisfaction and organizational commitment and reduced intentions to leave. Trust in the manager or supervisor is associated with more positive organizational citizenship behaviours.

Trust was introduced earlier as representing a willingness to be vulnerable. This involves coping with a degree of risk and uncertainty in the actions of others. Clark and Payne[38] define trust as a willingness to rely or depend on some externality such as an event, process, individual, group or system. Trust therefore implies the ability to take for granted many features of the social order,[39] and expect that actions will be beneficial rather than detrimental. Creed and Miles[40] distinguish *three* different facets of trust:

- *process-based* (personal experience of recurring exchanges which create ongoing expectations and norms of obligation about what is felt to be fair treatment);
- *characteristic-based* (beliefs about another's trustworthiness that result from a perception of their expertise, intentions, actions, words and general qualities);
- *institutional-based* (trust in the integrity and competence of informal societal structures).

The tensions that surround the perception of trust have become a central theme in recent psychological research. Sparrow and Marchington argued that all three of the facets outlined by Creed and Miles above have been challenged recently, but the HRM solutions to the breach and rebuilding of each facet are not as yet understood.[41] It is proving hard for managers to convince staff that they can be trusted to make decisions beyond short-term expedients. The behaviour of social groups, and the trusted divisions between them, has been thrown into confusion. The new HRM philosophy challenges age-old and trusted divisions between employer and employee or between managers and unions. The trust that employees placed in the HRM paradigm of the 1980s and 1990s and their belief that it would deliver greater benefit than a reliance on 'employee voice' achieved through formal union–management partnership has been questioned. The pursuit of flexibility has challenged the patterns of employee behaviour that managers assumed characterized full- or part-time workers, older employees or younger employees, men or women.[42] Indeed, Beardwell[43] argued that new social groupings of 'victims', 'accomplices' or 'conscious believers' are emerging at work.

At an anecdotal level, it is easy to see growing levels of mistrust. Do people trust presidents, politicians or political processes? Do they trust major institutions such as the police or the independence of their judiciary? Do they trust key professions such as food scientists or medical doctors? Do they trust the quality of information they have to deal with at work, or what they read or see on media such as television or the Internet? There has always been distrust in the employment contract, a sense of us and them, but it would seem that mistrust is highly evident again. Why is it legitimate to consider that there might have been a shift in the nature of trust? Consider the data in Figure 5.1. These reflect longitudinal studies from the opinion polling company MORI based on structured samples of 2000 general British public taken each year from 1969 to 2001.[44] When asked whether they agree that 'the profits of large companies help make things better for everyone who uses their products and services' in 1976 56 per cent of people would agree. By 1999 this figure had fallen to 28 per cent, and the latest data for 2001 show a further fall to 27 per cent – the lowest figure recorded in the time series. As far as the employment relationship is concerned, the issue concerns the perception of organizations as a good corporate citizen or not. MORI conducted the UK research as part of a global survey of public opinion – the Millennium Poll – in May 1999. When asked 'what are the things that matter most to you in forming an impression of a particular company?' 56 per cent of adults (based on a sample of 25 000 adults in 23 countries) spontaneously answer Responsibility (employee treatment, community commitment, ethics

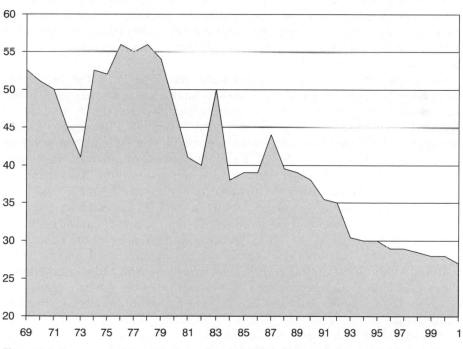

Figure 5.1 Percentage of population agreeing that 'the profits of large companies help make things better for everyone who uses their products and services' Source: MORI opinion poll data

and the environment). Integrity, fair treatment of employees, environmental responsibility and financial performance have become the crucial yardsticks by which an organization's trustworthiness is judged. The proportion of the British public for whom social responsibility is important when they form a decision about product or service has doubled in the last four years, from 24 per cent in 1997 to 46 per cent by 2001. Opinion poll organizations believe that:

> [Market research] has borne witness to major changes in public attitudes towards, and expectations of, big business. These trends raise fundamental questions about businesses' licence to oper- ate. . .as the deferential respect accorded to large companies – together with other major institutions – has declined over the years, so business needs to find a new basis of trust.[45]

Opinion survey firms are interested in such data in relation to brand management and corporate reputation, but for work psychologists they form part of the evidence that suggests that there is a shift in the nature of trust and/ or a deterioration in trust levels. The problem is that organizations are asking employees to trust *in* transition at the very time that the nature of employee trust *is itself in* transition.[46] Should the ability of organizations to re-establish high levels of trust be questioned? We will see in the next chapter with the example of Barclays Bank that it is possible for organizations to re-establish trust and develop a more positive employment relationship. However, we continue with the analysis that suggests that many organizations have to start from a base of having lost trust.

The impact of restructuring throughout the 1990s and the associated experiences of downsizing had much to do with this loss of trust. Indeed, many tensions in the employment contract surrounding the perception of trust can be expected to continue. American Management Association data show that 80 per cent of US firms that downsized were still profitable at the point of downsizing, and that on the day of the announcement of rationalization stock prices typically rose by 7 per cent. To test the proposition that victims of downsizing will be less likely to trust future employers than those who have not been laid off, Singh[47] examined data from the 1993 General Social Survey, which assesses the general disposition, satisfaction, happiness, racial attitudes and political views of 500 to 800 individuals representative of the US public. Items related to trust and self-interest versus organizational interest were analysed for those in full-time employment and those who had had experience of being laid off. Victims represented over 6 per cent of the general population, and were in fact significantly less trustful and had attitudes more inclined to self-interest.

Managerial attitude surveys also convey a sense of unease about the employment contract (see Box 5.2). However, they provide us with contra- dictory evidence over the level of trust that now exists and the likely consequences. When more reliable and representative surveys of the whole

Box 5.2   Managerial attitude surveys and levels of trust

Three recent managerial surveys in the UK suggest that negative attitudes have become a significant challenge for organizations. Evidence from the national surveys carried out by Guest and Conway[48] for the British Chartered Institute of Personnel and Development (CIPD) (the latest survey was the eighth one) show that deterioration in the psychological contract is restricted to around 25 per cent of the workforce, mainly less educated employees in more peripheral jobs. While 36 per cent of employees believed that their employer had no or at best low concern for their well-being and satisfaction at work, only around 5 per cent of employees would consider that the organization had not kept the promises made to them at all, and depending on the particular promise, from 62 per cent to 82 per cent would consider that the organization had fully kept its promises. However, work is no longer a dominant and central life interest. Only 37 per cent agreed that their personal goals were mainly work-related. For 59 per cent, however, what happens at work is still important to them. For the around three-quarters of the sample, change is far less stark than often suggested. Eighty-two per cent consider the promise to provide a reasonably secure job has been met, for example, 78 per cent trusted their immediate boss to look after their best interests somewhat or a lot, and 63 per cent felt the same about senior management. Interestingly, standard demographic items such as size of employer, sector, type of job, tenure, education level and union membership generally predicted very low levels of variance in people's answers to important work-related behaviours. Issues concerning the psychological contract are clearly more to do with either what psychologists would call within-person variables, i.e. personality, values etc., or the shape of HRM in the organization. HRM provision, organizational support (the most important predictor) and direct participation explained around three times as much variation in the state of the psychological contract as did the demographic factors.

Managers, as opposed to the general workforce, tend to have more concerned attitudes. A panel survey of 5000 British Institute of Management members by Worrall and Cooper[49] found that 52 per cent of managers feared that their company had lost essential skills and experience – up from 45 per cent of managers in 1997. Forty-one per cent of managers referred to a poverty of communication and consultation about strategic change in their organization. Attitudes to longer working hours were ambivalent; 45 per cent of senior managers thought that working long hours was acceptable; 22 per cent of junior managers felt it unacceptable, but had no choice over the matter; 70 per cent of managers reported working over 40 hours a week; 53 per cent regularly work in the evening; and 34 per cent regularly work over the weekend. Seventy-two per cent correctly sense that working long hours affected their relationship with their partner, 55 per cent perceive that long work hours damages their health, 55 per cent feel it actually makes them less productive and 49 per cent feel that they suffer from information overload.

Other large but unstructured surveys also tend to come up with a figure of from 20 per cent to 30 per cent highly dissatisfied individuals perceiving dysfunctional consequences to the new employment contract. For example, a Management Today/Ceridian survey of work–life balance of nearly 2000 managers[50] examined attitudes about what bothered managers in the new employment contract, what they would most like to change, and what the perceived consequences were. The conclusion was that British managers faced a 'strain drain' as a significant proportion of senior managers made sacrifices in their personal lives to keep up with the 'rat race', 49 per cent thought morale in their organizations was low, 55 per cent felt they faced frequent stress at work, 30 per cent felt their health was suffering because of this, half felt they had no time to build relationships out of work, 20 per cent admitted drinking to ease work pressure, and 8 per cent had resorted to therapy. Forty per cent were looking for a job over the next 12 months (whether they would get one is irrelevant, in their minds they were mobile). However, long work hours (12 per cent), workload pressure (18 per cent) and corporate culture (20 per cent) were not the main drivers for this. Rather it was lack of challenge (44 per cent), lack or recognition (37 per cent), lack of money (36 per cent) and poor work–life balance (35 per cent). However, while 81 per cent responded that 'I am very loyal to my organization', 71 per cent would seriously consider an approach from a head-hunter. Some loyalty!

workforce are taken, the evidence suggests that there are far more limited levels of breach of psychological contract or trust than we might assume. Yet, the general picture that emerges is one of uncertainty and the potential threat of future consequences.

The surveys noted in Box 5.2 suggest that emotions and rationality are currently rather confused. There has been a lack of examination of changes through the use of structured samples and much work has relied on anecdotal evidence, case studies in high-change industrial sectors, and unrepresentative surveys. However, while all surveys are not necessarily statistically representative[51] they do appear to capture a mood and a phenomenon that deserves further consideration.

Moreover, there will always be a limit to how much cross-sectional surveys can tell us about the changes taking place in the employment relationship. Surveys may simply pick up employee naivety – when faced with the enormous consequences of the radical economic and structural transitions taking place individuals act as though it will happen to others but not to them.

For example, Hallier and Lyon[52] found that middle management employees made responsible for downsizing lower echelons in their own organization still did not expect redundancy themselves, yet, as we have seen, this is a key target group. Hulin and Glomb note that there is also the problem of what psychologists call perceptual framing.[53] If times are tough, we learn to adjust our expectations downwards, reporting that perhaps things are not as bad as others make out. If the employee's frame is anchored in a context of no work, then even irregular work and income may be viewed positively. Therefore, some of the survey findings that show that reported levels of job satisfaction or trust are little altered might just be evidencing changes in the perceptual frame.

The downsizing phenomenon

The experience of redundancies is set to continue in the UK. The Chartered Institute of Personnel and Development (CIPD) latest survey of organizations that have made employees redundant, conducted across 563 organizations in May 2002, found that there were strong economic incentives to cut costs and restructure businesses.[54] Around 60 per cent of the FTSE 500 companies had made redundancies in the previous six months and 45 per cent of those organizations surveyed by the CIPD believed they would make further redundancies in the next 12 months. In most organizations redundancies accounted for around 6 per cent of the workforce, but in around 14 per cent of employers more than a fifth of the workforce were laid off. The 2001 Labour Force Survey shows that redundancy rates vary much across sectors, from 16 per 1000 in manufacturing, to 11 per 1000 in banking, finance and insurance and 2 per 1000 in public administration, education and health.[55] A range of impacts on employee relations are assumed to follow from this recent activity, with 52 per cent of the HR directors involved in the CIPD study anticipating a decline in the morale of remaining employees and 30 per cent a loss of trust from remaining employees.

We mentioned earlier in this chapter that trust has become a major issue in the employment relationship. The experience of downsizing throughout the 1990s was one of the main reasons for this. For example, data collected for the American Management Association show that 80 per cent of US firms that downsized were still profitable at the point of downsizing, and that on the day of announcement of rationalization their stock prices typically rose by 7 per cent.

By the mid-1990s most strategists were beginning to feel uncomfortable about the benefits of downsizing. Hamel and Prahalad used the phrase 'corporate anorexia' to refer to what they saw as leaner but not necessarily healthier (in strategic terms) organizations.[56] Organizational sociologists such as Budros and McKinley[57] have pursued the central question of why firms continue to downsize when the economic benefits are not evidenced (see Box 5.3).

Box 5.3   Dominant theories on why downsizing strategies have been pursued

Three dominant theories have been used to explain the attractiveness of downsizing strategies: Economic; Institutional, and Socio-cognitive.[58] The dominant theory has been the economic perspective.

Economic theory: This sees downsizing caused by a search for productivity, and efficiency and as a response to organizational decline, or as an attempt to increase profitability, i.e. a rational attempt to manipulate performance. This stream of research has examined the financial outcomes of downsizing and established the link to productivity, profitability and stock price.[59] This perspective has been questioned as more evidence emerges that it has failed to deliver the financial benefits expected.[60]

Institutional theory: This argues that it is social conventions that impel the pursuit of downsizing and view it as 'good management'.[61] Managers conform to this view in order to gain legitimacy[62] and downsizing decisions are seen as cloned and learned responses to uncertainty, reinforced by the rewards that exist within the internal career systems and external professional networks for senior managers. For example, survey data from the International Survey Research Corporation showed that US HRM professionals now show less objection to the pursuit of downsizing. The proportion who believe the process has 'gone too far' fell from 52 per cent to 39 per cent from 1996 to 1997.[63]

Socio-cognitive theory: This approach focuses attention on managers' mental models of downsizing and how these models are constructed.[64] Managers' decisions to downsize are based on shared mental models that define the causes and effects of downsizing, and indicate that it is effective way of conducting business better, faster and smarter, even though objective data might show that downsizing strategies may then be based on false assumptions of efficiency.

Source: Zhao *et al.*[64]

Life beyond downsizing: survivor syndrome

In recent years many organizations experiencing downsizing have designated certain job positions as redundant, leaving it up to the individuals declared redundant to find other positions. The focus of most existing research has been on those employees who have lost their jobs.[65] However, what of the impacts on those employees declared redundant but who manage to survive and remain with the organization? The survivors of organizational downsizing have to continue to help the organization function, often in a period when there are fewer staff around, but competitive pressures remain high.[66] In a post-layoff period, do the behaviours and attitudes of survivors change significantly? The reactions of survivors to downsizing were examined by several researchers throughout the 1980s.[67]

Doherty[68] argues that downsizing can have a profound impact on the survivors. They face a series of unsettling changes:

- Working in a new organization structure and design (organizational form)[69]
- New job sites, new bosses, new visions, new team roles, responsibilities and new policies[70]
- Taking on more work, managing ongoing cost reductions[71]
- Different progression opportunities[72]
- New rules for the employment relationship[73] and new rules for the negotiation processes within the relationship[74]
- The loss of peers and changes in the social fabric of their work life
- Ongoing fears about the survival of their own job.

As organizations have to resort to strategies based on control and containment, there is a lack of honest communication, resistance to change and decreased morale. Employees sense that there is more individualism at work, a loss of trust and confidence. This breeds a sense of increased vulnerability and insecurity. Commitment is assumed to suffer as a consequence of the politicization of the organizational climate. Decision making often gets recentralized and planning horizons become short term. Responses to change at all levels of the organization tend to have an ever-decreasing 'shelf life'.[75] Noer coined the phrase 'lay-off survivor syndrome' in 1990 to describe common feelings of guilt, lack of commitment and fear[76] seen across the managers who remain in the organization after a process of downsizing.

Considerable attention has been given to the phenomenon of job insecurity and the impact on the productivity and performance of those who survived the downsizing and delayering. A series of studies have looked at the attitudinal status of survivors and found that job satisfaction, organizational commitment, job involvement and intentions to turnover all become less favourable. Research has focused in particular on the content and causes of job insecurity,[77] the impact of layoffs on motivations, feelings and attitudes,[78] and the effects of role loss on job attitudes.[79] Downsizing has been found to be associated with:

- significant declines in job satisfaction within the nursing profession[80]
- reduced job performance among federal government managers[81]
- increased job insecurity[82]
- lower organizational morale[83] and
- decreased levels of trust and commitment[84]

In examining the evidence on reactions to downsizing, Kozlowski and colleagues[85] concluded that the '. . . pervasive impact of downsizing on organizations and its implications for our conceptions of career success, may be among the most profound legacies of the phenomenon'. Much attention has been given to the concept of employability in this regard. Moss-Kanter has argues that there is a set of skills and attitudes of self-reliance needed to master the new environment.[86]

However, the reactions of survivors to this environment are complex. They also vary markedly between individuals and organizations. We examine evidence on the emotional transitions that people go through later in the chapter. However, at this stage it is important to note that there are some important individual and organizational factors that moderate the impact of downsizing on individuals. The intensity of both individual reaction and the impact on productivity, loyalty and commitment is moderated at the organizational level by two main factors:

1 How the organization handles the layoffs
2 The extent to which the organization displays reciprocal commitment to both the leavers and the survivors

At the individual level, the most important moderating factors are:

1 Perceptions of fairness and the desire for equity
2 Status in the organization
3 Attitudes to work
4 Self-esteem
5 Coping mechanisms.

Job insecure or not?

Hartley and colleagues[87] define job insecurity as a discrepancy between the security employees would like their jobs to provide and the level they perceive to exist. They argue that the apparent demise of organizational commitment and stable and secure employment has led to job insecurity becoming a pervasive experience. Similarly, Herriot and Pemberton[88] argue that downsizing has transformed the employment relationship. However, there is much controversy as to the impact that insecurity has on individual employees and on important organizational outcomes.[89] Some would argue that insecurity can increase the amount of work effort and involvement, although the more traditional view as articulated by O'Driscoll and Cooper proposes that it is a source of burnout that produces stress and decreased performance.[90]

Another major issue to be resolved is how best to define, conceptualize and measure job insecurity. Distinctions can be drawn between hard, rational, objective definitions – which focus on external labour markets and use proxy measures of labour market stability such as job turnover and retention rates, or average level of employee tenure – and softer, perceptual and subjective definitions.

Does a more subjective view of job insecurity and labour market moves present a different picture? Jacobson noted that perceptual definitions of job insecurity range from those that are narrow in scope, such as the anticipation of a potential termination of a job,[91] to much broader definitions that stress the perceived powerlessness to maintain desired continuity of employment or loss of subjectively important features of the job, such as the theoretical model developed by Greenhalgh and Rosenblatt.[92]

The *objective* construct of job insecurity and supporting data suggests that the 'breach of contract' (labour market flexibility and job insecurity) position may be overstated. However, the HRM dynamics within organizations that flow from job insecurity are just as potent whether caused by subjective or objective factors. First, job security is subject to a significant perceptual gap. It carries more weight with employees than job interest in most OECD countries[93] but is rated eleventh out of fifteen items in terms of perceived satisfaction of need. Moreover, objective data on external labour market behaviour ignore the changes and disruptions caused within internal labour markets, generated by the changes in organizational form outlined at the beginning of the paper. Downsized and delayered organizations, even if not actually reducing the job tenure of survivors, certainly alter the 'rules of the game' for employees in terms of who gets promoted, how, and indeed what promotion means. When viewed as a subjective construct, job insecurity also includes assessments of the expected risk of job loss, and the consequences of job loss.

Support for there being greater risk of job loss in the future comes from analyses of shifts in the work of nations, international patterns of job creation, changes in employment conditions associated with the practice of social dumping, and changes in the level of organizational power and autonomy over the employment relationship. Support for there being significant financial adjustments and psychological transitions associated with job loss comes from analyses of the increased segmentation and structural nature of unemployment, increased duration of unemployment spells, political moves in many societies towards 'back to work' or 'work-fare' philosophies which can lead to significant reductions in earning power, and the reduced power of supportive institutions such as trades union collective bargaining power and welfare systems. Employees are probably *more objective in their subjective assessment of insecurity* than the external labour market and psychological outcome analysts give credence for.

The study of job insecurity forms part of the general investigation of psychological unwell-being. It is somewhere between the study of stress and burnout and the psychological consequences of unemployment and is concerned with people at work who fear they might lose their jobs and become unemployed.[94] The original questions that were asked were how important a stressor is job insecurity compared to other stressors, and how the impact of job insecurity compares to unemployment. Since these earliest questions about the topic in the late 1980s to this day, there has been significant debate about how best to measure and operationalize the phenomenon, what are the most important factors that lead to its creation (antecedents) and what important job-related outcomes follow if it is present (consequences). Related to this, there has been debate about what matters most – the continuation (or loss) of the actual job or of important features of the job?

The challenge facing those who have researched in the area of job insecurity is to unravel what is really happening. Klandermans and Van Vuuren started a recent debate from the following understanding:[95]

> . . . job insecurity is not just a matter of social construction, but related to actual changes in the company's situation. At the same time, it is also clear that not all the variance in job insecurity can be explained by the company's situation. Workers who are facing identical situations differ in their feelings of job insecurity . . . feelings of job insecurity, rather than the situation per se [impacts] on the workers' health, attitudes, and behaviour. Indeed, changes in the company's situation (be it an improvement or decline) only [result] in changes in psychological well-being, satisfaction, and intention to leave the company or to engage in collective action if workers experienced changes in their feelings of job insecurity.

Two different approaches to the measurement of job insecurity can be found in psychological research:

1 *Global definition*: This is seen in the work of Van Vuuren, Hartley, Jacobson and Klandermans.[96] Job insecurity is seen as an overall concern about the continued existence of their 'job as such' in the future. When considered this way, there are three important components: a subjective experience or perception; a sense of uncertainty about the future (as opposed, for example, to the certainty of being made redundant); and doubts about the continuation of the job as such.
2 *Multi-faceted definition*: This is seen in the work of Ashford, Lee and Bobko,[97] or Rosenblatt and Ruvio.[98] Job insecurity is related to concerns about the continued existence of the content or specific aspects of the job (such as a change in income or position in the organization) and the individual's ability to counteract these threats. A sense of powerlessness lies at its heart.

Common to both these approaches is the view that the anticipation of a stressful event can represent an equally important, if not more important, source of anxiety than the actual event.[99] In general, job insecurity is considered to be a stressor. It is associated with negative impacts on psychological well-being and also with dysfunctions in the way that individuals deal with this stress.[100] Both cross-sectional and longitudinal studies have shown that a causal relationship can be inferred between higher job insecurity and lower psychological well-being,[101] lower job satisfaction[102] and significant physical and psychosomatic strains.[103]

These negative impacts of job insecurity are explained using two theories developed in relation to the experience of unemployment. Jahoda's[104] *latent deprivation theory* considered the needs that are satisfied by work. These include acquiring income, social contacts outside the family, the structuring of time and both individual and social development. Unemployment – or the qualitative assessment of its possibility – frustrates these needs. The second theory is Warr's[105] *vitamin model*. He identified nine components in the work situation that have to be present to a degree, but which beyond that base level have little or no additional beneficial impact (hence the vitamin analogy). Two of these components can be related to the price of uncertainty. Joelson and Wahlquist[106] argue that the harmful impact of uncertainty comes from *unpredictability* and *uncontrollability*. The former relates to Warr's discussion of environmental clarity (clarity about the future and the expectations and behaviours to adopt) while the latter refers to Warr's powerlessness against the threat.

So several studies by psychologists have shown that at *any one point in time*, if individuals are found to be job insecure they are also more likely to suffer problems in terms of their well-being, job satisfaction and physiology. There are, however, two good reasons why these studies might overstate the impact of job insecurity on organizational effectiveness (see Box 5.3). Although discussed here in relation to job insecurity, these study design issues are equally applicable to other topics in this book such as survival syndrome, and also of course the study of the psychological contract *per se*.

In another longitudinal study of from 476 to 590 employees in three Finnish organizations, over a $2\frac{1}{2}$ year period, Kinnunen and colleagues[108] found that the more negative employees perceived job changes to be, the higher their job exhaustion a year later and the more absent from work due to sickness they were. The phenomenon of job insecurity among dual-earner families has also received attention. Mauno and Kinnunen[109] examined insecurity among a subsample of married dual-earner families in Finland. In only a small proportion of couples was job insecurity experienced by both partners. Perceptions of

---

Box 5.4   Problems with evidence from cross-sectional studies

Effects over time: It is not clear whether important outcomes such as lowered work attitudes and well-being hold true if the same outcomes are assessed in the same person at a later stage. Within-person longitudinal studies are needed to assess the duration and strength of the effects on potential outcomes.

Effects of mood disposition: Individuals who possess specific mood states are prone to evaluate themselves, others and events in overly positive or negative ways. This is known as *positive and negative affectivity*.[107] Positive affectivity reflects the principal personality tract of low anxiety/neuroticism. These individuals are characterized by high energy, excitement, enthusiasm and pleasurable engagement. Negative affectivity reflects low extraversion. These individuals are prone to evaluate themselves, others and the world in general in a more negative way.

economic stress crossed over from men to women and vice versa, but in general perceived insecurity resided more within the individual. Feeling job insecure is a lonely experience.

As noted earlier, the smaller number of longitudinal studies that have been done tend to show similar results. However, two recent studies reveal some interesting new insights. Hellgren and colleagues[110] studied 375 headquarter employees of a Swedish retail chain organization who had been retained after a 50 per cent downsizing exercise and who survived a series of subsequent reductions. Data were gathered at two intervals, a year apart. Importantly:

1 Insecurity about actually losing one's job was not related to the level of job satisfaction, but insecurity related to uncertainty over career prospects, stimulating job content and pay prospects, was significantly related to job satisfaction. Qualitative job insecurity predicted about 13 per cent of the variance in job satisfaction, a similar figure to that found in other longitudinal studies.
2 Insecurity also predicted turnover intentions (5 per cent of the variance), physical symptoms (7 per cent) and mental well-being (19 per cent).
3 Initially positive affectivity was associated with improved job satisfaction, but only accounted for a minimal effect.
4 Initially negative affectivity had more important relationships to turnover intentions (2 per cent of the variance) and physical symptoms (7 per cent) and (on combination with positive affectivity) accounted for 11 per cent of self-reported mental well-being.
5 However, once initial work attitude reactions were controlled for, the impact of personality disappeared, i.e. while job insecurity had a persistent effect over time, personality was more associated with initial reactions

The authors concluded that '. . . a concern about losing the job is intimately related to stress symptoms such as ill-health, sleeping problems, and distress, and that such problems also tend to transfer to the non-work setting. In contrast, perceived threats to important job features appear to relate primarily to altitudinal outcomes, such as dissatisfaction with the present job and propensity to leave it voluntarily'.[111]

Trust and security in abeyance?

A computer trawl of articles in British national newspapers found that, in 1986 when unemployment was higher, there were 234 stories on insecurity and just ten on job insecurity while, ten years later, there were 2778 stories on insecurity and 977 on job insecurity.[112] Within the UK, MORI opinion polls show that the proportion of people who feel secure in their jobs fell from 65 per cent to 54 per cent in 1990–95.[113]

Tensions in the employment contract surrounding the perception of trust can be expected to continue. American Management Association data show that 80 per cent of US firms that downsized were still profitable at the point of downsizing, and that on the day of announcement of rationalization stock prices typically rose by 7 per cent. To test the proposition that victims of downsizing will be less likely to trust future employers than those who have not been laid off, Singh[114] examined data from the 1993 General Social Survey, which assesses the general disposition, satisfaction, happiness, racial attitudes and political views of 500–800 individuals representative of the US public. Items related to trust, and self-interest versus organizational interest were analysed for those in full-time employment and those who had had experience of being laid off. Victims represented over 6 per cent of the general population, and were in fact significantly less trustful and had attitudes more inclined to self-interest when compared to those employees who had not experienced downsizing. Singh's study supports a transformational view, arguing that empirical evidence such as this shows that layoffs have had a marked and lasting impact on the psychological contract.

Hallier and Lyon argue that even the more systematic and proactive management of the downsizing process aimed at restructuring the employment relationship is achieved at a price. Their research demonstrates that organizational restructuring has a detrimental impact on the work attitudes and psychological contract of those who remain, as well as their ability to manage changes in their work role and to realize their careers over time. In short, many organizations are still struggling to achieve a successful renegotiation of the employment relationship.[115] In a subsequent longitudinal study of employee perceptions surrounding enforced work role changes before, during and after a redundancy event, Hallier[116] observed a temporary disturbance in employee behaviour – which they termed 'security abeyance'. The study showed that because employees were unable to arrive at convincing explanations of their organizational worth (or lack of it), there were clear changes in their information-scanning behaviour. Silence by management is seen as incompetence, lack of care or hidden intentions. When communication took place it generally resulted in the perception of contradictory valuations by managers of employee worth. This lack of communication or misperceived communication does not just reflect ignorant and poor management skills, but often a lack of comprehension of the end solution or clear managerial strategy towards it among managers who themselves are trying to find their way through a series of ambiguous, complex and little-understood changes. Most employers still place more emphasis on managing and legitimizing organizational changes rather than on the adaptation of employees. Consequently, employees hone their coping behaviours and tactics accordingly. For Hallier, contract breach should not be seen as a single episode attributable to specific signals sent by the employer. Rather, it operates as a longitudinal process of sense-making during which security is put into abeyance. Hallier uses the term 'security abeyance' to depict a state of chronic concern about an individual's security that results from ambiguous organizational change.

The self-adjusting animal? The view from longitudinal studies

Bridges[117] argued that in trying to manage the aftermath of downsizing, people and organizations have to work through two transitions – an external one to new job sites, new bosses, new team roles and new policies – and an internal psychological one – to come to terms with their own situation. The latter process – the internal transition to the new employment relationship – can take quite some time. We have discussed some of the evidence on survivor syndrome. Brockner[118] argued that there were no quick fixes to managing survivors in downsized organizations. The recovery periods are long, often running into years rather than weeks or months. Doherty and Horsted[119] focused on the processes needed to manage downsizing, arguing that any recovery requires a radical rethinking of organizational dynamics, often accompanied by the introduction of HR policies and practices designed to develop a more responsive and adaptable workforce, but also designed to meet the personal needs of the survivors.

What evidence is there to assess how long and in what ways people adjust to downsizing? Most research on survivor reactions to downsizing has been conducted in laboratory settings, or is based on cross-sectional surveys, or field case study settings. They all tend to be conducted at one point in time or over a relatively short period commencing shortly after downsizings have occurred. These sorts of study do appear to suggest consistently that there is then some quite considerable psychological impact on the survivors within organizations However, they pick up the immediate reactions to downsizing, but little else.

A number of researchers have pointed out that the longer-term effects of downsizing on the attitudes and behaviours of survivors is still relatively unknown and that we need to gather longitudinal data to see if any negative post-event relationships and effects actually hold over time[120]. What if employees are adaptable? Might they learn to adjust to the new realities at work without any significant negative consequences – or at least manageable changes in attitude? Do longitudinal studies provide us with different insights into the changes that take place within the psychology of individuals as they experience changes in the employment relationship? Fortunately, in recent years, a number of longitudinal studies have begun to emerge.

Marjorie Armstrong-Stassen has conducted a number of these. Her exploratory and small-scale study of 37 managers in a US telecommunications company found that those designated redundant but who eventually survived reported more job-related tension and burnout, lower perceived organizational support, and lower levels of proactive coping behaviours than those not affected by downsizing.[121] However, in this study data were only gathered 18–24 months after the last series of downsizings and not during the actual downsizings themselves. In a similar study of managers in public sector organizations moral and trust levels were seriously undermined by organizational downsizing.[122] More recently Armstrong-Stassen has conducted a three-year longitudinal study of 167 employees in a Canadian federal government workforce reduction programme in order to examine job-related changes in satisfaction, performance and job security over time, along with organization-related changes in morale, trust and commitment.[123] The change of attitudes and behaviours from a year post-announcement, through limited voluntary departures, and involuntary departures, was examined. In the initial downsizing phase, those declared redundant showed initially greater decreases in job satisfaction, organizational trust and commitment than those not declared redundant. However, after this initial phase and throughout the later stages of the downsizing process, those declared redundant then showed significantly higher increases in these outcomes than did the survivors (i.e. those not declared redundant). Intriguingly, the findings suggested that organizational downsizing did not have a long-term effect on survivors. Within a year of downsizing the negative effects began to dissipate. Perceived job insecurity began to recover once respondents had survived the involuntary downsizing. Armstrong-Stassen argues that it may well be that in certain occupations, retaining one's job after being designated redundant means that the organization is perceived as doing its best to maintain its obligations to the survivors under immediate threat, such that a re-establishment or renewal of the psychological contract becomes possible. Although this study demands replication with larger samples in a wider range of occupations, it serves to demonstrate that there are likely several important individual difference, job and organizational factors that moderate the impact of downsizing on the psychological contract.

The extent to which employees have a sense of choice or agency in the decisions that they make post-downsizing is clearly an important factor, as seen in the experiences of those who take early retirement or those who remain in the organization. For example, a recent study tracked the satisfaction, well-being, health and work centrality of nearly 400 senior employees aged 55 working for a Swedish insurance company.[124] Employees were invited to apply for early retirement on favourable terms. Both the early retirees and those continuing to work were tracked for 18 months following the downsizing. All the employees initially had the same work values. Those who were able to take early retirement voluntarily indeed showed more positive attitudes and lower levels of distress than those who stayed on in work. The effects of downsizing and the way the decision to retire or to continue working was taken affected the life of the individuals studied for longer than expected. Restricted individual choice had negative effects both on those forced into retirement and on those for whom retirement was denied.

Another study of 106 middle- and upper-level marketing-related managers in a large consumer packaged goods organization surveyed survivors one month after the downsizing, four months into the process and sixteen months after the layoffs.[125] Around one-third of the organization were made redundant. Data were collected on organizational commitment, role clarity, intent to leave, role overload, job involvement, satisfaction with senior management and job

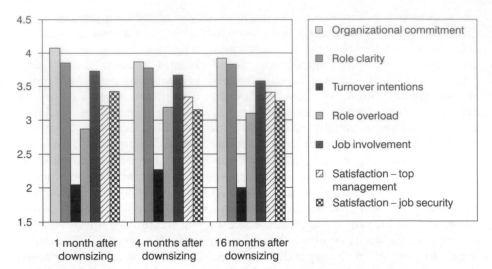

Figure 5.2 Longitudinal change in six post-downsizing outcomes. (Data from Allen *et al.*[125])

security. The complex patterns of change and adaptation are shown in Figure 5.2. Four months after the downsizing organizational commitment, intention to leave, role overload and satisfaction with job security were all more negative. However, one year after the downsizing three of the six attitudes had generally recovered to the levels immediately after the downsizing announcement (turnover intentions, satisfaction with job security and role overload). Organizational commitment recovered a little, but was still significantly lower one year later. The unexpected finding was that despite these cyclical phase changes, levels of satisfaction with top management increased seemed to increase over time while job involvement showed a continual linear decrease.

There seems to be a clear effect from this study. Those outcomes that reflect psychological *identification and engagement* with the actual job and organization (involvement and commitment) end up being worse one year post-downsizing and are the most difficult for an organization to recover. Those outcomes that reflect *feelings of discomfort* (job security, role overload and intention to leave), however, do tend to show a pattern of recovery. Nonetheless, post-downsizing adjustment can be managed more effectively. The researchers examined the extent to which the role overload, role clarity and satisfaction measures themselves predicted and explained the managers' organizational commitment and turnover intentions. As predicted, improvements in role overload and clarity and satisfaction were associated with higher levels of organizational commitment and lower intention to leave. Moreover, those managers who had demonstrated high levels of job involvement were particularly sensitive to changes in their work environment and responded more strongly. Upon discovering that their former psychological contract has been violated, survivors search for reasons to remain involved and committed to the organization. A new form of individual–organization attachment – a new psychological contract – has to be formed in the context of the newly restructured organization.[126]

The practical implications from this study also seem clear. If organizations focus on interventions that target employee commitment and involvement (these are called *occupational reinforcers*[127] and include such factors as advancement, co-workers, authority, social status and security) then the new psychological contract can be made more salient and survivors can be better equipped to move forward with the organization. It is important to note, however, that these recommendations can only be inferred from the longitudinal studies reviewed above. They have not been tested empirically yet.

References

1. See, for example, Settoon, R.P., Bennett, N. and Liden, R.C. (1996). Social exchange in organizations: perceived organizational support, leader–member exchange and employee reciprocity. *Journal of Applied Psychology, 81*, 219–227; Podsakoff, P.M. and MacKenzie, S.B. (1997). The impact of organizational citizenship behavior on organizational performance: a review and suggestions for future research. *Human Performance, 10*, 133–151; Wayne, S.J., Shore, L.M. and Liden, R.C. (1997). Perceived organizational support and leader–member exchange: a social exchange perspective. *Academy of Management Journal, 40*, 82–111.
2. Cropanzano R.S. and Kacmar, K.C. (1995). (Ed.), *Organizational politics, justice, and support: managing the social climate of the workplace*. Westport, CT: Quorum Books.
3. Cropanzano, R. (1993). *Justice in the workplace: approaching fairness in human resource management*. Hillsdale, NJ: Erlbaum.
4. Greenberg, J. (1990). Organizational justice: yesterday, today and tomorrow. *Journal of Management, 16*, 399–432.
5. Sheppard, B.H., Lewicki,, R.J. and Minton, J.W. (1992). *Organizational justice: the search for fairness in the workplace*. Lexington, MA: Lexington Books.
6. See, for example: Eisenberger, R., Huntington, R., Hutchison, S. and Sowa, D. (1986). Perceived organizational support. *Journal of Applied Psychology, 71 (3)*, 500–507; Shore, L.M. and Shore, T.H. (1995). Perceived organizational support and organizational justice. In R.S. Cropanzano and K.M. Kacmar (Eds.), *Organizational politics, justice and support: managing the social climate of the workplace*. Westport, CT: Quorum Books.
7. Settoon, R.P., Bennett, N. and Liden, R.C. (1996). Social exchange in organizations: perceived organizational support, leader–member exchange and employee reciprocity. *Journal of Applied Psychology, 81*, 219–227; Liden, R.C., Sparrowe, R.T. and Wayne, S.J. (1997). Leader–member exchange theory: the past and potential for the future. In G.R. Ferris (Ed.), *Research in personnel and human resources management, Volume 15*. Greenwich, CT: JAI Press, pp. 47–119.

8. Konovoksy, M.A. and Pugh, S.D. (1984). Citizenship behavior and social exchange. *Academy of Management Journal, 37*, 656–669; Whitener, E.M. (1997). The impact of human resource activities on employee trust. *Human Resource Management Review, 7*, 389–404.

9. Bradach, J.L. and Eccles, R.G. (1989). Price, authority, and trust: from ideal types to plural forms. *Annual Review of Sociology, 15*, 97–118.

10. Clark, M.C. and Payne, R.L. (1997). The nature and structure of workers' trust in management. *Journal of Organizational Behavior, 18 (3)*, 205–224.

11. Miles, R. and Creed, E.D. (1995). Organizational forms and managerial philosophies: a descriptive and analytical review. In L.L. Cummings and B.M. Staw (Eds.), *Research in organizational behavior, Volume 17*. Greenwich, CT: JAI Press.

12. Mayer, R.C., Davis, J.H. and Schoorman, F.D. (1995). An integrative model of organizational trust. *Academy of Management Review, 20*, 709–734.

13. Coyle-Shapiro and Kessler (in press). *Op. cit.*

14. Millward, L.J and Brewerton, P.M. (1999). Contractors and their psychological contracts. *British Journal of Management, 10*, 253–274.

15. Coyle-Shapiro, J. and Kessler, I. (2002). Contingent and non-contingent working in local government: contrasting psychological contracts. *Public Administration, 80 (1)*, 77–101.

16. Kickul, J., Lester, S.W. and Finkl, J. (2002). Promise breaking during radical organizational change: do justice interventions make a difference? *Journal of Organizational Behavior, 23*, 469–488, 470.

17. Noe, R.A., Hollenbeck, J.R., Gerhart, B. and Wright, P.M. (2000). *Human resource management: gaining a competitive advantage*. New York: Irwin-McGraw-Hill., p. 52.

18. See Folger, R. and Konovsky, M.A. (1986). Effects of procedural and distributive justice on reactions to pay raise decisions. *Academy of Management Journal, 82*, 115–130; McFarlin, D.B. and Sweeney, P.D. (1992). Distributive and procedural justice as predictors of satisfaction with personal and organizational outcomes. *Academy of Management Journal, 35*, 626–637; Cropanzano, R. and Greenberg, J. (1997). Progress in organizational justice: tunnelling through the maze. In C.L. Cooper and I. Robertson (Eds.), International review of industrial and organizational psychology. New York: Wiley, pp. 317–372.

19. Bies, R.J. and Moag, J.S. (1986). Interactional justice: communication criteria of fairness. *Research on Negotiation in Organizations, 1*, 43–55; Cropanzano and Greenberg (1997). *Op. cit.*, pp. 317–372. Colquit, J.A., Conlon, D.E., Wesson, M.J., Poter, C. and Ng, K.Y. (2001). Justice at the millennium: a meta-analytic review of 25 years of organizational justice research. *Journal of Applied Psychology, 86*, 425–445.

20. Adams, J. (1965). Inequity in social exchange. In L. Berkowitz (Ed.), *Advances in experimental social psychology. Volume 2*. New York: Academic Press, pp. 267–299.

21. Leventhal, G. (1980). What should be done with equity theory? In K.

Gergen, M. Greenberg and R. Wills (Eds.), *Social exchange: advances in theory and research*. New York: Plenum, pp. 27–55.

22. Bies, R. and Moag, J. (1986). Interactional justice: communication criteria in fairness. In R. Lewicki, B. Sheppard and B. Bazerman (Eds.), *Research on negotiation in organizations. Volume 1*. Greenwich, CT: JAI Press, pp. 43–55.

23. Morrison, E.W. and Robinson, S.L. (1997). When employees feel betrayed: a model of how psychological contract violation develops. *Academy of Management Review, 22*, 226–256.

24. Paterson, J.M., Green, A. and Cary, J. (2002). The measurement of organizational justice in organizational change programmes: a reliability, validity and context-sensitivity assessment. *Journal of Occupational and Organizational Psychology, 75 (4)*, 393–408.

25. Brockner, J. and Weisenfeld, B.M. (1996). An interactive framework for explaining reactions to decisions: interactive effects of outcomes and procedures. *Psychological Bulletin, 120*, 189–208.

26. Kickul *et al*. (2002). *Op. cit.*

27. Thibaut, J. and Walker, L. (1975). *Procedural justice: a psychological analysis*. Hillsdale, NJ: Erlbaum.

28. McFarlin, D.B. and Sweeney, P.D. (1992). Distributive and procedural justice as predictors of satisfaction with personal and organizational outcomes. *Academy of Management Journal, 35*, 626–637.

29. Lamertz, K. (2002). The social construction of fairness: social influence and sense making in organizations. *Journal of Organizational Behavior, 23*, 19–37.

30. Greenberg, J. (1990). Looking fair versus being fair: managing impressions of organizational justice. *Research in Organizational Behavior, 12*, 111–157; Mossholder, K.W., Bennett, N., and Martin, C. (1998). A multilevel analysis of procedural justice context. *Journal of Organizational Behavior, 19*, 131–141.

31. Van den Bos, K., Bruins, J., Wilke, H.A.M. and Dronkert, E. (1999). Sometimes unfair procedures have nice aspects: on the psychology of the fair process effect. *Journal of Personality and Social Psychology, 77*, 324–337.

32. Lamertz (2002). *Op. cit.*

33. Konovoksy, M.A. and Pugh, S.D. (1984). Citizenship behavior and social exchange. *Academy of Management Journal, 37*, 656–669; Whitener, E.M. (1997). The impact of human resource activities on employee trust. *Human Resource Management Review, 7*, 389–404.

34. Aryee, S., Budhwar, P.S. and Chen, Z.X. (2002). Trust as a mediator of the relationship between organizational justice and work outcomes: test of a social exchange model. *Journal of Organizational Behavior, 23*, 267–285.

35. McAllister, D.J. (1995). Affect- and cognition-based trust as foundations for interpersonal cooperation in organizations. *Academy of Management Journal, 38*, 24–59.

36. Shore, L.M. and Shore, T.H. (1995). Perceived organizational support and organizational justice. In R.S. Cropanzano and Kacmar (Eds.). *Op. cit.*; Pearce, J.L., Branyiczki, I. and Bakacsi, G. (1994). Person-based reward systems: a theory of organizational reform practices in reform-communist organizations. *Journal of Organizational Behavior, 15,* 261–282.

37. Aryee, S., Budhwar, P.S. and Chen, Z.X. (2002). Trust as a mediator of the relationship between organizational justice and work outcomes: test of a social exchange model. *Journal of Organizational Behavior, 23,* 267–285.

38. Clark, M.C. and Payne, R.L. (1997). The nature and structure of workers' trust in management. *Journal of Organizational Behavior, 18 (3),* 205–224

39. Miles, R.E and Creed, W.E.D. (1995). Organizational forms and managerial philosophies: a descriptive and analytical review. In L.L. Cummings and B.M. Staw (Eds.), *Research in organizational behaviour, Vol. 17.* Greenwich, CT: JAI Press.

40. Creed, W.E.D. and Miles, R.E. (1996). Trust in organizations: a conceptual framework linking organizational forms, managerial philosophies and the opportunity costs of control. In R.M. Kramer and T.R. Tyler (Eds.), *Trust in organizations: frontiers of theory and research.* London: Sage.

41. Sparrow, P.R. and Marchington, M. (Eds.) (1998). *Human resource management: the new agenda.* London: Financial Times/Pitman Publishing.

42. Emmott, M. and Hutchinson, S. (1998). Employment flexibility: threat or promise? In P. Sparrow and M. Marchington (Eds.), *Human resource management: the new agenda.* London: Financial Times/Pitman Publishing.

43. Beardwell, I. (1998). Bridging the gap? Employee voice, representation and HRM. In P. Sparrow and M. Marchington (Eds.), *Human resource management: the new agenda.* London: Financial Times/Pitman Publishing.

44. We are indebted to Stewart Lewis, a Director of MORI for the release of the 2001 figure for inclusion in this book.

45. Lewis, S. (2002). Who's in charge of the brand? Reflections on brand and reputation. *MORI Internal Report,* p. 2.

46. Sparrow, P. and Cooper, C.L. (1998). New organizational forms: The strategic relevance of future psychological contract scenarios. *Canadian Journal of Administrative Sciences, 15 (4),* 356–372.

47. Singh, R. (1998). Redefining psychological contracts with the US work force: a critical task for strategic human resource management planners in the 1990s. *Human Resource Management, 37 (1),* 61–70.

48. Guest, D. and Conway, N. (2002). *Pressure at work and the psychological contract.* London: Chartered Institute of Personnel and Development.

49. Worrall, L. and Cooper, C. (1998). *The quality of working life – the 1998 survey of managers' changing experiences.* Institute of Management/UMIST.

50. Davis, E. (1999). Does your life work? The Management Today Work Life Survey, *Management Today,* August, 48–55.

51. Guest, D. (1998). Is the psychological contract worth taking seriously? *Journal of Organizational Behaviour, 19*, Special Issue, 649–664.

52. Hallier, J. and Lyon, P. (1996). Job insecurity and employee commitment: managers' reactions to the threat and outcomes of redundancy selection, *British Journal of Management, 7 (1)*, 107–123.

53. Hulin, C.L. and Glomb, T.M. (1999). Contingent employees: individual and organizational considerations. In D.R. Ilgen and E.D. Pulakos (Eds.), *The changing nature of performance: implications for staffing motivation and development*. San Francisco: Jossey-Bass.

54. Chartered Institute of Personnel and Development (2002). *Redundancy: Survey Report.* London: Chartered Institute of Personnel and Development.

55. Labour Market Trends (2002). Redundancies by Industry (C.43). *Labour Market Trends*, February, *110 (2)*, S65.

56. Hamel, G. and Prahalad, C.K. (1994). *Competing for the future: a breakthrough strategy for seizing control of your industry and dominating the markets of tomorrow*. Boston, MA: Harvard University Press.

57. Budros, A. (1997). The new capitalism and organizational rationality: the adoption of downsizing programs, 1979–1994. *Social Forces, 76 (1)*, 229–250; Budros, A. (1999). A conceptual framework for analysing why organizations downsize. *Organization Science, 10 (1)*, 69–82; McKinley, W.C., Sanchez, C. and Schick, A. (1995). Organizational downsizing: constraining, cloning, learning. *Academy of Management Executive, 9 (3)*, 32–44.

58. Zhao, J., Rust, K.G. and McKinley, W. (1997). A socio-cognitive interpretation of organizational downsizing: toward a paradigm shift. Paper presented at the 23rd European International Business Academy Conference on Global Business in the Information Age, Stuttgart, 14–16 December.

59. Bruton, G., Keels, J.K. and Shook, C. (1996). Downsizing the firm: answering the strategic questions, *Academy of Management Executive, 10 (2)*, 38–45; Worrell, D., Davidson, W. and Sharma, V. (1991). Layoff announcements and stockholder wealth. *Academy of Management Journal, 34*, 662–678.

60. See, for example, De Meuse, K., Vanderheiden, P. and Bergmann, T. (1994). Announced layoffs: their effect on corporate financial performance, *Human Resource Management, 33*, 509–30; Mentzer, M. (1996). Corporate downsizing and profitability in Canada. *Canadian Journal of Administrative Sciences, 13*, 237–250.

61. McKinley *et al.* (1995). *Op. cit.*

62. DiMaggio, P. and Powell, W. (1983). The iron cage revisited: institutional isomorphism and collective rationality in organizational fields. *American Sociological Review, 48*, 147–160.

63. International Survey Research Corporation (1997). Downsizing not such a downer. *HR Focus, 74 (12)*, 6.

64. Zhao *et al.* (1997). *Op. cit.*

65. See, for example, DeFranck, R.S. and Ivancevich, J.M. (1986). Job loss: an individual level review and model. *Journal of Vocational Behavior, 28,* 1–20; Fryer, D. and Payne, R. (1986). Being unemployed: a review of the literature on the psychological experience of unemployment. In C.L. Cooper and I. Robertson (Eds.), *International review of industrial and organizational psychology.* New York: Wiley; Hanisch, K.A. (1999). Job loss and unemployment research from 1994 to 1998: a review and recommendations for research and intervention. *Journal of Vocational Behavior, 55,* 188–220; Hartley, J. and Fryer, D. (1987). The psychology of unemployment: a critical appraisal. In G. Stephenson and J. Davis (Eds.), *Progress in applied social psychology, Volume 2.* London: Wiley; Leana, C.R. and Feldman, D.C. (1994). The psychology of job loss. *Research in Personnel and Human Resources Management, 12,* 271–302; Swinburne, P. (1981). The psychological impact of unemployment on managers and professional staff. *Journal of Occupational Psychology, 54,* 47–64.

66. Kozlowski, S.W.J., Chao, G.T., Smith, E.M. and Hedlund, J. (1993). Organizational downsizing: strategies, interventions and research impli-cations. In *International review of industrial and organizational psychology, Volume 8.* Chichestor: Wiley.

67. For a review see Kozlowski, S.W.J., Chao, G.T., Smith, E.M. and Hedlund, J. (1993). Organizational downsizing: Strategies, interventions and research implications. In *International review of industrial and organizational psychology, Volume 8.* Chichester: Wiley.

68. Doherty, N. (1996). Surviving in an era of insecurity. *European Journal of Work and Organizational Psychology, 5 (4),* 471–478.

69. Curtis, R.L. Jr (1989). Cutbacks, management and human relations: Meanings for organizational theory and research. *Human Relations, 22 (8),* 671–689.

70. Bridges, W. (1991). *Managing transitions.* New York: Addison-Wesley.

71. Doherty (1996). *Op. cit.*

72. Inkson, K. and Coe, T. (1993). *Are career ladders disappearing?* London: Institute of Management.

73. Hirsch, W., Jackson, C. and Jackson, C. (1995). Careers in organizations: Issues for the future. *Report No. 287.* Brighton: Institute for Employment Studies.

74. Herriot and Pemberton (1995). *Op. cit.*

75. Conner, D. (1993). *Managing at the speed of change.* New York: Villard Books.

76. See Noer, D.M. (1990). Layoff survivor sickness: a new challenge for supervisors. *Supervisory Management,* March, 3; Noer, D.M. (1993). *Healing the wounds.* San Francisco, CA: Jossey-Bass; Noer, D.M. (1997). Layoff survivor sickness: what it is and what to do about it. In M.K. Gowing, J.D. Kraft & J.C. Quick (Eds.), *The new organizational reality: downsizing, restructuring and revitalization.* Washington, DC: American Psychological Association.

77. Ashford, S.J., Lee, C. and Bobko, P. (1989). Content, causes, and consequences of job insecurity: a theory-based measure and substantive test. *Academy of Management Journal*, 32, 803–829.

78. See, for example, Brockner, J., Davy, J.A. and Carter, C. (1985). Layoffs, self-esteem and survivor guilt: Motivational, affective and attitudinal consequences. *Organizational Behavior and Human Decision Consequences*, 36, 229–244; Davy, J.A., Kinicki, A.J. and Scheck, C.L. (1991). Developing and testing a model of survivor responses to layoffs. *Journal of Vocational Behavior*, 38, 302–317; Olson, D.A. and Tetrick, L.E. (1988). Organizational restructuring. *Group and Organization Studies*, 13 (3), 374–388; Tombaugh, J.R. and White, L.P. (1990). Downsizing: an empirical assessment of survivors' perceptions in a post lay-off environment. *Organization Development Journal*, Summer, 32–43.

79. Schlenkar, J.A. and Gutek, B.A. (1987). Effects of role loss on work-related attitudes. *Journal of Applied Psychology*, 72, 287–293.

80. Armstrong-Stassen, M., Cameron, S.J. and Horsburgh, M.E. (1996). The impact of organizational downsizing on the job satisfaction of nurses. *Canadian Journal of Nursing Administration*, 9, 8–32.

81. Armstrong-Stassen, M. (1998). Downsizing the federal government: a longitudinal study of managers' reactions. *Canadian Journal of Administrative Sciences*, 15, 310–321; Jalajas, D.S. and Bommer, M. (1996). The effect of downsizing on the behaviors and motivations of survivors. *Organization Development Journal*, 14 (2), 45–54.

82. Cameron, K.S., Freeman, S.J. and Mishra, A.K. (1993). Organizational downsizing. In G.P. Huber and W.H. Block (Eds.), *Organizational change and redesign: ideas and insights for improving performance*. New York: Oxford University Press.

83. Worrall, L., Cooper, C.L. and Campbell-Jamison, F. (2000). The impact of organizational change on the work experiences and perceptions of public sector managers. *Personnel Review*, 29, 613–636.

84. Kets de Vries, M.F.R. and Balazs, K. (1997). The downside of downsizing. *Human Relations*, 50, 11–50.

85. Kozlowski, S., Chao, G.T., Smith, E.M. and Hedlund, J. (1993). Organizational downsizing: strategies, interventions, and research implications. *International review of industrial and organizational psychology, Volume 8*. Chichestor: Wiley, p. 316.

86. Moss-Kanter, R.M. (1993). *Men and women of the corporation*. Oxford: Macmillan.

87. Hartley, J., Jacobson, D., Klandermans, B. and Van Vuuren, T. (1991). *Job insecurity: coping with jobs at risk*. London: Sage.

88. Herriot, P. and Pemberton, C. (1995). *New deals: the revolution in managerial careers*. Chichester: Wiley.

89. Jalajas, D.S. and Bommer, M. (1999). A comparison of the impact of the threat of future downsizings on workers. *Journal of Social Behavior and Personality*, 14, 89–100.

90. O'Driscoll, M.P. and Cooper, C.L. (1996). Sources and management of

excessive job stress and burnout. In P.B. Warr (Ed.), *Psychology at work*. Harmondsworth: Penguin.

91. Jacobson, D. (1987). A personological study of the job security experience. *Social Behavior, 2*, 143–155; Jacobson, D. (1991). The conceptual approach to job insecurity. In J.F. Hartley, D. Jacobson, B. Klandermans and T. Van Vuuren (Eds.), *Job insecurity: coping with jobs at risk*. London: Sage.

92. Greenhalgh, L. and Rosenblatt, Z. (1984). Job insecurity: toward a conceptual clarity. *Academy of Management Review, 9*, 438–448.

93. White, G. (1997). How real is job insecurity? *Flexible Working Practices*, Issue No. 20, 22 December, 10–11.

94. De Witte, H. (1999). Job insecurity and psychological well-being: review of the literature and exploration of some unresolved issues. *European Journal of Work and Organizational Psychology, 8 (2)*, 155–177.

95. Klandermans, B. and Van Vuuren, T. (1999). Job insecurity: Introduction. *European Journal of Work and Organizational Psychology, 8 (2)*, 145–153, pp. 145–146.

96. See, for example, Van Vuuren, T. (1990). *Met ontslag bedreigd. Werknemers in onzekerheid over hun arbeidsplaats bij veranderingen in de organisatie*. Amsterdam: VU Uitgeverij; Hartley, J. Jacobson, D., Klandermans, B. and Van Vuuren, T. (1991). *Job insecurity: coping with jobs at risk*. London: Sage.

97. Ashford, S., Lee, C. and Bobko, P. (1989). Content, causes and consequences of job insecurity: a theory-based measure and substantive test. *Academy of Management Journal, 32 (4)*, 803–829.

98. Rosenblatt, Z. and Ruvio, A. (1996). A test of a multidimensional model of job insecurity: the case of Israeli teachers. *Journal of Organizational Behaviour, 17*, 345–359.

99. Lazarus, R.S. and Folkman, S. (1984). *Stress appraisal and coping*. New York: Springer.

100. De Witte (1999). *Op. cit.*

101. See, for example, Burchell, B. (1994). The effects of labour market position, job insecurity and unemployment on psychological health. In D. Gallie, C. Marsh and C. Vogler (Eds.), *Social change and the experience of unemployment*. Oxford: Oxford University Press.; Roskies, E. and Louis-Guerin, C. (1990). Job insecurity in managers: Antecedents and consequences. *Journal of Organizational Behaviour, II*, 345–359; Roskies, E., Louis-Guerin, C. and Fournier, C. (1993). Coping with job insecurity: how does personality make a difference? *Journal of Organizational Behaviour 14*, 617–630; Dekker, S. and Schaufell, W. (1995). The effects of job insecurity on psychological health and withdrawal: a longitudinal study. *Australian Psychologist, 30 (1)*, 57–63; Orpen, C. (1993). Correlations between job insecurity and well-being among white and black employees in South Africa. *Perceptual and Motor Skills, 76*, 885–886; De Witte, H. (1999). Job insecurity and psychological well-being: Review of the literature and exploration of some unresolved issues. *European Journal of Work And Organizational Psychology, 8 (2)*, 155–177.

102. See, for example, Ashford, S., Lee, C., and Bobko, D. (1989). Content, causes and consequences of job insecurity: a theory-based measure and substantive test. *Academy of Management Journal, 32 (4)*, 803–829; Landsbergis, P. (1988). Occupational stress among health care workers: a test of the job demands – control model. *Journal of Organizational Behaviour, 9*, 217–239; Heaney, C., Israel, B. and House, J. (1994). Chronic job insecurity among automobile workers: effects on job satisfaction and health. *Social Science and Medicine, 38 (10)*, 1431–1437; O'Quin, K. and Lotempio, S. (1998). Job satisfaction and intentions to turnover in human service agencies perceived as stable and non-stable. *Perceptual and Motor Skills, 76*, 885–886; Lim. V. (1996). Job insecurity and its outcomes: moderating effects of work-based and non-work based social support. *Human Relations, 49 (2)*, 171–194; Lim, V. (1997). Moderating effects of work-based support on the relationship between job insecurity and its consequences. *Work and Stress, 11 (3)*, 251–266.

103. See from the above, Landsbergis (1988); Heaney *et al.*, (1994) and Roskies and Louis-Guerin (1990). In addition to these see Catalano, R., Rook, K., and Dooley, D. (1986). Labor markets and help-seeking: a test of the employment security hypothesis. *Journal of Health and Social Behaviour, 27*, 227–287; Siegrist, J., Peter, R., Junge, A., Cremer, P., and Siedel, D. (1990). Low status control, high effort at work and ischemic heart disease: prospective evidence from blue-collar men. *Social Science and Medicine, 31 (10)*, 1127–1134.

104. Jahoda, M. (1982). *Employment and unemployment: a social-psychological analysis*. Cambridge: Cambridge University Press.

105. Warr, P. (1987). *Work, unemployment and mental health*. Oxford: Clarendon Press.

106. Joelson, L. and Wahlquist, L. (1987). The psychological meaning of job insecurity and job loss: results of a longitudinal study. *Social Science and Medicine, 25 (2)*, 179–182.

107. See, for example, Brief, A.P., Burke, M.J., George, J.M., Robinson, B.S. and Webster, J. (1988). Should negative affectivity remain an unmeasured variable in the study of job stress? *Journal of Applied Psychology, 2*, 193–198; Costa, P.T. and McCrae, R.R. (1980). Influence of extraversion and neuroticism on subjective well-being: happy and unhappy people. *Journal of Personality and Social Psychology, 4*, 668–678; Roskies, E., Louis-Guerin, C. and Fournier, C. (1993). Coping with job insecurity: how does personality make a difference? *Journal of Organizational Behavior, 14*, 617–630; Schaubroeck, J., Ganster, D.C. and Fox, M.L. (1992). Dispositional affect and work-related stress. *Journal of Applied Psychology, 3*, 322–335; Watson, D. and Pennebaker, J.W. (1989). Health complaints; stress and distress. Exploring the central role of negative affectivity. *Psychological Review, 2*, 234–254.

108. Kinnunen, U., Mauno, S. Natte, J., and Happonen, M. (1999). Perceived job insecurity: a longitudinal study among Finnish employees. *European Journal of Work and Organizational Psychology, 8 (2)*, 243–260.

109. Mauno, S. and Kinnunen, U. (2002). Perceived job insecurity among dual-earner couples: do its antecedents vary according to gender, economic sector and the measure used? *Journal of Occupational and Organizational Psychology, 75 (3)*, 295–314.
110. Hellgren, J., Sverke, M. and Isaksson, K. (1999). A two-dimensional approach to job insecurity: consequences for employee attitudes and well-being. *European Journal of Work and Organizational Psychology, 8 (2)*, 179–195.
111. *Ibid.*, pp. 190–191.
112. Smith, D. (1997). Job insecurity and other myths: the employment climate. *Management Today*, May, 38–41.
113. Sparrow, P.R. (1996). Transitions in the psychological contract: some evidence from the banking sector, *Human Resource Management Journal, 6 (4)*, 75–92.
114. Singh, R. (1998). Redefining psychological contracts with the US work force: a critical task for strategic human resource management planners in the 1990s. *Human Resource Management, 37 (1)*, 61–70.
115. Hallier, J. and Lyon, P. (1996). Job insecurity and employee commitment: Managers' reactions to the threat and outcomes of redundancy selection. *British Journal of Management, 7*, 107–123.
116. *Ibid.*
117. Bridges, W. (1991). *Managing transitions*. New York: Addison-Wesley.
118. Brockner, J. (1992). Managing the effects of layoffs on survivors. *California Management Review*, Winter, 9–28.
119. Doherty, N. and Horsted, J. (1995). Helping survivors to stay on board. *People Management*, 12 January, 26–31.
120. See, for example, Ashford, S.J., Lee, C. and Bobko, P. (1989). Content, causes and consequences of job insecurity: a theory-based measure and substantive test. *Academy of Management Journal, 32*, 803–829; Bergh, D.D. (1993). Watch time carefully: the use and misuse of time effects in management research. *Journal of Management, 19*, 683–705; Mishra, A.K. and Spreitzer, G.M. (1998). Explaining how survivors respond to downsizing. The roles of trust, empowerment, justice and work redesign. *Academy of Management Review, 23*, 567–588.
121. Armstrong-Stassen, M. (1997). The effect of repeated management downsizing and surplus designation on remaining managers: an exploratory study. *Anxiety, Stress and Coping, 10*, 377–384.
122. Armstrong-Stassen, M. (1998). Downsizing the federal government: a longitudinal study of managers' reactions. *Canadian Journal of Administrative Sciences, 15*, 310–321.
123. Armstrong-Stassen, M. (2002). Designated redundant but escaping lay-off: a special group of lay-off survivors. *Journal of Occupational and Organizational Psychology, 75*, 1–13.
124. Isaksson, K. and Johansson, G. (2000). Adaptation to continued work and early retirement following downsizing: long-term effects and gender differences. *Journal of Occupational and Organizational Psychology, 73*, 241–256.

125. Allen, T.D., Freeman, D.M., Russell, J.E.A., Reizenstein, R.C. and Rentz, J.O. (2001). Survivor reactions to organizational downsizing: does time ease the pain? *Journal of Occupational and Organizational Psychology, 74,* 145–164.
126. Rousseau, D.M. and Wade-Benzoni, K.A. (1995). Changing individual– organization attachments. In A. Howard (Ed.), *The changing nature of work.* San Francisco, CA: Jossey-Bass.
127. Dawis, R.V. and Lofquist, L.H. (1984). *A psychological theory of work adjustment.* Minnesota, MN: University of Minnesota Press.

6

Work and Career Transitions

Introduction: new patterns of career behaviour?

In this chapter, we focus on the impact that changes in the employment relationship have had for career behaviour and the resultant challenges that this creates for organizations. However, what is a career? It is defined by Arthur, Hall and Lawrence as 'the evolving sequence of a person's work experiences over time'.[1] Arthur and colleagues have recently pointed out that work takes up perhaps 50 hours a week of an individual's time and unfolds over a 40–50-year timespan.[2] The impact of the changing employment relationship on careers and the individual become clear from this.

Traditional career theory has always recognized the connection between careers and personal fulfilment. Employment and legal systems are still pervaded by the post-war concept of a career even though there is increasing pressure for new career behaviours. Indeed, much of the career management literature is still written in the light of internal labour markets. For example, Arthur and Rousseau[3] noted that a review of five interdisciplinary journals found that 75 per cent of the research articles published were looking at traditional intra-company rather than inter-company movements within large organizations. The majority of articles presumed a static host organization environment. The essence of traditional career theory has been to understand the sequences of behaviour that take place over time, discerning a series of 'career stages' that individuals characteristically go through, such as Super's observation that there were periods of exploration, advancement and maintenance.[4] These models were of course based largely on the experiences of males in the post-war period.

Arthur and colleagues draw attention to some early psychologically grounded developments in work on careers, which give far more weight to the role of personality and individual agency in shaping careers, such as the idea that people act as 'sculptors' of their own careers and that careers serve to create meaning in an individual's life.[5] However, it has been the boundaryless career perspective that has proved to be the most popular in articulating the new career challenges. By the mid-1990s speculation about the consequences of employability for careers took centre-stage, with discussion of the 'boundary-less career' by DeFillippi and Arthur[6] and the 'boundaryless organization' by Ashkenas and colleagues.[7] These discussions argued that the employing organization is simply one of several stakeholders in an individual's career development. Age-bound stereotypes such as 'new kid on the block', 'fast-track', 'climbing the ladder', 'at home looking after babies', 'career woman' and 'faithful company servant' seemed to be increasingly irrelevant.

A series of new prescriptions for career behaviour emerged in the 1990s as a series of books and journal papers brought a new vocabulary into the field of HRM, describing future careers under the labels of 'intelligent careers',[8] 'career resilient workforce',[9] and 'post-corporate careers'.[10] Peiperl et al. have recently summarized the implications of these changing concepts of working lives.[11] Even though evidence on the true level of inter-firm mobility outlined in Chapters 3 and 4 suggests that the boundaryless career might be an overstatement for many, critics could still look at the 'self-adjusting animal' and 'reconfigured diversity' stances noted in Figure 1.1 (which both stress more limited and evolutionary change in the psychological contract) and argue that the difference today from previous generations is that while researchers such as Super argued that historically the process of psychological disengage-ment from work was seen to begin at the age of 60[12], now for the majority of employees the process starts a good deal earlier. Proponents of the *boundaryless career* perspective argue that careers now cross multiple employment bound-aries. Consequently, as individuals we validate our experiences in a much wider range of employment situations, sustain a wider set of inter-company networks and develop and implement our careers in an arena that offers the choice of multiple employers. The yardstick by which we assess whether to stay with an employer is more to do with the successive accommodations that they can make to our personal learning and lifestyle agendas rather then because of simple loyalty. We are encouraged more to think of careers in terms of breaking through traditional work boundaries such as hierarchy, status, occupation, trade and job, as well as breaking through traditional social boundaries to do with family and home. It has been linked in particular to project-based organizations such as in semiconductors and the film industry.[13]

Arthur and colleagues are well aware that some of the more extreme behaviours are not indicative of the employment relationship for the economically disadvantaged or people marginalized in more insecure jobs. They argue, however, that the concept provides the opportunity for fresh solutions whereby individuals can be valued as retaining careers with an organization not for length of service or because of layers of privilege negotiated by job incumbents, but for the market value of their skills. They studied a group of 75 individuals from a range of occupational groups over a ten-year period[14] over which the 75 participants had held 265 jobs with 217 employers. Average job tenures typically ranged between 3 and 5 years. Rather than careers being characterized by a pattern of 'onwards and upwards' most of the voluntary job changes did not involve career advancement. Most cases of traditional career advancement occurred with moves between companies, not within companies, although even so the majority of inter-company moves did not involve advancement. Career moves were non-linear, with several lateral, diagonal or apparent downward shifts to adapt to changing situations. Individuals 'cycled' around activities without apparent progression, or 'spiralled' around different activities so that progression was apparent in terms of personal fulfilment, learning or earnings.

Negotiating career contracts

Given such emerging career patterns, although research on changes in the employment relationship reviewed in Chapters 3 and 4 shows that we are faced with a slow and incremental change process in the employment relationship, in some sectors the level of breach of psychological contract has been high and the emergence of new individual patterns of career behaviour are developing, as new contours within internal labour markets begin to emerge.

Research in sectors that have undergone significant amounts of rationalization, such as financial services does seem to suggest a more individually diverse attitudinal response to changes in the employment relationship and set of career preferences (see Table 6.1). Studies by Hartley, Herriot and Pemberton and Sparrow[15] have teased out quite different attitudinal and contractual stances held by segments of the workforce. For example, Sparrow[16] studied a major change initiative aimed at understanding the 'deal' sought by a structured sample of 200 employees in a large UK retail bank. Attitudes to pay, promotion, tenure, and flexibility were measured from the three attitudinal dimensions:

- What do you expect to happen?
- How do you feel about this?
- What do you intend to do?

Ninety-five per cent of the workforce expected less opportunity for promotion, only 7 per cent expected that promises about their career would be kept, 35 per cent expected actively to seek out a new job outside the company, and 43 per cent thought there was some possibility that they might be made compulsorily redundant in the future. When their expectations, feelings and intentions were factor analysed, it became clear that there were eight different *contractual stances* within this workforce.

Table 6.1 Diverse contractual stance or career contract frameworks

Sparrow's[17] contractual stances	Herriot and Pemberton's[18] career contracts
Still ambitious: understood the realities of the new deal but felt that some advancement was still possible for them	*Development or core deal:* organization seeks high flexibility, high commitment and work hours involvement, added-value in the skills the individual possesses. Individuals sign up to this deal in return for as much trust and security that the firm can offer, the provision of employability, and development of core skills.
Frustratedly mobile: had disengaged mentally and were hoping for and seeking a job elsewhere, but only because they were frustrated that their manager did not understand their needs	*Autonomy or project deal:* organization seeks specific but cross-organization skills for short time. Individuals capable of delivering high performance with low supervision or management. Individuals sign up to this deal in return for the provision of autonomy, freedom over how they design their work, and the provision of interesting and challenging work.
Passively flexible: expected to have to be more flexible in most areas, but had little enthusiasm for it or sense of agency in it	*Lifestyle or part-time deal:* organization seeks flexibility to match work and time pattern demands, part-time individuals with skills of a full-timer, and performance levels to match high levels of customer service. Individuals sign up to this deal in return for a willingness from their employer to balance their work with other lifestyle roles, and provision of work patterns matched to their lifestyle.
Lifers: respected the old deal, not impressed with performance pay, and thought that time-served and technical competence were a legitimate way to decide on advancement	
Buy me outers: had a price to buy them out of their job, waiting for right deal to come along	
Guidance seekers: needed help and assistance to understand what the changes meant for their careers and future course of action	
Don't push me too fast: understood and would go along the changes, but felt it was happening too fast and being asked to change too soon	
Just pay me more: transactional outlook, would take on most flexibilities at a negotiated price	

Source: Sparrow.[19]

The important point about the contractual stances discussed by Sparrow is that they do not represent different people (although people can be typed as holding a dominant attitudinal stance) but rather dimensions along which the attitudes held towards the new employment contract varied within the workforce. In principle, an individual might hold several of these positions to varying degrees, might be disengaged now, but be capable of redemption and re-engagement. The different contractual stances make it clear that a 'Lycra' or 'one-size-fits-all' brand of HRM, or the pursuit of high-commitment practices, is not something that will suit all of the workforce. The armoury brought to bear (cafeteria benefits, empowerment, performance-related pay, high-involvement teams and so forth) will not work for many segments of this workforce – 31 per cent of this workforce had disengaged in any event. The contractual stances were a source of major individual difference, and could not be predicted significantly by traditional internal labour market segmenting variables. Age, length of service, sex, and grade level together accounted for generally no more than 16 per cent of variance in contractual stances. Anyone could be a 'buy me outer'. Perceptions about the new employment contract are clearly relative, and responses highly variable.

Hartley's[20] survey analysis of 587 bank employees similarly found marked differences in job satisfaction and trust (not commitment) between key-time employees who chose to join a union and those who did not. The least satisfied, least trusting employees were more inclined to join the union. They had least faith in the intentions of managers, in their abilities or competence. The contours of change in insecurity are not straightforward as we saw in the previous chapter.

An indication of the transactions through which trust has to be re-established at the individual level can be gleaned from the recent book and model of career contracting processes by Herriot and Pemberton[21] (see Figure 6.1). There is a new context for organizational careers. The increased use of information technology and e-enablement of HR services has rendered the role of managers increasingly redundant as a channel for communication about careers and the devolution of budgets and decisions to lower levels of the hierarchy has reduced the need for supervisory and management control. The assumption that individuals only progress or best progress through internal labour markets within the organization and predictable movements up a hierarchy can no longer be made and expectations of security of employment are increasingly untenable. They argue that the new organizational context for careers means that individual employees should negotiate and renegotiate explicit understandings of what they expect to give and receive (see Box 6.1).

The challenge is to educate HR practitioners about the processes of individual career (or psychological) contracting – managing socialization, feelings, commitment and trust – and not just learning about the HR techniques that are associated with establishing a contract (the reward and performance management systems, training techniques and so forth). For researchers, an area of future clarification is whether it will be more important

Box 6.1 Contracting careers

Herriot and Pemberton's model of career contracting assumes a series of relationships. The business environment affects the strategy, structure and business process within the organization (see the discussion of new organizational forms in Chapter 1). This determines what the organization wants from their employees and what they are able to offer them. For the individual their career represents a fundamental part of their identity (see the discussion of organizational identification in Chapter 8). This career identity enables the individual to arrive at and prioritize their values and this in turn helps them decide which roles they will accept or reject, as well as helping them estimate their capabilities, self-esteem and self-efficacy. From their career identity emerges the wants they have of the organization, and what they have and are prepared to offer. A negotiating process lies at the heart of modern careers. Two things happen. First, the organization's wants are cognitively matched with the individual offers and vice versa. Second, each party is perceived to have made promissory offers (we discussed the nature of promises in Chapter 2) and a bargain is struck. This negotiation does not take place in a vacuum, as individuals might be vested with power from there being a seller's labour market, or the organization might have the benefit of a buyer's market. The exchange is also informal such that the clearer the communication, the fewer misunderstandings about wants, offers and contracts. An organizational career is then a repeated negotiation of the psychological contract.

Source: Herriot and Pemberton.[21]

to understand whether fulfilment of the *content* of the contract most predicts employee behaviour, i.e. whether the different 'contractual stances' noted earlier are in fact associated with different HRM preferences, or whether the *process through which it is negotiated*, as highlighted in this last section, are more important and predictive of eventual outcomes.[22]

Herriot and Pemberton have theorized about this question. We talked about the social climate that surrounds the psychological contract in the previous chapter and discussed the role of equity, fairness or justice. Herriot and Pemberton argue that two sorts of career contract result from the process outlined in Box 6.1. The individual may develop a transactional contract whereby the career exchange is purely instrumental – services in exchange for compensation. In such circumstances the individual's primary concern is whether the outcomes from the career deal continue to represent a fair exchange. They are most concerned about distributive justice. The second outcome is that the individual develops a relational career contract. This implies mutual commitment. In this case the individual is more concerned with the fairness of the procedures used to negotiate the career contract –

procedural justice. Not only do the two types of career contract result in different perceptions of what is fair treatment, the outcomes that result from fair treatment and honouring of the contract also differ. For transactional career individuals, the perception of a fair distribution of rewards will simply mean they continue on a transactional basis, but if the distribution is unfair they will renegotiate the terms of the contract or exit. For relational career individuals the key determinant is the fairness of procedures. If fair procedures are used and honoured then the outcome is mutual loyalty, trust and commitment and both parties offering each other benefits over and beyond the agreed contract. The perception of unfair procedures leads to much stronger emotional reactions of anger, grief and mistrust, however, a need to make sense of these emotions, defence mechanisms and an unpredictability of subsequent behaviours. This process is cyclical and continuous. The psychological contract formed might be between individuals and others who represent the organization's interests, but in knowledge-based organizations it might be between teams and the organization. Arnold points out that the model outlined above and in Box 6.1 means that:

> . . . both sides need to take a career perspective. Not a lifetime-of-employment type career, but career in the sense of a sequence of work-related experiences, roles, positions.[23]

There is a clear set of questions that have to be answered by both the employing organization and the individual as part of negotiating the career deal (see Table 6.2). The benefit of this is that rather than operate in what Schein[25] called a climate of mutual selling, both parties have to be honest about how they see themselves, what they want and what they are willing to offer. Even in a climate of distrust mutually satisfactory relationships between employee and organization can be negotiated. These negotiations clearly require negotiation skill as well as insight into one's own situation and an appreciation of the other's situation.

The need for more individually aware career contracting is evidenced by a number of special category employees. For example, we noted in Chapter 3 that boundaryless temporary employees are quite different from other temporaries. Human resource practices will have to vary to meet the needs of this type of employee.[27] Indeed, Marler and colleagues conclude:

> . . . managing the employment relationship with temporary employees is no less complex than with regular employees and perhaps slightly more challenging because the relationship is not directly with the employee but also with the temporary help agency. . . Boundaryless temporaries expect to earn higher market wages but may accept less in return for flexible assignments that also improve their marketability outside the organization. On the other hand, when demand for their skill is high, they will be less inclined to join an organization and more discriminating about the nature of their work.[28]

Table 6.2 Doing the career deal

Questions for the employing organization	Questions for the individual employee
How do employees discover what's expected of them now and in the future?	Do you know the organization's current business strategy, and what this means for its staffing policies?
How do employees learn about how the business is going?	Do you actively seek out information about what is happening in the organization, through official and unofficial routes?
How can they understand the implications for their career?	Do you know what is happening in other organizations in the same sector?
How does top management learn how employees are thinking?	Do you know who has the power base in the organization to help you get what you want?
Are individual differences in wants discovered and considered?	Do you know what mindset you are bringing to your own career, and how this could affect your approach to negotiation?
Does the organization ever engage in career negotiations – i.e. does it change its offers to accord with employees' wants and offers?	How well developed are your negotiating skills?
What types of employee wants is the organization prepared to consider (e.g. family situation, functional preference, external employability)?	Do you know what your own boundaries are for negotiating purposes, what is negotiable and what is not?
What sort of employee offer is the organization prepared to consider (i.e. existing expertise, development willingness)?	When moving job, do you consider the psychological contract you are seeking as well as the benefits package?
Who negotiates on behalf of the organization, and by what process?	What timespan are you operating with in your negotiation? Are you sure it is realistic?
Does the organization check whether it already has the skills and knowledge to meet its present needs? If so, how?	From the organization's point of view, what are your strengths and weaknesses?
	Can you use your strengths to offset your weaknesses?
Does the organization check whether it is developing the skills and knowledge to meet its future needs? If so, how?	Have you rehearsed selling your case in terms of business benefits rather than personal ones?

Table 6.2 continued

Questions for the employing organization	Questions for the individual employee
Does the organization review the nature of what it offers employees?	Do you know with whom you should be negotiating?
Does the organization monitor labour market trends in order to discover the likely availability of skills and knowledge?	Are you monitoring the operation of the contract, including any ways in which you and/or your family and/or the organization are changing?
Does the organization check up on the fulfilment of the contract? If so, how?	Do you monitor how much support the organization gives you, and whether this is enough to enable you to deliver your side of the contract?
Does the organization monitor the satisfaction of both parties with the contract? If so, how?	Do you monitor changes in the prominence and satisfaction you get from your various life roles?
Does the organization monitor the satisfaction of both parties with the contract? If so, who does this, and what resources do they need?	How does your organization signal that you are valued? Are you the recipient of these signals?
	Do you monitor the external environment, so that you can put your experiences and skills into a wider context?

Source: Arnold.[24]

The need to pursue different HR strategies for such employees is clear. As Marler and colleagues found, job characteristics and incentive systems had different motivating effects on boundaryless as opposed to traditional temporaries. Little, however, is known about the productivity effects of different HR strategies for different types of employee as defined by their psychological contract. Moreover, there is a conflict between the desire to better match HR systems to the unique needs and motivations of certain groups of employee, and the increasing legal scrutiny and regulation of the employment contract.

Re-engaging the workforce

Many organizations now see themselves faced with the challenge of re-engaging their workforce – winning back their hearts and minds. There are two important strategies that organizations have to pursue. They need to:

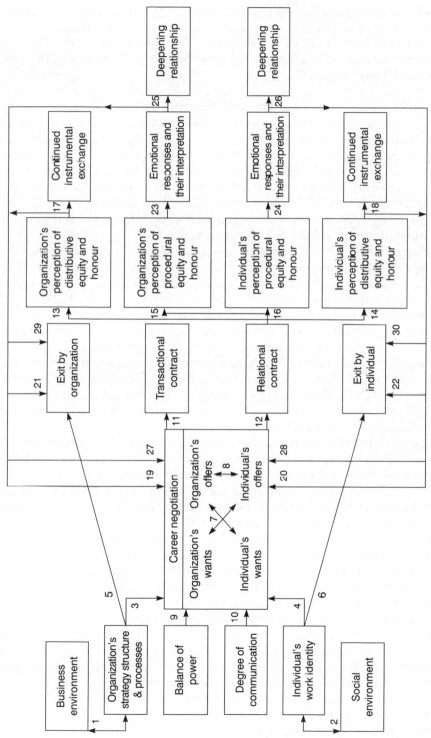

Figure 6.1 A contractual model of careers.
(*Source*: Herriot and Pemberton.[26])

1 Attend to the delivery of the basic mutualities of the contract to re-engage many employees, and to institute a process of individual dealing.[29]
2 Predict new internal labour market groupings on the basis of the different 'contractual stances' and develop different brands of HRM to suit the new internal labour markets.[30]

We use two examples from the retail banking sector to demonstrate the attention that can be given to recontracting the workforce as a whole, above and beyond initiating an individual contracting process. In the 1990s there were four threats to banking. There was saturation of mass markets for retail banking products. New economic agents such as supermarkets were bypassing the banking system and entering the market. Information technology was raising the level of competition leading to new product and service innovations. Finally, there were heightened customer performance expectations and this made it more difficult to cross-subsidize loss-incurring products.

The response in the industry was generic.[31] Banks attempted to provide customers with convenience. They sought precision in delivering their services, seeking to be able to launch new products quickly and in a variety of places. They ensured cost efficiency in their delivery channels. They sought greater market penetration by making front-line staff into sales agents (with an impact on the identity of these staff who had seen themselves as protecting the interests of banking clients rather than being a conduit for other financial services). The culture in branches became more technocratic, performance and sales orientated, flexible, and commercially driven. Finally, they refurbished branches, pushed ATM transactions, automated the back-office operations, set up regional service centres, and introduced more office reception and counselling space into branches.

There were two HR strategies that could be pursued. One was to use an empowerment strategy in which the investments in staff capability and high-performance work systems would be recouped theoretically by the fact that staff would become more productive, meet higher quality standards, make fewer mistakes, requiring less rework, build their customer relationship skills and therefore improve levels of customer retention. The second HR strategy was a control strategy. Here banks would maintain a tight cost control. They would avoid any detrimental declines in quality or lost sales opportunities through tight monitoring of performance. They would provide tightly targeted incentives to focus behaviour and rely on technology to deliver the majority of new products and services. The reality was that they pursued an unclear mix of both strategies, creating a rather divided level of organizational identity (we discuss the problems created by a schizophrenic organizational identity in Chapter 8). In the meantime the HR environment was one in which there was significant rationalization and downsizing, new performance-related pay initiatives, different performance criteria introduced into appraisal systems, customer-service checks by mystery shoppers, a squeeze on across-the-board pay rises and collective bargaining, a drive for greater productivity but a reduction in career promotion opportunities.

One of the better known responses was that made by the National Westminster Bank.[32] External research showed them that there was a dissatisfaction among the workforce at the rate at which they were driving out costs from the business through business process redesign initiatives. Staff considered that if they were to be innovative, they needed a more confident environment in which to develop new income streams. There was also low staff turnover, but this was indicative of the fact that there was nowhere for staff to go given that the whole sector was undergoing change. NatWest decided to initiate what it called A Proposition For Staff. They needed to know what were staff perceptions of the current 'deal' – what was the psychological contract? What was it that staff ideally required in return for the commitment and performance being asked of them? What would be commercially viable and acceptable for the organization to provide?

The organization held a series of one-to-one meetings with around 30 per cent of the most senior staff. It also ran focus groups with another 400 staff drawn from the heartland of the organization. These were intended to obtain views on their own and their staff's perceptions of and requirements in the employment relationship. The process was facilitated by an external agency and the report for the managing director was fed back to all staff. The organization decided that it had to segment its HR strategies across the different businesses. It concentrated on the identification and development of future capability requirements. The HR strategy was to influence and manage the behavioural and attitudinal changes needed through recruitment, development, reward, and retention policies. These policies were designed to facilitate the motivation needed for optimum business performance. A series of initiatives were introduced successively to build on this strategy. These included:

- a partnership relationship with the union allowing for greater access to information and wider territory for involvement
- a 'Staff as customers' programme, driven by the principle that all staff should be treated in the same way as customers
- a staff survey to monitor key indicators from a balanced scorecard perspective, in an attempt to remove the 'information filters' that exist in some organizations between employee feelings and management acknowledgement of the issues associated with this
- a flexible approach to working hours, with annualized hours (set at 1826 per year) and staff having the right to determine their own rosters within the team
- a confrontation of the long work hours culture and overtime practices
- more flexibility over job-sharing and offers of part-time work
- use of flexible rewards and a review of benefits, with the option to switch elements of salary increments to bonuses
- structural changes in some units in order to ease workloads and job pressures
- a revised career development approach, with increased levels of proactivity and a partnership approach to career development.

In explaining the impact that their approach to people management had had, the HR professionals at NatWest concluded '. . . we are still in the early stages of this development and recognize that changes may take place in our marketplace and/or internally which could either impact on the rate of introduction or indeed change the shape of the programme'.[33] However, the fragility of the above efforts should not be understated. The hostile takeover bid for NatWest on 29 November 1999 forced the organization to initiate further cost savings of £525 million. This meant that another 5000 jobs had to go on top of the 11 650 job losses that had already been earmarked. The final share dividends had to be increased by 25 per cent for the year. Moreover, there was an expectation of up to 18 000 more job losses after the takeover and more pressure was expected on the branch network. Nonetheless, the logic behind the strategy of re-engagement seems clear. Indeed, it has recently been emulated in another bank (see Box 6.2 for an outline of the initiatives taken at Barclays Bank).

The HR strategists at NatWest identified two primary influences that will shape the speed and ease with which organizations can re-engage their workforce through a psychological contracting strategy (see Figure 6.2).

In the best situation, the devolution of responsibility for HR would be very high and the line management would be very skilled in handling the

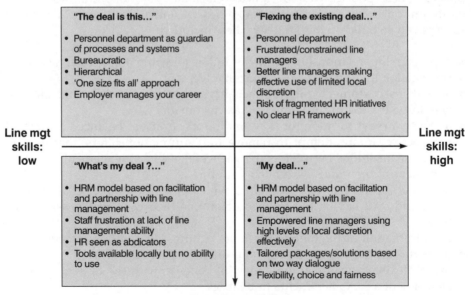

Figure 6.2 Four different psychological contracting scenarios.
(*Source*: Bendall *et al.*[34])

workforce. The role of HR would simply be one of facilitating the deal-creation process through partnership with managers. The same situation would apply if there was high devolution of HR to line managers but their skills in people management were low. The problem here, however, would be a sense of frustration among employees about the ability of managers to handle and discuss the real issues involved in negotiating an individualized deal, poor and variable levels of psychological contracting leading to perceptions of unfairness and inadvertent breach, and a risk that the HR function would be seen as having abdicated responsibility. If the HR department did not have trust in the skills of managers to conduct a psychological contracting process and HR was consequently relatively centralized, then the HR department would be seen as the guardian of career processes and systems. The risk would be an overly bureaucratic environment where the organization was seen as the manager of individuals' careers. In an environment of more individualized career demands the tensions that this would create seem obvious. Finally, the worst situation of all as far as managers would be concerned would be a scenario where they felt that they were skilled in managing individuals and in handling a sensitive and sophisticated contracting process, but the HR department had not devolved responsibility to them and still ran centralized systems. The better line managers would try to use their discretion effectively but there would be a risk of a series of fragmented initiatives and a lack of clear frameworks by which the employee could judge whether the organization had kept to its side of the deal. Put bluntly, an individualized psychological contracting process within organizations is critically dependent on there being a sophisticated set of people management skills distilled throughout the organization. The level of competency, capability and desire among line managers to be made responsible for formally managing a psychological contracting approach becomes a critical determinant of an organization's ability to respond to some of the challenges faced in the employment relationship. As Sparrow has noted: '. . . critical decisions have to be made about the rate of devolution of HRM policies and the rate of upskilling of managers'.[35]

Theoretical insights into work transitions

Herriot argues that the experience of the organizations such as NatWest and Barclays above raises a fundamental challenge for HR functions: '. . . Structural change is now so frequent an event that organizations are permanently in a state of transition.' This means that the role of the HR function will be one of '. . . enabling the organization to prepare for, encounter and adjust to new structures and processes. And that will in turn require them to help employees make the individual transitions which these organizational transitions imply.'[37]

Transitions at work are considered to involve a series of changes. The most notable changes are in: how a person understands the world; where he or she locates themselves within this world; what he or she does day by day; and how

Box 6.2   Satisfaction guaranteed at Barclays[36]

In the late 1990s Barclays had a very demoralized workforce. It had initiated an ill-judged branch closure programme and had charged non-Barclays customers for use of cash machines. A protracted pay dispute in 1997 meant that industrial relations with the Unifi union were very negative. A new chief executive, Matthew Barrett, launched a strategy of doubling the value of the banking group every four years. Radical restructuring and cost cutting was involved – for example, the HR function moved to a shared service centre supported by six centres of excellence while cutting costs by 34 per cent and headcount by 46 per cent. Barclays Business Banking wants to be a low-cost producer of products and services that it creates. It considers that its differentiation comes from the quality of people who deliver these products and services. The new strategy involved a model based on relationships and customer service, putting HR issues at the heart of commercial decision making. By 1999 the first groupwide staff survey identified widespread concerns about job security and organizational leadership. A 21-day communication programme involved the executive team in addressing 12 000 employees at a variety of events. Follow-up events were run for thousands of team leaders under the theme of 'Climbing the big mountain'. Teamworking behaviours, which included a customer focus and business awareness, were incorporated into a new pay mechanism. Money was targeted at high-performers who were at the lower end of the salary ranges in order to bring them up to market level, rather than at the highly visible well-paid stars. In 2001 a three-year pay deal was negotiated with the unions and a partnership agreement reached. Money was put aside to develop employees with a £150 individual grant to spend on any form of learning, a state-of-the-art learning centre and a Barclays University to act as a gateway to higher education and training providers. The impact on employee engagement has been dramatic. In October 2001, when the first roadshows took place, 54 per cent of employees would recommend Barclays Business Banking to friends and relatives as a good place to work. By mid-2002 that figure was 73 per cent. The most recent staff survey shows a 19 per cent improvement in employees' perception of the impact the business has on society. The financial results are also improving with operating profits up from £830 million to £984 from 1999 to 2001. At its Investors' day 50 front-line staff are now at hand to answer questions and demonstrate the quality of the workforce.

Source: Arkin and Allen.[36]

he or she relates to other people.[38] These transitions can also include non-events – failing to achieve an expected promotion can require just as many changes above as changing employer. Our discussion of job insecurity in the previous chapter should be seen in the same light. Insecurity might not be supported by any detrimental actual event, but subtle psychological changes even beyond those measured by insecurity researchers might nonetheless take place. However, it should be noted that most of the work transition literature concentrates on how people respond and adapt to events.[39]

A number of psychologists have examined the way in which individuals learn to cope and adapt to change at work. The most notable of these have been the work of Hopson and colleagues[40] on managing personal change, Kubler-Ross[41] and Parkes[42] on adjustment to loss and grief reactions, and Nicholson on cycles of transition at work.[43] The experience of transitions is considered to be a stressful life event and while the majority of models describe major change as a negative event, most also propose that transition from one state to another can culminate in psychologically beneficial outcomes. The experience of individual change can be described as a psychological adjustment involving movement from one state to another. It should be emphasized, however, that individual change cannot be explained according to any one particular model. This is because people change at different rates and do not go through every 'phase' described in every model. Most people also oscillate between the stages. In order to understand the nature of these changes, psychologists tend to draw on two broad types of theory.

The first source of understanding draws upon the long-standing interest that psychologists have shown in understanding how people cope with the trauma of major life-spanning events, such as bereavement. Kubler-Ross articulated a model that described reactions after a divorce or the loss of a loved one.[44] Much of the literature on downsizing and survivor reactions has adopted the *Bereavement Phase Model* theoretical perspective. Closely associated with this work on bereavement are Adams, Hayes and Hopson[45] (see Box 6.3).

One difficulty with the bereavement or traumatic life event phase theories is that they might tend to overstate the negative emotions associated with career and work transitions. Moreover, there are a number of questions that need to be resolved.[47] It is by no means certain whether all people have to go through all stages, whether they may have to recycle through certain stages, whether the emotions at one stage have to be resolved before emotions at a subsequent stage can be, or whether unresolved stages may be repressed.

The second source of understanding is Nicholson and West's *Work role transition theory*[48] (see Box 6.4). Work role transitions are initiated by significant changes in:

1 the role requirements or job context, such as changes in the job itself (new responsibilities, modified reported relationships, new co-workers, or new policies and procedures) or
2 a requirement to move within or between organizations (frequently triggered by job loss, promotion, or decisions to leave the organization).

Box 6.3 Personal transition phases

Adams, Hayes and Hopson consider that all transitions – even those welcomed by an individual – are traumatic and stressful. They identified seven stages that an individual passes through in any transition:

1 Immobilization. The person is unable to make any plans, to reason, or to understand what is happening. Everything is problematic.
2 Minimization. The person denies that change is happening, or at least attempts to make it seem as small as possible.
3 Depression. The reality of change is now acknowledged, but the person feels powerless to do anything about it, and is uncertain about how to cope.
4 Letting go. The person fully accepts that his or her old situation really is a thing of the past, and cannot be re-created.
5 Testing. The person starts trying out new ways of coping; new patterns of living. At first he or she may need to see things in overly simplistic ways in order to make them understandable.
6 Searching for meaning. The person tries to understand how and why things are the way they are.
7 Internalization. The person now takes on the new reality as his or her own. Self is seen more in terms of his or her new role.

Emotions (in the form of general morale) change significantly over these stages. They begin at moderate levels during immobilization and minimization, fall drastically during depression and acceptance of reality, and begin a slow recovery during testing and subsequent stages, eventually surpassing the start point during the search for meaning, and ending at a more positive level once internalization is reached. The most appropriate strategy for people experiencing a difficult transition is to:[46]

1 Handle one crisis at a time – don't try to deal with everything at once.
2 Seek information from multiple sources.
3 Formulate specific, attainable goals.
4 Rehearse new behaviours in 'safe' situations.
5 Monitor your own reactions – feelings as well as thoughts.
6 Have contingency plans.
7 Look after yourself – give yourself treats now and then.
8 Get reasonable amounts of sleep and exercise.
9 Look out for gains made, things that are going well.
10 Reflect on past experiences of transitions and learn from them.

Source: Adams *et al.*[45]

Nicholson and West argued that there are important distinctions between each stage. This can be seen in Box 6.4 by the different areas of focus, common problems and strategic solutions typical at each stage. The stages are interdependent, in that what happens in one stage influences the next stage. Positive resolution of issues in a previous stage facilitates progress in the next stage. Nicholson and West noted that by the late 1980s around 33 per cent of managers were experiencing significant business reorganizations or organizational changes and that 46 per cent of newly created jobs originated from such changes. The speed of change in role focus these days means that the traditional role of being a custodian, and indeed also being an innovator, mean that the adjustment phase is becoming a major challenge. Indeed, newcomers increasingly have to find their own way of doing things, and need the organization simply to facilitate this. The model produced three important insights into transitions.[49] Notably:

1 Transitions begin well before the first day that an individual is put into the new environment
2 Newcomers and the organization benefit from appreciating 'the lie of the land' before understanding how they will deal with it, and emotions are minimized by this
3 Organizations foolishly try to squeeze performance from new role incumbents immediately, but encounter and adjustment are needed in order to avoid mistakes, duplication, and subversion of effort.

Some of the limited negative outcomes revealed by recent longitudinal studies of downsizing might be explained by work role transition theory. For example, in the popular business press at the end of the 1980s it was noted that new and different career opportunities might emerge after the elimination of dead wood[50] and reduced layers of the hierarchy might actually result in higher levels of autonomy.[51]

Herriot warns that in considering the organizational and individual transitions taking place, the danger that we face is that the opportunity for stabilization has often been removed:

> . . . Our habitual analysis has always assumed that stabilization was the norm, and that the other three stages simply punctuated periods of stability. Yet there is an argument for saying that the stability stage actually seldom occurs. Rather, organizational life today consists increasingly only of preparation, encounter and adjustment. Many would assert that there is little or no opportunity to prepare, since many changes are forced on organizations by external events . . . and those who allow that preparation is usually possible nevertheless admit that preparation for the next change has to occur while they are still adjusting to the previous one.[53]

Just as organizational transitions are truncated such that preparation and stabilization are frequently omitted, so individual transitions are also fre-

Box 6.4   Nicholson's work role/ job transition theory

Work role transitions cover four stages:

1 *Preparation:* Period before starting a new job, when the fact that it is going to happen is known or expected. Immediate antecedents and consequences of change events. Period of psychological readiness. *Focus*: Expectations and motives. *Common problems*: unrealistic expectations, unreadiness, fearfulness. *Strategies*: self-appraisal, making advance contacts, realistic job previews.

2 *Encounter:* First few days and weeks following transition. Task for newcomer and organization is to develop basic understanding of roles, relationships, expectations and behaviours associated with new situation. Psychological defence mechanisms appear such as denial and withdrawal. *Focus*: Emotions and perceptions. *Common problems*: shock, rejection, regret. *Strategies*: social support, freedom to explore, information gathering.

3 *Adjustment:* Approach person takes to doing their job. Newcomer and organization seek ways of handling the new situation to mutual satisfaction. Change assimilated and adjusted to. Shock and surprise subsides and new priorities emerge. Work roles, changed interactions and new work culture begin to appear. *Focus*: Changes made in self and other party. *Common problems*: misfitting, grieving. *Strategies*: useful work, feedback.

4 *Stabilization:* Each side has fairly constant and rarely disconfirmed experience of each other. The individual strives to maintain valued elements of their current role, making fine adjustments, and either enjoys success or suffers from failure. The pace of change in some jobs means this stage is never reached. *Focus*: performance. *Common problems*: failure, boredom, stagnation. *Strategies*: goal-setting, project work.

Work role transitions are stressful during the initial encounter period, but positive feelings can return depending on the freedom, challenge and the opportunity to grow in the new job. However, healthy adult development depends on periods of both change and discontinuity, as well as on stability and continuity.[52]

Source: Nicholson.[43]

quently only allowing for encounter and adjustment, with preparation for the next change taking place while some adjustment to the last is still happening. If organizations are to manage this individual transition process successfully, Herriot argues that they have to engage with employee feelings associated with five discussions:

- *Outcomes for the individual*: is a role change seen as an opportunity, a cross-functional move as an irrevocable step, or redundancy as a personal disaster or freedom at last? What is the balance between more time but less money or more money but less time on feelings of survival, lifestyle and health?
- *Predictability of the transition*: has change been signalled in advance and do people know when it is going to happen? What is the balance between feelings of helplessness and anxiety as opposed to preparation and mental practice or rehearsal for the event?
- *Optionality of the decision:* has the individual any say in whether a transition happens for them and the nature of the change? What is the balance between perceived imposition and feelings of resentment and helplessness, or choice in commitment to the transition and motivation to make it succeed?
- *Clarity of the post-transition role*: has it been described? What is the balance between an outline that is so specific that inhibits its adaptation, or an outline that is so loose that it raises anxiety?
- *Justification or purpose of the transition*: have the reasons been clarified to the individual? Are the attributions for the reason for change external, with dangers of powerlessness, or are the attributions to the individual, with dangers for self-esteem?

Career adjustments: underemployment and relative deprivation

In Chapter 5 we examined a series of studies that all focused on the immediate and medium-term consequences of layoffs on *the survivors within organizations*. What of those who have to make more significant readjustments and find re-employment? Most of the research on job loss has taken the attainment of re-employment as its end-point. Once laid-off workers find another job, they cease to be the focus of research attention, despite the fact that there may be long-term effects on the their careers.[54] One way of gaining insight into whether there are any longer-term shifts in attitudes and behaviours at work is to examine the experiences of the re-employed. This is because evidence suggests that it is the quality of replacement jobs and not just the attainment of re-employment which becomes the major determinant of future career trajectories and psychological well-being.[55] Where laid-off workers become re-employed in lower-quality jobs they tend to have more negative attitudes towards their new employers, invest less energy in their new jobs, and remain more likely to keep searching for different jobs even after accepting positions.[56]

The work of Feldman has become associated with the issue of under-employment – jobs which the job-holders perceive as being lower in quality in some way.[57] Jobs may be perceived as being of lower quality because they:

1 Are considered to be lower in the hierarchy of employment, e.g. employees laid off from permanent full-time jobs find themselves working in part-time or temporary jobs at lower levels of the hierarchy.
2 Involve a loss of wages, e.g. research on re-employment problems after the Great Depression used a rate of income loss of 33 per cent as the standard for underemployment,[58] and more recent research considers that if current earnings fall by 20 per cent compared to the previous job then under-employment exists.[59]
3 Do not fully utilize the skills and abilities for which the job-holder has been officially trained or educated, e.g. jobs taken by teenage school leavers or qualified graduates.[60]

Work in the late 1980s by O'Brien and Feather indicated that the psychological consequences of *underemployment* can be as detrimental as those of unemployment itself.[61] During the 1990s the issue of underemployment gained attention through studies on two main groups of employees: laid-off manual workers[62] and underemployed graduates.[63] The latter group became the centre of attention because of concerns either about the persistence of high levels of youth unemployment and the detrimental effect of make-work employment schemes or over the mismatch between the high expectations of an MBA-educated set of work entrants and subsequent low-quality employ-ment experiences. For example, in studies of MBA graduates individuals who had their psychological contracts violated were more likely to be cynical about the relationship between hard work and career success[64] and were less likely to stay two years with their employers or give advance notice before leaving.[65] In short, research on MBAs shows that underemployment among the more competent leads to more careerist attitudes towards work and an increased reliance on non-performance tactics such as networking and impression management.[66] More generally, underemployment has been associated with: higher levels of job dissatisfaction; lower organizational commitment; lower trust (expectations of another's goodwill, willingness to reciprocate and honouring of commitments); and greater job-searching behaviour.[67]

A recent study of 517 senior managers who had been laid off from their jobs within the past twelve months but who had subsequently found re-employment[68] tested for the effects of underemployment on subsequent work attitudes, and for the mediating impact of relative deprivation (see Box 6.5 for an outline of *relative deprivation theory*). The managers had all been found new jobs, on average after a period of five months, through the services of an outplacement organization. Three forms of underemployment were measured – *hierarchical loss, pay loss,* and *inferior skill utilization* – and their impact on job satisfaction, commitment, trust, job searching and careerism examined. The impact of pay cuts has dominated the underemployment literature but in each

Box 6.5   Relative deprivation theory

Early organizational research considered that job satisfaction worked on a discrepancy basis. Lawler argued that an individual's satisfaction with their job was not just a function of how positive the *actual* job conditions were but were also a function of what job conditions the employee felt *should exist*.[70] Equity theory, as proposed by Adams, considered that an individual's satisfaction with, for example, pay was determined by how the ratio of the job rewards to job inputs that they received (reward–effort bargain) stacked up against the ratio of job rewards to job inputs that their colleagues received.[71]

It is the process of comparisons that shapes an individual's attitudes. Relative deprivation theory builds on this observation, but argues that it is not just the individual's assessment of specific jobs that is important, but also their sense of injustice with various societal conditions. The concept was first introduced to explain levels of satisfaction among soldiers after the Second World War which did not seem to coincide with their objective job conditions.[72] It differs from equity theory in some important ways. Equity theory examines how employees assess the fairness of job rewards relative to their *present* colleagues, but relative deprivation theory concerns assessments in relation to *previous injustices* and frustrated hopes with regard to *future employment*. It has been used to explain a series of social problems where people's subjective feelings and objective circumstances do not match, such as race and gender discrimination[73] and also perceived inequities in pay rises and promotion decisions.[74] The concept of relative deprivation refers to an individual's *subjective* reactions to their employment predicament, and argues that how individuals react negatively to a situation such as underemployment will depend on how much the individual wants job rewards, feels entitled to those rewards, and the standards that they use to compare and assess the fairness and justness of the rewards that they receive.[75] Two components of relative deprivation – wanting more and feeling entitled to more – appear to be the most predictive of impact on other behaviours.[76]

Source: Feldman *et al.*[56]

case, it was the *skill utilization* form of underemployment that was significantly related to the various outcome measures. Pay loss had no impact on subsequent work outcomes and hierarchical loss only impacted commitment negatively. The importance of skill underutilization has been examined in the re-employment of expatriates, but it clearly is an important variable to examine in more general re-employment situations.[69] Moreover, the effects of underemployment were mediated by relative deprivation. Underemployment generates feelings of relative deprivation which then impacts adversely on the attitudes that the individual holds both towards their present job and their careers in general.

This study has many practical implications, not least of which is that outplacement firms looking for replacement positions for managers should track the level of skill utilization in replacement jobs. Even among downsized executives with significant financial resources, underemployment creates feelings of relative deprivation which do not automatically disappear when they obtain new jobs. The researchers concluded that while dominant models of job satisfaction generally suggest that employees' reactions to their jobs are largely a function of their experiences with their *present* employers, their results showed that the job attitudes of laid-off managers may be due as much to their experiences with their *past* employers as to any ill behaviour on the part of their current employers. Future research will undoubtedly consider how other factors – such as procedural justice and psychological contract violations – may create perceptions of relative deprivation and lead to fundamental conscious or unconscious changes in the psychological contract.

This process of individualization creates some significant challenges for managing the employment relationship. We examine some of these challenges in more detail in the next chapter.

References

1. Arthur, M.B., Hall, D.T. and Lawrence, B.S. (1989). (Eds.) *Handbook of career theory.* Cambridge: Cambridge University Press, p. 8.
2. Arthur, M.B., Inkson, K. and Pringle, J.K. (1999). *The new careers: individual action and economic change.* London: Sage Publications.
3. Arthur, M.B. and Rousseau, D.M. (1996). Introduction: the boundaryless career as a new employment principle. In M.B. Arthur and D.M. Rousseau (Eds.), *The boundaryless career.* Oxford: Oxford University Press.
4. Super, D.E. (1957). *The psychology of careers.* New York: Harper and Row.
5. Bell, N.E. and Staw, B.M. (1989). People as sculptors versus sculpture: the roles of personality and personal control in organizations. In M.B. Arthur, D.T. Hall and B.S. Lawrence (Eds.), *Handbook of career theory.* Cambridge: Cambridge University Press.
6. DeFillippi, R.J. and Arthur, M.B. (1994). The boundaryless career: a competency-based prospective. *Journal of Organizational Behavior, 15 (4),* 307–324.
7. Ashkensas, R., Ulrich, D., Jick, T. and Kerr, S. (1995). *The boundaryless organization.* San Francisco: Jossey-Bass.
8. Arthur, M.B., Claman, P.H. and DeFillippi, R.J. (1995). Intelligent enterprise, intelligent careers. *Academy of Management Executive, 9 (4),* 7–22.
9. Hind, P., Frost, M. and Rowley, S. (1996). The resilience audit and the psychological contract. *Journal of Managerial Psychology, 11,* 18–29; Waterman, R.H. Jr, Waterman, J.A. and Collard, B.A. (1994). Toward a career-resilient workforce. *Harvard Business Review, 72 (4),* 87–95.

10. Peiperl, M.A. and Baruch, Y. (1997). Back to square zero: the post-corporate career. *Organizational Dynamics, 25 (4)*, 7–22.
11. Peiperl, M.A., Arthur, M., Goffee, R. and Morris, T. (2000). (Eds.) *Career frontiers: new conceptions of working lives.* Oxford: Oxford University Press.
12. Super, D. (1980). A life span, life space approach to career development. *Journal of Vocational Behaviour, 16,* 282–298.
13. See, for example, Saxenian, A.L. (1996). Beyond boundaries: open labour markets and learning in Silicon Valley. In M.B. Arthur and D.M. Rousseau (Eds.), *The boundaryless career.* Oxford: Oxford University Press; Jones, C. (1996). Careers in project networks: the case of the film industry. In M.B. Arthur and D.M. Rousseau (Eds.), *The boundaryless career.* Oxford: Oxford University Press.
14. Arthur, M.B., Inkson, K. and Pringle, J.K. (1999). *The new careers: individual action and economic change.* London: Sage Publications.
15. See, for example, Hartley, J. (1995). Challenge and change in employment relations: issues for psychology, trade unions and managers. In L.E. Tetrick and J. Barling (Eds.), *Changing employment relations: behavioural and social perspectives* Washington, DC: American Psychological Association; Herriot, P. and Pemberton, C. (1996). Contracting careers. *Human Relations, 49 (6),* 757–790; Sparrow, P.R. (1996). Transitions in the psychological contract in UK banking, *Human Resource Management Journal, 6 (4),* 75–92.
16. Sparrow (1996). *Op. cit.*
17. *Ibid.*
18. Herriot and Pemberton (1996). *Op. cit.*
19. Sparrow, P.R. (2000). The new employment contract. In R. Burke and C.L. Cooper (Eds.), *The organization in crisis.* London: Basil Blackwell.
20. Hartley (1995). *Op. cit.*
21. See Herriot, P. and Pemberton, C. (1995). *The career management challenge.* Sage: London; and Herriot, P. and Pemberton, C. (1996). Contracting careers. *Human Relations, 49 (6),* 757–790.
22. Sparrow, P.R. and Marchington, M. (1998). Re-engaging the human resource management function: rebuilding work, trust and voice. In P.R. Sparrow, P.R. and M. Marchington, M. (Eds.), *Human resource management: the new agenda,* London: Financial Times/Pitman Publishing.
23. Arnold, J. (1997). *Managing careers into the 21st century.* London: Paul Chapman Publishing, p. 44.
24. *Ibid.* pp. 44 and 45.
25. Schein, E. (1978). *Career dynamics.* Reading, MA: Addison-Wesley.
26. Herriot and Pemberton (1996). *Op. cit.*
27. McLean Parks, J., Kidder, D.L. and Gallagher, D.G. (1998). Fitting square pegs into round holes: mapping the domain of contingent work relationships onto the psychological contract. *Journal of Organizational Behavior, 19,* 697–730.
28. Marler, J.H., Barringer, M.W. and Milkovich, G.T. (2002). Boundaryless and traditional contingent employees: worlds apart. *Journal of Organizational Behavior, 23,* 425–453, p. 448.

29. Herriot, P., Manning, W.E.G. and Kidd, J.M. (1997). The content of the psychological contract. *British Journal of Management, 8 (2),* 151–162.
30. Sparrow, P.R. and Marchington, M. (1998). (Eds.), *Human resource management: the new agenda,* London: Financial Times/Pitman Publishing.
31. Sparrow, (1996). *Op. cit.*
32. Bendall, S.E., Bottomley, C.R. and Cleverly, P.M. (1998). Building a new proposition for staff at NatWest UK. In P.R. Sparrow and M. Marchington (Eds.), *Human resource management: the new agenda,* London: Financial Times/Pitman Publishing.
33. Bendall *et al.* (1998). *Op cit.,* p. 105.
34. *Ibid.*
35. Sparrow, P.R. (1998). New organizational forms, processes, jobs and psychological contracts: resolving the HRM issues. In P.R. Sparrow and M. Marchington (Eds.), *Human resource management: the new agenda,* London: Financial Times/Pitman Publishing, p. 137.
36. Arkin, A. and Allen, R. (2002). Satisfaction guaranteed. *People Management, 8 (21),* 40–42.
37. Herriot, P. (1998). The role of the HR function in building a new proposition for staff. In P.R. Sparrow, P.R. and M. Marchington, M. (Eds.), *Human resource management: the new agenda,* London: Financial Times/Pitman Publishing, p. 113.
38. Arnold (1997). *Op. cit.*
39. Schlossberg, N.K. (1981). A model for analysing human adaptation to transition, *The Counseling Psychologist, 9 (2),* 2–18.
40. Hopson, B (1984). Transition: understanding and managing personal change, In C.L. Cooper and P.J. Makin (Eds.), *Psychology for managers.* London: Macmillan; Adams, J.D., Hayes, J. and Hopson, B. (1976). *Transition: understanding and managing personal change.* London: Martin Robertson.
41. Kubler-Ross, E. (1969). *On death and dying.* New York: Macmillan.
42. Parkes, C M (1996). *Bereavement: studies of grief in adult life, 3rd edition.* London: Penguin.
43. Nicholson, N. (1990). The transition cycle: Causes, outcomes, processes and forms in S. Fisher & C.L. Cooper (Eds), *On the move: the psychology of change and transition,* Chichester: Wiley.
44. Kubler-Ross (1969). *Op. cit.*
45. Adams, J.D., Hayes, J. and Hopson, B. (1976). *Transition: understanding and managing personal change.* London: Martin Robertson.
46. See, for example, Hamburg, D., Coelho, G. and Adams, J. (1974). Coping and adaptation: steps toward a synthesis of biological and social perspectives. In G. Coelho, D. Hamburg and J. Adams (Eds.), *Coping and adaptation.* New York: Basic Books; Hopson, B. (1984). Transition: understanding and managing personal change, In C.L. Cooper and P.J. Makin (Eds.), *Psychology for managers.* London: Macmillan.
47. Arnold (1997). *Op. cit.*
48. Nicholson, N. and West, M.A. (1988). *Managerial job change: men and women in transition.* Cambridge: Cambridge University Press.

49. Arnold (1997). *Op. cit.*
50. Isabella, L.A. (1989). Downsizing: survivors' assessments. *Business Horizons*, May, 35–41.
51. Stewart, T.A. (1989). New ways to exercise power. *Fortune*, 6 November, 52–66.
52. Levinson, D.J. (1986). A conception of adult development. *American Psychologist, 41*, 3–13.
53. Herriot, (1998). *Op. cit.*
54. Leana, C.R. and Feldman, D.C. (1995). Finding new jobs after a plant closing: antecedents and outcomes of the occurrence and quality of re-employment. *Human Relations, 48*, 1381–1401.
55. Kaufman, H. (1982). *Professionals in search of work.* New York: Wiley.
56. Feldman, D.C., Leana, C.R. and Bolino, M.C. (2002). Underemployment and relative deprivation among re-employed executives. *Journal of Occupational and Organizational Psychology, 75 (4)*, 453–472.
57. Feldman, D.C. (1996). The nature, antecedents and consequences of underemployment. *Journal of Management, 22*, 385–409.
58. Elder, G. (1974). *Children of the Great Depression: Social change in life experiences.* Chicago: University of Chicago Press.
59. Zvonkovic, A.M. (1988). Underemployment: Individual and marital adjustment to income loss. *Lifestyles: Family and Economic Issues, 9*, 161–178.
60. See Clogg, C.C., Sullivan, T. and Mutchler, J. (1986). Measuring underemployment and inequality in the work force. *Social Indicators Research, 18*, 375–393; Humphrys, P. and O'Brien, G.E. (1986). The relationship between skill utilization, professional orientation and job satisfaction for pharmacists. *Journal of Occupational Psychology, 59*, 315–326.
61. See O'Brien, G.E. (1986). *Psychology of work and unemployment.* New York: Wiley; O'Brien, G.E. and Feather, N.T. (1990). The relative effects of unemployment and quality of employment on the affect, work values and personal control of adolescents. *Journal of Occupational Psychology, 63*, 151–165.
62. Leana and Feldman (1995). *Op. cit.*
63. Feldman, D.C. and Turnley, W.H. (1995). Underemployment among recent business college graduates. *Journal of Organizational Behavior, 16*, 691–706; Winefield, A. and Tiggemann, M. (1990). Employment status and psychological well-being: a longitudinal study. *Journal of Applied Psychology, 75*, 455–459; Winefield, A., Winefield, H., Tiggemann, M. and Goldney, R. (1991). A longitudinal study of the psychological effects of unemployment and unsatisfactory employment on young adults. *Journal of Applied Psychology, 76*, 424–431.
64. Rousseau, D.M. (1990). New hire perceptions of their own and their employer's obligations: a study of psychological contracts. *Journal of Organizational Behavior, 11*, 389–400.
65. Robinson, S.L., Kraatz, M.S. and Rousseau, D.M. (1994). Changing obligations and the psychological contract: a longitudinal study. *Academy of Management Journal, 37*, 137–152.

66. Feldman (1996). *Op. cit.*
67. Borgen, W.A., Amundson, N.E. and Harder, H.G. (1988). The experience of underemployment. *Journal of Employment Counselling*, 25, 149–159; Rousseau, D.M., Sitkin, S.B., Burt, R.S. and Camerer, C. (1998). Not so different after all: A cross-discipline view of trust. *Academy of Management Review*, 23, 393–404.
68. Feldman *et al.* (2002). *Op. cit.*
69. Bolino, M.C. and Feldman, D.C. (2000). Increasing the skill utilization of expatriates. *Human Resource Management*, 39, 367–380.
70. Lawler, E.E. III (1973). *Motivation in work organizations*. Monterey, CA: Brooks/Cole.
71. Adams, J.S. (1976). Equity theory revisited: Comments and annotated bibliography. In L. Berkowitz (Ed.), *Advances in experimental social psychology, Volume 9*. New York: Academic Press.
72. Stouffer, S.A., Suchman, E.A., DeVinney, L.C., Star, S.A. and Williams, R.M. (1949). *The American soldier: adjustments during army life. Volume 1*. Princeton, NJ: Princeton University Press.
73. Crosby, F. (1976). A model of egoistical relative deprivation. *Psychological Review*, 83, 85–113; Crosby, F. (1982). *Relative deprivation and working women*. New York: Oxford University Press.
74. See, for example, Buunk, B.P. and Janssen, P. (1992). Relative deprivation, career issues, and mental health among men in midlife. *Journal of Vocational Behavior*, 40, 338–350; Martin, J. (1981). Relative deprivation: a theory of distributive injustice for an era of shrinking resources. In B.M. Staw and L.L. Cummings (Eds.), *Research in organizational behavior, Volume 3*. Greenwich, CT: JAI Press; Sweeney, P.D., McFarlin, D.B. and Inderrieden, E.J. (1990). Using relative deprivation theory to explain satisfaction with income and pay level: a multistudy examination. *Academy of Management Journal*, 33, 423–436.
75. Feldman, D.C. Leana, C.R. and Turnley, W.H. (1997). A relative deprivation approach to understanding underemployment. In C.L. Cooper and D.M. Rousseau (Eds.), *Trends in organizational behavior. Volume 4*. New York: Wiley.
76. Olson, J. and Hafer, C.L. (1996). Affect, motivation, and cognition in relative deprivation research. In R.M. Sorrentino and E.T. Higgins (Eds.), *Handbook of motivation and cognition, Volume 3*. New York: Guilford Press; Olson, J., Roese, N., Meen, J. and Robertson, D. (1995). The preconditions and consequences of relative deprivation: two field studies. *Journal of Applied Social Psychology*, 25, 944–964.

7

Individualization of Human Resource Management

Individualization of work

The previous chapter on work and career transitions demonstrated how individualized the employment relationship has become. The theme that cut across that chapter was the management of more diverse relationships. In this chapter we concentrate and build upon the theme of individualization of the employment relationship. Why is individualization so important? We argue that individual capability (talent) and individual engagement (hearts and minds) is now becoming a key differentiator for many organizations in the effectiveness of the employment relationship. Yet, in saying this, as individuals, organizations and societies we face immense challenges in responding to this individualization without destroying the benefits that are derived from community and collectivism. The individual risks are high. For example, in Chapter 3 we outlined the view of labour economists on the growth of non-standard employment. Mangan[1] pointed out that non-standard employment covers a wide range of income levels and is associated with a range of experience in terms of desirability and job satisfaction. At the upper end of the desirability scale might be the self-employed, independent contractors and permanent part-time workers (where firms allow this option for retention reasons). These individuals might enjoy relatively attractive combinations of income, job stability and autonomy at work. At the opposite end of the desirability scale are those in precarious employment with low wages, low job security and little workplace discretion.

As has been seen throughout this book so far, the *individualization of work* has been presented in two contrasting ways:[2]

1 Critical management writers present it as a powerful ethic, force and ideology. They see individualization of work as part of a political economy of insecurity in which risk is redistributed 'away from the state and the economy and towards the individual'.[3] The impacts of individualization are contrasted with those that arise from a social welfare perspective.[4]

2 The boundaryless career perspective acknowledges the shift that organizations have made towards the pursuit of flexibility and offer of employability rather than employment security, but highlights the supply-side motivations and rising demands for more career flexibility from an increasingly diverse workforce;[5] and the opportunities now afforded to break the mould.[6]

Taking the first perspective, a number of writers from the critical management tradition, such as Beck, Gephart, Perlow, Rogers and Trice, have summarized the essence of the individualization ethic. Although presenting individualization in a generally negative way, their work demonstrates a flow of logic that might come to dominate many work environments. Why is individualization presented as an ideology? Trice[7] argued that individualization provides Western societies with a morally based and credible understanding of events and relations within the world of work. It includes assumptions about how best to maintain the social world and distribute resources, and helps us justify why individualist values and individualized ways of action should be considered natural. Gephart[8] argues that there is a profound transformation taking place in the logic of modern industrial society. He describes the ideology as follows.[9] People place their personal interests first and feel that they have to be at the centre of their own planning and conduct, must be expected to care for themselves, and therefore should accept and interpret outcomes in terms of their own personal agency (or be aware of and take responsibility for their own lack of it). He points out that accounts of biographies, leadership and careers tend to reflect this sense of personal agency and serve to demonstrate the importance of personal competencies and talent. Perlow[10] has drawn attention to the link between individualism and time paucity. He argues that people at work – especially professionals and technical employees – focus on completing individual deliverables and on doing high-visibility work to demonstrate their talent in return for personal advancement and reward. The time investment needed to do this, however, is high. Self-management, employment uncertainty and cultural assumptions about what creates organizational performance all lead employees towards extended workplace presence. Although the work process has become more complex and inter-dependent and workplace interruptions are inevitable as a result, the ethic of individualization means that helping others is a personal cost and a potential waste of time relative to meeting one's own deliverables. Although most people are unaware of it, in a competitive environment behaviours become shaped in dysfunctional ways. Interrupting others to complete your own task is considered acceptable, but interruptions to your own work by others are seen as counter-productive. Indirectly, this reinforces more early and late working to complete tasks.

Beck[11] argues that another way to judge whether employment has become more individualized is to consider how crises within it are evaluated. He argues that they are seen increasingly as individual problems with individual causes. Several key behaviours at work – for example, leadership, influence, adaptability and resilience – are seen as the result of psychological dispositions. Organizational success is therefore considered to be linked to the efforts of key individuals and, by implication, to their extended workplace influence (which is often assumed to require actual workplace presence). Too many long hours worked are evidence of this effort and commitment. Extreme pressures on time are therefore created, yet a failure to cope with this is again seen as an individual problem and not a systemic one – a personal inability to manage the demands of home and work life. Sustained unemployment too is seen as a personal dysfunction. Finally, it is argued that people seek individualized solutions to their reward needs in what is a multi-activity society. As work through employment, paid labour and non-work life can be redefined and changed more easily, then the informal economy tends to become more prominent in the lives of many people. Income generation goes unregulated by social institutions, reinforcing the pressure on them to gain sufficient state funds through formal taxes, distancing the individual even more from the personal gain that they feel results from the collective provision of employment benefits compared to what they might negotiate based on their own talents. The risks become individualized. Rogers[12] uses temporary work as an example of this and considers the nature of risk – defined here as the chances that people take to gain or not gain income. He argues that risk has become more individualized as employees become more prepared to expend their own resources to manage and mitigate workplace and career risks. We shall be discussing the challenges created by the debate about work–life balance in Chapter 9, but despite the growth of family-friendly policies, many employers still have a preference for what Hochschild[13] calls the 'zero-drag employee' – unencumbered by social ties and available to work or relocate at any time. Employees with a home life find that this can increase their employment risk, so the temptation is to avoid strong time commitments to family, community and society.

Indeed, several governments have now shifted their strategy away from providing universal and acceptable benefit levels to those outside employment (a safety net strategy) to emphasizing individual responsibilities (as well as rights) and *social citizenship*. The British government, in emulating 1990s US policy, now sees itself needing to enable citizens actively to engage in paid employment and to achieve a degree of prosperity for doing so. This is a moral strategy based on '. . . individual emancipation through a code of rights and obligations in the labour market'.[14]

A rebalancing of the individual risks of employment is clearly necessary, for at the moment social scientists see widely diverging types of citizen. In terms of risk, Beck sees four social classes of employee emerging:

1 What he calls the *'Columbus'* class, including those employees who increasingly own and manage capital (for example, senior managers

incentivized by stock options), receiving a greater share of economic benefits associated with organizational membership, but at the expense of time poverty

2 *Precarious employees*, possessing high skill levels and high earnings, but exposed to high risks of being pushed out by other rival talented employees and moving into the temporary or contingent sectors of the economy

3 *Working poor*, who find it necessary to hold several jobs or employment relations at one time

4 *Hopeless people*, living in poverty with abandoned hope of returning to the workplace either through loss of motivation or immense gaps between their capabilities and the demands of jobs.

Coming more from a labour process, flexible specialization and dual-labour market perspective, Smith[15] argues that it is too simplistic to divide work into 'bad' contingent jobs and 'good' permanent standard jobs. Nonetheless, she concludes that the balance of evidence suggests that 'uncertainty and unpredictability, and to varying degrees personal risk, have diffused into a broad range of post-industrial workplaces'. Indeed, the analysis of historical trends in Chapters 3 and 4 supported this conclusion.

The second perspective then argues that the employing organization is simply one of several stakeholders in an individual's career development. A series of books and journal papers brought a new vocabulary into the field of human resource management about the nature of individual careers and has created a series of new prescriptions for career behaviour. Notable among these have been descriptions by Ashkenas and colleagues[16] of the 'boundaryless organization', DeFillippi, Arthur and Rousseau's characterization of future careers within these organizations as being 'boundaryless' or 'intelligent',[17] and Waterman and colleagues' outline of the consequent development of 'career resilient workforces'.[18] What cuts across all these prescriptions is the idea that organizations are competing increasingly for talent.

War for talent thinking and employee value propositions

While many different classes of employees can be recognized dependent on their desirability to the organization, those who argue that organizations need to respond to there being a war for talent would probably take a more positive view of the situation facing at least the high skill level employees – doubting whether their situation is quite so precarious as intimated in the opening sections of this chapter. In 1997 a group of McKinsey consultants asked how firms built a strong managerial talent pool and whether such talent helped to drive organizational performance. They produced a report that seemed to capture the spirit of the times based on a survey of nearly 6000 managers from 27 large companies and 18 case studies, including Enron, Intel, General Electric, Johnson & Johnson, Harley-Davidson, Hewlett-Packard, Monsanto, the US Marine Corps and the Home Depot. Three years later they worked in 35 large companies and 19 medium-sized companies. The survey results were separated into those from the top quintile of performing firms by sector and those from the middle quintile (based on total shareholder return) in order to identify the characteristics of better-performing firms.

In the book that resulted from the project, Michaels, Handfield-Jones and Axelrod[19] argued that it was not sophisticated HR processes concerned with succession planning, recruitment and compensation that made the difference, but rather the mindset of leaders throughout the organization. They held, it was argued, a fundamental belief in the importance of individual talent. The title of the report – *The War For Talent* – it was felt vividly captured '. . . the new realities of the talent market'.[20] The US economy was at the height of the economic bubble, organizations were scrambling to recruit and retain the people they needed, they were offering large signing-on bonuses, offering pay rises every three months, and talented managers were moving away from companies to new start-up operations. Once the economic bubble was over, the authors argued that drive to attract and retain individual talent had not diminished. Organizations were considered to have gone through a 'strategic inflexion' point – a critical point in time when the dynamics of a business shift permanently – and were then, and will for the next 20 years, operate in a labour market driven by war for talent thinking.

In their context, *talent* is defined as the sum of a person's abilities (widely defined as gifts, skills, knowledge, experience, intelligence, judgement, attitude, character and drive). Although the profile is different from organization to organization, it involves a combination of '. . . sharp strategic mind, leadership ability, emotional maturity, communications skills, the ability to attract and inspire other talented people, entrepreneurial instincts, functional skills, and the ability to deliver results'.[21] The challenge for organizations is to improve this, given that overall only 19 per cent of senior managers strongly agreed that their organization brought in highly talented people, 8 per cent believed that they retained almost all of their high performers, and only 3 per cent considered that the organization developed people quickly and effectively, or removed low performers. *Talent management* is seen as a central focus of chief executive activity, requiring them to set the standards for progression, become actively involved in the decisions over individuals, drive a probing review process, instil a culture that manages talent in their organization, invest money in talent and hold themselves accountable for the pool of talent (and the actions of this pool). The example often cited is Jack Welch's 'Session C process' (General Electric's talent review process), in which he spent 30 days each year chairing the reviews for the top 20 to 50 general managers against critical business priorities. The process actually predated Welch's tenure as CEO and continues after his departure. It is supported by a policy of 20 per cent external recruitment at top level (roughly 75 out of the top 500 positions at GE become vacant every year).

A central tenet of this war for talent thinking is the *employee value proposition* (EVP). This touches upon the psychological contract, in that it conveys a clear statement of some of the more explicit obligations to which the organization commits. However, it is a human resource management policy influenced very much by marketing thinking that cuts across the whole of the employment experience and applies to all individuals in the organization. It is the application of a customer value proposition – why should you buy my product or service? – to the individual – why would a highly talented person work in my organization? It differs from one organization to another, has to be as distinctive as a fingerprint, and is tailored to the specific type of people the organization is trying to attract and retain. An employee value proposition is defined as:

> . . . the holistic sum of everything people experience and receive while they are part of the company – everything from intrinsic satisfaction of the work to the environment, leadership, colleagues, compensation and more. It's about how well the company fulfils people's needs, their expectations, and even their dreams.[22]

Building EVPs has become a central focus of HRM in many large organizations. The McKinsey research on what managers are looking for identified a series of factors that drove their decision to join and stay with an organization and the link between these factors and satisfaction. Intriguingly, in relation to lifestyle and work–life balance (discussed in Chapter 9), being able to meet personal/family commitments was the second-highest drive after interesting and challenging work, but it *was not* correlated to reported satisfaction. The factors in the EVP that were key elements of satisfaction levels were exciting work, a great company to work for (culture and values, leadership and well managed), development (growth and advancement, company committed to the individual) and wealth and rewards.

The new expectations were to be faced with: new challenges and exciting businesses: a flat, fluid and flexible organization; a five-year rewards horizon with wealth linked to value-creation; and a career that involved 'jumping from one rock face to another'. It should be remembered, however, that this is a sample of middle to senior managers in large US corporate organizations! It would not be an attractive EVP for all workforces. The challenge, however, is identify what it is that drives attraction and retention behaviour and to create aligned EVPs for each major unit *within the organization*. For one unit it might be state-of-the-art technology, for another it might be a corporate role within eighteen months, the opportunity to choose job or location, a risk-loving and aggressive culture, or a love of science and notion of improving the quality of people's lives. This reinforces the points made by the study of employees in a major UK retail bank by Sparrow[23] and the need to understand the new internal labour markets within the organization driven by the different attitudes to the psychological contract (see the previous discussion).

Another central tenet of the war for talent thinking is the shift towards more immediate rewards and the proposition that organizations break the compensation rules and pay what other firms might think the individual is worth, or pay even more to ensure employee delight. The price of talent is considered to be rising. Starting pay for MBA graduates from the top 25 US universities rose by 36 per cent from 1996 to 2000[24] while chief executive compensation rose by a factor of 10 from 1990 to 2000 from $1.2 million to an average of $12.4 million.[25] Michaels and colleagues argued that in order to support an EVP based on the management of talent, organizations will have to change their reward systems to a pay-for-the-person approach (based on shareholder value creation) so that high performers are paid significantly more than average performers. Indeed, talent agents have become a new intermediary for executives, building business deals around CEO clients. They also operate for high-technology teams in Silicon Valley (see the discussion of 'no brand' people in Chapter 4). The dynamics between talented individuals and the organization are expected to come under increasing pressure as these new intermediaries provide advice on compensation and the practice slowly spreads down the hierarchy of the organization.

The final tenet of war for talent thinking is the strict management of under-performance – *dealing with the C players*. The philosophy argues that there is immense cost to keeping these individuals, considerable frustration among the talented that their organization does not take action and act decisively, that a lack of action perpetuates a vicious circle whereby untalented people recruit and promote low-risk and low-personal-challenge individuals and perform-ance is driven down. The argument is that if good management is a key factor of the employee value proposition, then the retention of poor talent soon destroys the proposition and demotivates the talented. It is a philosophy of meritocracy as judged by the recently successful and it takes individualism to a logical, if harsh, endpoint (see the critical discussion of this philosophy later in the chapter).

Career success and social capital

We noted towards the end of Chapter 4 that the networks of relationships and contacts of employees in Silicon Valley appeared to be as important as their skill levels in maintaining employability. The individualization of HRM and focus on talent – or on competency or capability – is then forcing organizations to think deeply about what is really meant by such words. What is more important – the skills and know-how of the individual or the resources that they can muster based on other attributes that they bring – such as who they know and what information and insight they can broker into the organization based on their position in an information market? What the popular management press would call 'know-who', academics label 'social capital'. The work of Burt[26] has become most associated with this latter proposition. 'Social capital' has become viewed as a critical business competence, and as such a critical goal for organizations. It has also been used as a loose metaphor for the principles of coordination, creativity, leadership, learning and teamwork that the new organizational forms discussed in the opening chapter engender.

While *human capital theory* assumes that people, groups or organizations do better (i.e. receive higher returns for their efforts) because of their personal traits and characteristics (such as intelligence and competence), *social capital theory* assumes that they do better because they are better 'connected'. Bourdieu and Wacquant define social capital as '. . . the sum of the resources, actual or virtual, that accrue to an individual or group by virtue of possessing a durable network of more or less institutionalized relationships of mutual acceptance or recognition'.[27]

There are many loose definitions as to what social capital is and the most important outcomes that it leads to. As a theory, *social capital theory* has mainly been the preserve of economists[28] and sociologists.[29] It has been established through the analysis of networks and network mechanisms associated with the market exchange of goods or ideas necessary for the delivery of effective business performance. A recent review by Adler and Kwon noted 20 definitions, but the construct in general is said to concern '. . . the good-will that is engendered by the fabric of social relations and that can be mobilized to facilitate action'.[30] Certain network structures, or certain locations in this set of exchange relationships, become an asset in their own right, and it is this asset that it the social capital. This 'connection' might be realized in the form of trust, obligation or dependency. We have seen how trust, obligation and dependency play a critical role in the creation and fulfilment of psychological contracts in previous chapters. This goodwill that others have towards us is a valuable resource and consequently the relevance of this social structure and its social ties is now being recognized by organizational theorists in relation to a wide range of work issues. At the very least, we can draw a connection between an individual's social capital and the influence that they can have on the fulfilment or breach of psychological contract of others.

Social capital theory seems to have most relevance for the design of work teams and network forms of organization[31] because it helps to explain the workings of such designs and organizational forms. We discuss it here because it has also been linked to: the career behaviour of individuals pursuing a psychological contract based on employability by Adler and Kwon;[32] and the implications of network destruction on survivor reactions to downsizing by Shah[33] (we discussed the survivor syndrome in Chapter 5); and the formation of virtual organizations and the behaviour of teleworkers by Sparrow and Daniels.[34] It is, however, also considered an essential feature of innovation and new forms of work organization because it informs the creation of inter-organizational linkages and the design of knowledge-based organizations. For example, Harryson[35] studied knowledge management and innovation processes in a number of leading firms including ABB, Canon, Eastman Kodak, Ericsson, HP, IBM, Lucent, Nokia, Philips, Sony, Toyota, Unilever and Xerox. He argues that the knowledge and innovation process is no longer limited to intra-corporate 'know-how' (the solving of problems efficiently based on accumulated knowledge, experience and skills). Today it is leveraged more by global 'know-who' (the ability to acquire, transform and apply know-how across networks). The importance of social capital and the position of the

Box 7.1   Social capital theory and individual career power

Social capital serves a powerful production role in that it makes possible the achievement of certain ends that would not be attainable in its absence. Building upon the view outlined in the opening chapter that organizations operate as information markets, Podolny[36] argues that the nature of these network structures affects or replaces the flow of information and therefore shapes what people can do with that information. It is an advantage when the social structure conveys the beliefs and practices that prove to be appropriate, or when the unit or individual has a position of *network dominance*. Examination of the behaviour of networks shows that prior relationships speed up communications, opportunity or insight and therefore who knows early. Such information also circulates within groups before it circulates between groups or spreads across people in a market (which may be work groups, divisions, or industries). Individuals can then gain a significant advantage because their social capital provides them with advantage in such brokering of valuable information.

Brokerage opportunities exist in relation to participation in, and control of, information diffusion. Central to this process is the concept of what Burt[37] calls 'structural holes' (holes in the social structure of a network that might not reflect a total unawareness of the other parties but do reflect a lack of attention to them). Structural holes are implicit in the boundaries between cohorts of employees, teams, divisions, and between firms. Individuals, units or organizations that have relationships that span these holes can create a competitive advantage depending on the nature of their brokerage. Holes act as buffers with people on either side of the hole circulating in different flows of information. They therefore offer an opportunity to broker the flow of information between people and to control the projects that bring people together from opposite sides of the hole. A number of structural features have been measured including 'network bridges', 'constraints' (redundant contacts) and 'betweenness' (brokerage of indirect connections). A wide range of research has demonstrated benefits that accrue to individuals, units and organizations that span structural holes. At the individual level these include salary values, positive peer and supervisor evaluations, promotion, information and control benefits to the teams which they serve, relationships between team performance and the average social capital of members. At the organizational level benefits demonstrated include patent outputs, innovation levels, organizational learning and survival rates.

Source: Podolny.[36]

individual in the network of information that flows within an organization is highlighted in Box 7.1.

Not surprisingly, individual career success and social capital have formed the attention of much recent research, given the discussion of the importance of networking for the achievement of career goals. A study by Seibert, Kraimer and Liden[38] examined the career success of 773 MBA and engineering alumni from a US university who has graduated from 3 to 30 years prior to 2000. Career sponsorship, career satisfaction, access to resources, social capital, access to information and objective career success were examined. As shown in Figure 7.1 social capital was very important to career success. Note in particular the fact that social capital features such as weak ties or bridging a structural hole precede access to information and it is access to information that generates access to resources. It is the access to resources and sponsorship (itself generated by social capital) that most predict career success. Much more work needs to be done in this area, but the linkage between social capital and psychological contract fulfilment in the more individualized organizational culture of modern organizations seems self-evident.

In many organizations then, the need to create a unique 'deal' with a particular individual reflects not just their 'talent' but also the 'social capital' that they bring. In a more individualized environment, what challenges does the need to work with such people create?

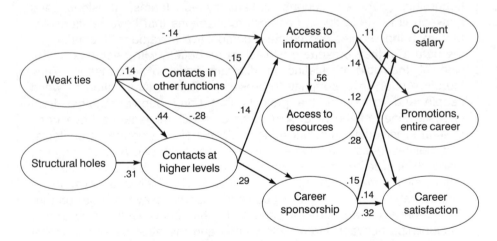

a Fit: x^2 = 165.25, df = 82, $p <$ .01; AGFI = .91, NFI = .92, CFI = .96. Parameter estimates are from the completely standardized solution and are significant at $p <$ .05. Hypothesized relationships are represented by bold arrows, and relationships that were not hypothesized are represented by light arrows. Hypothesized paths that were not significant were eliminated from the model. Control variables and their paths are not shown for the sake of clarity. Current salary was a logarithm.

Figure 7.1 Social capital effects on individual career success. (*Source*: Seibert *et al.*[38])

Idiosyncratic dealing

In Chapter 2 we noted that psychological contract theory demonstrates that different people doing comparable work are working to different 'deals' and that there is more evidence of employees seeking greater flexibility at work and negotiating work arrangements that better suit their personal needs. This trend is part of a more individualized arrangement between valued – or rather those who are valuable and powerful – employees and their employer. Rousseau[39] calls this organizational negotiation the *idiosyncratic deal* (see Box 7.2 for an outline of five reasons that she argues lie behind the growth of idiosyncratic dealing).

The idiosyncratic deal is related to but distinct from the psychological contract. We noted in Chapter 2 that the psychological contract is an idiosyncratic set of reciprocal expectations. However, just because two individuals might create their own view of what is implied by their employment relationship, it does not mean that an idiosyncratic deal has actually been established. Idiosyncratic deals only arise when employees negotiate different treatment from their employers than that received by comparable others. Rousseau concludes that '... it is the difference in treatment, not the difference in perception, which defines the idiosyncratic deal'.[40] Examples might include having more choice in job duties than newer workers, negotiating educational leave, shifting to periods of homework, negotiating personal time to use the organization's resources, or a marked reduction in work time in order to increase time for personal activities. The negotiation is around features of the job beyond pay, such as hours, location, travel, skill development and mobility. There are some significant challenges to be faced by organizations going down an idiosyncratic dealing route.

In some senses it might appear that there is nothing new in this. Any HRM textbook defines a series of non-monetary rewards that a supervisor might offer in the interests of effective performance management, such as unofficial time off, preference over vacation scheduling, favourable job or project assignments, in-group membership (inside information), and participation in unit decision making that is not formally required. However, the main difference between the creation of such personalized deals in the past as opposed to those created today is that they now become part of the official deal rather than an implicit arrangement. They often result from there being a legitimate need to recruit in a tight and competitive labour market. Also, rather than being seniority perks, such arrangements today are much more person-specific. In theory at least, the negotiation is a result of particular qualities of the employee rather than the political needs of the employer. They must serve the functional interests of the employee and the organization. The leverage that individuals have to make their own idiosyncratic deals depends on a series of factors:

- the individual's willingness to negotiate – an individual predisposition
- credentials

Box 7.2   Five reasons behind the growth of idiosyncratic dealing

1 In a hypercompetitive marketplace those knowledge workers who have distinctive competencies have greater labour market power and more opportunity to negotiate employment conditions suited to their tastes and preferences. The value of non-human assets as a factor of production is assumed to have declined. Although control over non-human assets such as plants, patents and client lists can give an employee power, more valuable assets reside within the unique capabilities of the individual – such as their ability to take a whole project and its team members to another organization. This social capital – or residual assets – is increasingly difficult for the host organization to control in functions that involve knowledge work.

2 Employees are in a better position to create idiosyncratic deals given that they now are more likely to have access to financial information regarding the organization. Organizations in knowledge-based sectors have disseminated financial information in order to align the motivations of employees with their financial goals. Where employees have an understanding of how to use that information and have demonstrated valued performance, they can enhance their bargaining position.

3 The weakening of the job security model of organizational careers and erosion of power of trades unions has led to less standardized conditions of employment. Knowledge workers have been educated into seeing themselves as an asset in which they and their employers invest in order to reap benefits in the marketplace. Without the guarantees of seniority-based rewards employees are less motivated to contribute above and beyond the present value of their compensation in anticipation of future reward. Rather, they are motivated to demand a reward now.

4 Mobility is made more attractive because of the stigma that starts to become associated with 'too long a stay' in one organization (whether or not actual mobility occurs). This mobility mindset creates a pressure on employees to differentiate themselves from each other by developing distinctive competencies and generating options within the organization to pursue personal and career goals.

5 Expanded choices over the type of work carried out and more diversified products and services has led to rising expectations among the workforce for customization of their work arrangements. In the same way that employees as consumers have been encouraged to exercise individual tastes and preferences in buying behaviour, so too have they developed parallel expectations of this expression in their work life.

Source: Rousseau.[39]

- occupation
- status
- marketability.

There is clearly considerable risk, however, in this organizational trend. As with pay secrecy, idiosyncratic deals are seldom made public and reflect local arrangements between managers and employees. While it can be a new source of flexibility and innovation, it can also create a vehicle for excessive unfairness and inconsistency. What to one person might be a sensible and constructive negotiation of flexibility can prove to be simply an opportunity for favouritism and cronyism to another. The consequences of a poorly managed idiosyncratic dealing process are that employees place little trust in the way rewards are allocated, people performing essentially the same work do not have equal access to flexibility, the ability to negotiate an idiosyncratic arrangement becomes very dependent on who is the manager, and status differences become evident in the opportunities for idiosyncratic arrangements.

Rousseau acknowledges that there is no 'quick fix' to resolve the inevitable tension between the need for flexibility and consistency. The process has to be managed in a strategic way. This involves specifying employment arrangements immediately, showing that idiosyncratic deals act as a source of innovation in workplace flexibility (and therefore indirectly benefit others because idiosyncratic deals will be shared and adopted by the rest of the firm), requiring supportive relations with co-workers where workers are inter-dependent, assessing and providing the job-related support necessary to sustain the idiosyncratic deal on a regular basis, and keeping track of the accommodations that have been negotiated to ensure that future innovations provide equity for others. It is also clear that this form of idiosyncratic dealing will only work in a 'receptive environment' (see Box 7.3).

While the conditions noted in Box 7.3 are clearly beneficial to idiosyncratic dealing, the reality in most work settings is that these conditions do not exist. Therefore, idiosyncratic dealing should be approached with some caution.

Rousseau also argues that there is a *zone of negotiability* that has to be managed. This refers to the conditions of employment available for negotiation by workers and their employer, established through the constraints and guarantees built into the employment relationship. We pick this issue up in the last chapter, but at this point it is important to note that there are of course wide cross-national differences in the level – or rather lack of – *a priori* conditions of employment as dictated by government regulation, legislation, and collective bargaining arrangements. The USA has perhaps the highest level of negotiability around the employment arrangement, closely followed by New Zealand and the UK. Countries such as France and Belgium have relatively small zones of negotiability. The amount of societal tolerance for unequal outcomes varies markedly around the world.

Box 7.3.   The preconditions for effective idiosyncratic dealing

Denise Rousseau[41] argues that there are a number of important conditions that are necessary to support an idiosyncratic dealing approach:

- High-quality relationships between employees and managers
- Responsibilities and role requirements well understood and agreed to
- Performance criteria clear and well specified
- Shared understanding regarding the performance-appraisal process
- Workers trusting the performance process
- Co-workers having mutually supportive relations
- Co-workers trusting the managers
- Convey legitimate reasons where job conditions limit flexibility
- Idiosyncratic deals viewed as a source of innovation that can be shared and adopted by the rest of the firm.

Trust and confidence in the role definition and performance management processes are critical factors.

Source: Rousseau.[39]

Limits: the price of individual stars

In Chapter 4 we discussed evidence on the emergence of a new employment model in California and considered whether we will see one group of individuals who can market themselves as a 'personal brand' and another class of 'no-brand' individuals. While still in the realms of California, a classic example of a high-risk–individual star business culture is, of course, Hollywood. Six out of ten films produced by Hollywood lose money. The industry is based on a system in which massive options are granted to lead actors such that they get paid whether the film is produced or not. Ridley Scott, of *Bladerunner* and *Gladiator* fame, began filming *Gladiator* without having completed the script. The scriptwriter was fired with one week to shooting on the say-so of the lead actor Russell Crowe. The actors now have immense power over directors above and beyond providing the venture with their acting skills. Given that it is the one in ten film that makes a sufficiently large return to boost the overall rate of return for the industry to 4 per cent (little more than would be made by putting money in a building society) the temptation to pander to the individual star is self-evident.

Perhaps one of the best-known critics of the 'war for talent' and individualized HRM thought process is Jeffrey Pfeffer. He recently marshalled a series of arguments that signal not just some of the challenges that will be faced by organizations going down this route, but also some of the significant risks. He argues that the essence of the 'war for talent' thought process is to emphasize the top 10 per cent for recruitment but also for retention and cultivation once they are inside the organization. The argument coming out of war-for-talent consulting is as follows:[42]

> . . . Identify the top ten and bottom 10 per cent. The top 10 per cent of your people should be lavished with rewards, interesting job assignments, fast-track opportunities, and special training and mentoring. The bottom 10 per cent should either be removed from the organization or helped to improve. Implicitly, such recommendations suggest ignoring everyone else.

This fools organizations into implicitly categorizing their people as the stars, the dogs and everyone else. It assumes that there are some relatively stable attributes such as talent and drive which continue to differentiate people over their careers. Moreover, it assumes that such attributes outweigh the myriad other production factors. Yet in modern organizations, the interdependence among individuals is such that productivity is affected by the capabilities and actions of collectives. What is most important is not so much individual motivation or abilities, but the attributes of the system within which the person works. Fighting a war for talent and individualizing HRM not only means that organizations are fighting the wrong war with the wrong methods, but Pfeffer argues that it also will unleash negative consequences in itself (see Box 7.4). The essence of his argument, contained in a number of publications, is that emphasizing individual performance and rewarding the stars diminishes teamwork, creates destructive internal competition, retards learning and reduces the spread of best practice throughout the organization.[43]

The language of talent assumes that there are individual stars within and outside organizations and that these stars are best served by the provision of differentiated rewards, i.e. if you do not pay inordinate rewards then someone else will. It creates another pressure for idiosyncratic dealing, but without the counter-balancing promise of innovation for all that Rousseau argues is necessary to avoid issues of unfairness. Pfeffer places internal competition created by zero-sum rewards systems at the heart of the problem. Differentiated pay means paying the best more and the worst less. However, when used to extremes it creates a negative behavioural dynamic. General Motors is criticized as exemplifying an organization that spent hundreds of millions of dollars on technologies to collect and distribute knowledge but then creating an internal competition organization culture in which knowledge sharing was unlikely to occur – as exemplified in the problems that it had in diffusing lean manufacturing processes. A plant manager with performance problems will not seek to ask for help and make problems visible. In a competition for salary, status and the attribution of being 'talented' failures are career limiting. Moreover, when employees are competing for zero-sum rewards of promotions, recognition as a winner and performance-related financial rewards, self-interest overrules the desire to help others. Pfeffer cites IBM and Motorola as organizations exemplifying an

---

Box 7.4   The unplanned consequences of a war for talent?

Jeffrey Pfeffer argues that waging a war for talent and individualizing HRM leads to a number of negative consequences for organizations. Notably:

● Highlighting the recruitment challenge leads to a glorifying of the talents of those outside the organization and a downplaying of the skills and abilities of insiders, leading in turn to a loss of motivation of internal employees and higher turnover, inadvertently making the recruitment challenge that much harder.

● Having uncovered people through effortful activity a commitment response to the likely value of that person is triggered along with a tendency to assume that they are better than those inside. Familiarity breeds contempt. The scarcity and 'reputational' value of outsiders – and mystique of 'will they come or won't they' – places a higher financial value on them beyond their true worth. Moreover, people who come for money leave for money.

● Concentrating on individual talent de-emphasizes the need to fix the systemic, cultural and business process issues that have a larger impact on business performance. Best-practice studies show that in most sectors even where products are produced using the same machines there is more variation in performance between their own plants and sites than there is between organizations. Intra-organizational learning suffers at the expense of internal competition.

● Having competed and apparently won the war for talent an elitist and arrogant attitude can develop which makes building a wise organization (one where people know what they don't know as well as what they do know) more difficult.

Source: Pfeffer.[42]

---

alternative approach, with edicts sent from the top ensuring that practices ensured cooperation over internal competition, business results rather than manoeuvring to be on the right project or team that ensures visibility, and cooperative objectives rather than bonuses achieved at the expense of fights over internal transfer pricing. A war for talent mindset inevitably over-emphasizes the individual over organizational effectiveness:

> . . . not only are such individual, zero-sum reward practices encouraged by virtually all those who have written about talent wars, but even if they weren't, rewarding the individual is what logically follows from the belief that it is individuals who make the difference.[44]

The self-fulfilling prophecy and its effects on expectations of behaviour was well documented during the 1970s and 1980s.[45] Pfeffer argues it has been overlooked in the recent attention given to differential rewards and incentives. It holds that high expectations increase performance and low expectations decrease performance. Labelling only a few people in the organization as stars will cause the majority to underperform. If you aren't going to succeed anyway, why expend effort that will just be wasted? Yet the resources that you get – and the extent to which you might be able to negotiate an idiosyncratic deal – depend upon judgements about your talent and what people expect of you. Superiors save their precious time for those who have a real chance of benefiting. These 'resource-allocation' opportunities have a real impact on performance, creating a virtuous circle. However, this virtuous circle can also be exposed as having little solid foundation. Enron, now the focus of many attacks on 'guru prescriptions', has been used to highlight some of the negative and extreme consequences of a war for talent mentality (see Box 7.5).

Broad-reaching events such as the collapse and total destruction of shareholder value of one of the top ten largest firms in the world (with the loss of retirement funds, job security and tainted employability of former employees) can only result from a pattern of errors allowed to happen by a culture and value-set based on badly designed and flawed reward, training and performance management systems. In the post-Enron era professional commentary among HR executives began to ask the question 'did HR cause the downfall of Enron?' and a raised the need for a strategic reevaluation of the role of the HR function. Enron failed '. . . because of the people it hired (or failed to terminate) and the HR systems it implemented that incorrectly appraised and incented risky and unethical behaviour'.[49] The challenge for the HR function is how best to mobilize and unleash talent while also giving attention to systems and people management processes that balance the need for talent with the needs to protect long-term shareholder value, and the stake of employees via their pensions, security and employability.

It has been argued then that war-for-talent theory implicitly causes us to view organizational performance as the aggregate of a series of individual performances – hence the argument that being able to recruit and retain talented individuals helps an organization win its competitive battle. This understates the importance of the system of organizing, which, as for example, in the case of Nissan, Toyota and Honda, can permit ordinary people to achieve world-class results on a consistent basis over a long period of time. All three of these Japanese manufacturers make more than half their profits in the USA and whereas General Motors makes about $330 profit per car, Toyota and Nissan make $1000 and Honda over $1600.[50] Japanese vehicle production has risen year on year from 1 per cent to 19 per cent of US vehicle production from 1983 to 2001 as a result of attention to product quality, inventory control and market research systems. Nissan's plant in Smyrna, Tenessee is the most efficient car factory in the world.

War-for-talent theory can also lead to overattention to the more charismatic leadership-orientated competencies at the expense of the more enduring

Box 7.5   Enron and the talent myth

A recent critique of Enron in the *The Times* argued that its collapse was not in spite of its talent policy, but because of it.[46] McKinsey had a very close relationship with Enron. It conducted 20 projects with fees topping $10 million a year. A McKinsey director regularly attended board meetings and the chief executive was a former McKinsey partner. The *War For Talent* approach forwarded by McKinsey argues that organizations have to have leaders that are obsessed with talent, a deep-seated belief that having better talent at all levels enables an organization to outperform its competitors, and HR systems that differentiate and affirm this talent, hiring assumed talented people and paying them more than they think they are worth. Enron, along with several other firms including General Electric, used what became known as the 'rank and yank' internal performance review system. Employees were categorized as A's (to be challenged and rewarded with bonuses two-thirds higher than the next level of performance), B's (needing to be encouraged and their talent affirmed) and C's (who receive no bonuses and no extra stock options and are encouraged to leave). The principle of 'fluid movement' and an open market for hiring meant that anyone could apply for any job they wanted and poaching was encouraged. Project Quick Hire was used to attract 50 of the firm's top performers to the new Global Broadband unit within a week.[47] In general, managers were allowed to move towards the business units that they found the most exciting and attractive, thereby shaping the business in the direction of those activities that people found the most rewarding (as opposed to those that customers and shareholders might have wished to be resourced) and leaving holes in the organization where managers had been poached. The culture that McKinsey created in Enron, however, meant that annual turnover from promotions was running at nearly 20 per cent, so that performance was being rated on very low levels of tenure and sustained effectiveness. During the 1990s Enron was hiring 250 fresh MBA graduates every year. In 1998 Enron hired 10 Wharton MBAs while McKinsey hired 40. In 1999 Enron hired 12 from Wharton while McKinsey hired 61. The critique ends by arguing '. . . The consultants at McKinsey were preaching at Enron what they believed about themselves. They were there looking for people who had the talent to think outside the box. It never occurred to them that, if everyone had to think out of the box, may be it was the box that needed fixing'.[48]

Source: Gladwell.[46]

attributes of wisdom – what Pfeffer outlines as an attitude that '. . . permits an organization to take action even as it doubts what it knows, so that it continues to learn even as it acts'.[51] Pfeffer's analysis, then, warns of the unforeseen consequences that a war-for-talent mentality might have on the psychological contract of the non-stars. It is useful and helpful in this regard. It does, however, paint scenarios based on extreme behaviour within organizations. Pfeffer acknowledges that organizations can both pursue an individualized HR strategy *and* attend to the systemic and cultural issues required for superior organizational effectiveness.

In noting that we shall see a return to understanding and empowering systems within organizations and not just individuals, it is important not to ignore and turn attention away from useful work that is being conducted in the area of individual capability. In truth, the top 10 per cent of an organization *can* make a significant difference to both organizational performance – and indeed the general well-being of the workforce. The whole field of strategic leadership and its associated literature demonstrates this. Yet the impact of a talented elite on the organization depends, of course, on what your definition of what 'talent' is. The competencies that are sought by the more forward-thinking organizations in fact include many of the attributes – wisdom, listening, error tolerance – that Pfeffer argues get designed out of the system by the single-minded pursuit of 'stars'. By making more purposeful attempts to engineer the behaviour of talented people such that it brings out the talents throughout the organization, and by balancing the flexibility of idiosyncratic dealing with the demands for fairness and innovation in the overall HRM system, an individualized HR strategy can still deliver effectiveness. Hodgkinson and Sparrow[52] have outlined the nature and content of this strategic competence.

References

1. Mangan, J. (2000). *Workers without traditional employment: an international study of non-standard work.* Cheltenham: Edward Elgar.
2. This distinction has been drawn by Marler, J.H., Barringer, M.W. and Milkovich, G.T. (2002). Boundaryless and traditional contingent employees: worlds apart. *Journal of Organizational Behavior, 23,* 425–453.
3. Beck, U. (2000). *The brave new world of work.* Cambridge: Polity Press, p. 3.
4. Smith, V. (2001). *Crossing the great divide: worker risk and opportunity in the new economy.* Ithaca, NY: Cornell University Press.
5. See, for example, Arthur, M.B. and Rousseau, D.M. (1995). *The boundaryless career as a new employment principle.* New York: Oxford University Press; Capelli, P. (1999). *The new deal at work.* Cambridge, MA: Harvard Business School Press.
6. Bailyn, L. (1993). *Breaking the mold.* New York: Free Press.
7. Trice, H. (1993). *Occupational subcultures in the workplace.* Ithaca, NY: Cornell University Press.

8. Gephart, R.P. Jr (1996). Management, social issues and the postmodern era. In D.M. Boje, R.P. Gephart Jr and T.J. Thatchenkery (Eds.) *Postmodern management and organization theory*. Thousand Oaks, CA: Sage.

9. Gephart, R.P. Jr (2002). Introduction to the brave new workplace: organizational behavior in the electronic age. *Journal of Organizational Behavior*, 23, 327–344.

10. Perlow, L. (1997). *Finding time: how corporations, individuals and families can benefit from new work practices*. Ithaca, NY: ILR Press.

11. Beck (2000). *Op. cit.*

12. Rogers, J.K. (2000). *Temps: the many faces of the changing workplace*. Ithaca, NY: ILR Press.

13. Hochschild, A. (1997). *The time bind: when work becomes home and home becomes work*. New York: Henry Holt and Company.

14. Taylor, R. (2002). *The future of work–life balance*. Swindon: Economic and Social Research Council, p. 8.

15. Smith, V. (2001). *Crossing the great divide: worker risk and opportunity in the new economy*. Ithaca, NY: Cornell University Press.

16. Ashkensas, R., Ulrich, D., Jick, T. and Kerr, S. (1995). *The boundaryless organization*. San Francisco, CA: Jossey-Bass.

17. See DeFillippi, R.J. and Arthur, M.B. (1994). The boundaryless career: a competency-based prospective. *Journal of Organizational Behavior, 15 (4)*, 307–324; Arthur, M.B., Claman, P.H. and DeFillippi, R.J. (1995). Intelligent enterprise, intelligent careers. *Academy of Management Executive, 9 (4)*, 7–22; Arthur, M.B. and Rousseau, D.M. (1995). (Eds.) *The boundaryless career as a new employment principle*. New York: Oxford University Press

18. Hind, P., Frost, M. and Rowley, S. (1996). The resilience audit and the psychological contract. *Journal of Managerial Psychology, 11*, 18–29; Waterman, R.H. Jr, Waterman, J.A. and Collard, B.A. (1994). Toward a career-resilient workforce. *Harvard Business Review, 72 (4)*, 87–95.

19. Michaels, E., Handfield-Jones, H. and Axelrod, B. (2001). *The war for talent*. Boston, MA: Harvard Business School Press.

20. *Ibid.*, p. x.

21. *Ibid.*, p. xii.

22. *Ibid.*, p. 43.

23. Sparrow, P.R. (1996). Transitions in the psychological contract in U.K. banking. *Human Resource Management Journal, 6 (4)*, 75–92.

24. Interview by authors of Michaels *et al.* (2001). with Jennifer Merritt of *Business Week*, December 2000.

25. Bianco, A. and Lavelle, L. (2000). The CEO trap. *Business Week*, 11 December, 88.

26. Burt, R.S. (2000). The network structure of social capital. In B.M. Staw and R.I. Sutton (Eds.), *Research in organizational behavior: an annual series of analytical essays and critical reviews. Volume 22*. New York: JAI Press.

27. Bourdieu, P. and Wacquant, L.J.D. (1992). *An invitation to reflexive sociology*. Chicago, IL: University of Chicago Press, p. 119.

28. See, for example, Woolcock, M. (1998). Social capital and economic

development: toward a theoretical synthesis and policy framework. *Theory and Society*, 27, 151–208.

29. See, for example, Burt, R.S. (1997). The contingent value of social capital. *Administrative Science Quarterly*, 42, 339–365; Portes, A. (1998). Social capital: its origins and applications in modern sociology. *Annual Review of Sociology*, 24, 1–24; Lin, N. (1999). Social networks and status attainment. *Annual Review of Sociology*, 25, 467–487.

30. Adler, P.S. and Kwon, S.-W. (2002). Social capital: prospects for a new concept. *Academy of Management Review*, 27 (1),17–40.

31. Nahapiet, J. and Ghoshal, S. (1998). Social capital, intellectual capital, and the organization advantage. *Academy of Management Review*, 23, 242–266.

32. Adler, P.S. and Kwon, S-W. (2000). Social capital: the good, the bad, the ugly. In E.L. Lesser (Ed.), *Knowledge and social capital*. Boston, MA: Butterworth-Heinemann. p. 17.

33. Shah, P.P. (2000). Network destruction: the structural implications of downsizing. *Academy of Management Journal*, 43 (1), 101–112.

34. See Sparrow, P.R. and Daniels, K. (1999). Human resource management and the virtual organization: mapping the future research issues. In C.L. Cooper and D. Rousseau (Eds.), *Trends in organizational behavior, Volume 6*. London: Wiley; Sparrow, P.R. (1999). Teleworking and the psychological contract: a new division of labour? In K.Daniels, D. Lamond and P. Standen (Eds.), *Managing teleworkers*. London: Sage.

35. Harryson, S.J. (2000). *Managing know-who based companies: a multi-networked approach to knowledge and innovation management*. Cheltenham: Edward Elgar.

36. Podolny, J.K. (1993). A status-based model of market competition. *American Journal of Sociology*, 98, 829–872.

37. Burt, R.S. (1992). *Structural holes*. Cambridge, MA: Harvard University Press.

38. Seibert, S.E., Kraimer, M.L. and Liden, R.C. (2001). A social capital theory of career success. *Academy of Management Journal*, 44 (2), 219–237.

39. Rousseau, D.M. (2001). The idiosyncratic deal: flexibility versus fairness? *Organizational Dynamics*, 29 (4), 260–273.

40. *Ibid.*, p. 261.

41. *Ibid.*

42. Pfeffer, J. (2001). Fighting the war for talent is hazardous to your organization's health. *Organizational Dynamics*, 29 (4), 248–259, p. 252.

43. See also Pfeffer, J. (1998). *The human equation: building profits by putting people first*. Boston, MA: Harvard Business School Press; O'Reilly, C.A. and Pfeffer, J. (2000). *Hidden value: how great companies achieve extraordinary results with ordinary people*. Boston, MA: Harvard Business School Press.

44. Pfeffer (2001). *Op. cit.*, p. 251.

45. See, for example, Archibald, W.P. (1974). Alternative explanations for self-fulfilling prophecy. *Psychological Bulletin*, 74–84; Eden, D. (1984). Self-fulfilling prophecy as a management tool: harnessing Pygmalion. *Academy*

   of Management Review, 64–67; Livingston, J.S. (1969). Pygmalion in Management. *Harvard Business Review*, July-August, 81–89.
46. Gladwell, M. (2002). The talent myth. *The Times*, 20 August, 2–4.
47. See Michaels *et al.* (2001). *op. cit.*, p. 50 for an outline of this initiative at Enron.
48. Gladwell (2002). *Op. cit.*, p. 4.
49. Sullivan, J. (2002). Did HR cause the downfall of Enron? *Vice President of HR Newsletter*, 1–10, p. 4.
50. *The Economist* (2002). Japanese car makers in America: Twenty years down the road. *The Economist*, *364*, No. 8290, 68–69.
51. Pfeffer (2001). *Op. cit.*, p. 256.
52. Hodgkinson, G. and Sparrow, P.R. (2002). *The competent organization: a psychological analysis of the strategic management process*. Milton Keynes: Open University.

8

Managing the New Individual–Organization Linkages

Individual differences in the relationship with the organization

Herriot[1] points out that: '... the employment relationship is ultimately a relationship between human beings and as such is subject to the same fundamental psychological constraints and influences as are other human relationships'. He argues that it is possible to use metaphors drawing upon a wide range of other relationships to capture the essence of the employment relationship. Table 8.1 summarizes eight different types of employment relationship from a psychological sense that exists between the individual and the organization. Each relationship can be characterized by a series of key features and each has a negative side – what Herriot calls a 'flip-side' that can come to the fore if the mutual obligations embodied in the contract are not met and trust drains away from the relationship. As we saw in the previous chapter, the important features of the employment relationship can be destroyed. The flip-side is what it feels like when the relationship goes wrong. Sadly, many people will only understand the deal to which they have been working within their organization by recognizing the flip-side perceptions of their deal having gone wrong.

How can we capture the relationship between the individual and organization? At this point we return to the psychological contract and the issue of individual differences that can influence its nature. We noted in Chapter 2 that *by definition* the psychological contract is different for each individual and, as Table 8.1 shows, it is different for each type of employment relationship. However, are there some individual difference factors that can help organizations to categorize this complexity and spot patterns in overall shape and content of psychological contracts, and therefore devise HR strategies that are

Table 8.1 Employment relationship metaphors

Metaphor	Core elements and feelings	Flip-side perceptions	Typical location
Family	Care and support from the employer; dependence, security and trust from the employee	Care too much (dominance, dependence) or too little (mistrust and injustice) leading to family feud (abuse, bullying or desire for revenge)	Small and medium sized enterprise, family or local firm
Crusade	Mission, vision, values, leadership and charisma from the employer; commitment and authenticity from the employee	Narcissism (corruption, abuse of power) or collusion (disillusionment, cynicism, pretence) leading to play-acting	Voluntary organization, public sector, 'excellence' culture
Contract	Promises, obligations, and reciprocity from the employer; agency and transactions from the employee	Ambiguity and exercise of power (domination); violation (abuse); anger (survival); and litigation and redress (fear and greed); all leading to a jungle	Short-term organizations
Club	Formation, membership, belonging, and standards from the employer; knowledge, value, collegiality and fitting in from the employee	Over-exclusivity, cloning and groupthink (stereotype, being devalued) or exclusion, powerlessness, isolation, polarization (organized opposition) leading to being an outsider	Professional organizations
Resource	Value as assets, utilization, conservation and deployment from the employer; contribution and development from the employee	Exploitation and control (use up, exhaust); performance and drive (stress and survival) leading to being a discard	Large private sector organizations

Democracy	Justice in procedures and interactions from the employer; rights, responsibilities and voice from the employee	Rhetoric (surveillance); power (repression, outflanking); acceptance and compliance (fear) leading to dictatorship	Public sector
Partnership	Participation, shared and mutual interests and co-ownership from the employer; commitment, quality, Improvements from the Employee	Rhetoric and retention of Power (assertion of own interests) and attribution of cynical motives (disputes, internalization) leading to conflict	Unionized workplaces
Customer	Consumer, customer service, stakeholder and support from employer; initiative and identification from the employee	Marketing (abuse); total engagement (overstretch, anger at selling lies, regret); consumer (see through the rhetoric) leading to rip-off	Retail sector

After Herriot.[2]

more able to cope with the twin challenges of creating flexibility and fairness? There are very good reasons to consider that some important aspects of the psychological contract can be gleaned from individual measures.

One of the major challenges facing employers is to better understand the individual factors that are associated with, shape and better explain the employee's relationship with the organization. We have seen the development of a number of ideas in this area. An individualized work relationship by definition means that people give more expression to their individualism and their self-identity. Possessions are an important and symbolic expression of this self-identity. In an individualized world, it is not surprising therefore that increasing attention has been given to the topic of psychological ownership. It has long been assumed that a psychological sense of ownership, and the associated need for personal control, is an integral part of an employee's relationship with the organization. A number of different types of relationship, bond, or attachment to the organization seem to capture the human experience of organizations. Four such employee–organization linkages have served as an increasing focus of recent attention:

1 *Organizational commitment:* reasons for social membership and the desire to maintain this, the feelings and/or beliefs regarding the reasons why an individual wants to maintain a relationship with or membership of the organization, seen, for example, in the work of Meyer and Allen[3]
2 *Organizational identification:* the use of characteristics of the organization to define oneself, the social classification of oneself in terms of what one believes are distinctive and admirable attributes of the organization, seen, for example, in the work of Mael and Tetrick[4] and Wan-Huggins and colleagues[5]
3 *Internalization:* the adoption of the values and goals of the organization, seen, for example, in the work of O'Reilly and Chapman,[6] and Mael and Ashforth[7]
4 *Psychological ownership:* an attitudinal state of mind involving feelings of possessiveness and of being psychologically tied to an object, seen, for example, in the work of Pierce, Kostova and Dirks.[8]

For each of these, one can imagine the search for more sophisticated measurement and assessment approaches in order to make the individual differences in these areas more amenable to assessment – whether for selection, development or attitudinal monitoring reasons. They are all considered to be learned responses, more than they are inherited predispositions.[9] The most important consequences linked to each of these four factors are shown in Table 8.2.

Organizational commitment

We noted in Chapter 4 that longitudinal data on *organizational commitment* in the UK suggests that overall it has remained fairly stable, but that this hides some a complex set of reactions to both positive and negative changes in work practice.[10] Organizational commitment has been studied for years and is perhaps the most measured employee–organization linkage. As an employee–organization linkage it is considered alongside related constructs such as identification, internalization and psychological ownership. It is also treated as an important work-related attitude, in which case it tends to be discussed together with satisfactions and involvements. We treat it here in its broader role as a form of employee-organization linkage. The study of commitment has been central to understanding both individual and organizational performance and considerable attention has been given to trying to understand:

- What causes it
- The different types of commitment that exist
- The form that this commitment takes
- The outcomes that result when it exists.

In this first section we draw upon a critical review of this work, developed recently by Swailes.[11] He first draws attention to the historical importance given to what we now consider to be organizational commitment in a number of classical management texts. The concept can be traced back to early work by Fayol on the principles of management, by Weber on bureaucracy, by Burns and Stalker on organic forms of organization, and by Etzioni on power and control systems. Fayol argued that in order for the interests of the organization to take precedence over those of the individual or the group, there must be a degree of internalization of its goals by its employees and time in order for them properly to understand job requirements. While Weber did not use the term commitment, he talked about the importance of rational actions and identification in relational to goals (*zweckrational*) and values (*wertrational*). Burns and Stalker noted that in order successfully to cope with a changing environment, structures have to generate a spread of commitment to the organization and its tasks.

By the early 1960s commitment had emerged as a distinctive construct. Throughout the 1970s and 1980s it was used by work and organizational psychologists to study a range of attachments. What are these different attachments and how does commitment work across them? Morrow[12] identified 29 separate constructs that were being used to measure individual commitment to five different referents related to work (subsequently called different *foci* of commitment):

- the nature of *work* itself regardless of the organization
- to specific *jobs*
- to a *union* or staff association
- to a *career* or profession
- to an employing *organization*.

This section focuses on the latter concept – organizational commitment – but some general principles about commitment must first be understood.

Table 8.2 Comparison of psychological ownership with commitment, identification, and internalization

Dimensions of distinctiveness	Psychological ownership	Commitment	Identification	Internalization
1 Conceptual core	Possessiveness	Desire to remain affiliated	Use of element of organization's identity to define oneself	Shared goals or values
2 Questions answered for individual	What do I feel is mine?	Should I maintain membership?	Who am I?	What do I believe?
3 Motivational bases	• Efficacy/effectance • Self-identity • Need for place	• Security • Belongingness • Beliefs and values	• Attraction • Affiliation • Self-enhancement • Holism	• Need to be right • Beliefs and values
4 Development	Active imposition of self on organization	Decision to maintain membership	Categorization of self with organization • Affiliation • Emulation	Adoption of organization's goals or values
5 Type of state	Affective/cognitive	Affective	Cognitive/perceptual	Cognitive/objective

6 Select consequences/ correlates	• Rights and responsibilities • Promotion of/resistance to change • Frustration, stress • Refusal to share • Worker integration • Alienation • Stewardship and OCBs	• Organization Citizenship Behaviours (OCBs) • Intent to leave • Attendance	• Support for organization and participation in activities • Intent to remain • Frustration/stress • Alienation • Anomie	• Organization Citizenship Behaviours • Intent to leave • In-role behaviours
7 Rights	• Right to information • Right to voice	• None	• None	• None
8 Responsibilities	• Burden sharing • Active and responsible voice • Becoming informed • Protecting • Caring for and nurturing • Growing/enhancing	• None	• Maintain the status of the admired attribute	• Goal and value protection

Source: Pierce et al.[8]

Employees have multiple commitments across these different foci and although one or two of these referents might come to dominate their attitudes and behaviour, none are mutually exclusive. Moreover, as we shall see when we discuss work–life balance in the next chapter, at times the main focus of commitment can be outside work to other spheres of life such as family or religion. Do individuals have a finite amount of commitment to share across these different areas or can the total level of commitment increase across them? The answer has important implications for organizations. Opinion seems divided. *Zero-sum theory* argues that there is a finite level of commitment such that increases in commitment to one focus mean that it will decrease in other areas. While it appears that there are some direct trade-offs – for example, low demands outside work (such as a lack of family commitments) can increase the energy and investment available at work[13] – the bulk of studies seem to show that the total sum of commitment can go up and down. T.E. Becker[14] concludes that strong multiple commitments are possible and commitment to each focus can either be unrelated to changes in commitment in different foci, or positively enhanced by activity in different foci. Work commitment has been shown to be unrelated to non-work ties, positively related to non-work and career satisfactions, and increased by organizational support for non-work activity.[15] In short, the relationship is complex, but commitment can be managed up or down across the different spheres of work and life.

Early work by sociologists also established that as well as commitment being directed at different objects (work, the job, union, career or organization) there are a number of distinct *forms* or *types* of commitment. For example, in the 1960s Etzioni[16] argued that employees lower down the organization form different types of involvements (or rather evaluate other 'actors' such as the organization) and that compliance with these involvements is associated with the use of different types of power:

- Moral involvement (internalize the organization's norms and values either by acting individually or under pressure from other social groups), usually associated with power derived from established norms of behaviour
- Calculative involvement (develop a relationship with the organization on the basis of an exchange in which the employee trades off what they give to the organization and what the organization offers in return), usually associated with the use of power based on the manipulation of remuneration
- Alienative involvement (a negative orientation that arises if behaviour is constrained through enforced membership of an organization), usually associated with the power based on use coercion.

At the same time H.S. Becker[17] established his *side-bets theory* of commitment behaviour. Employees become committed to and embody the 'costs' associated with leaving an organization. As they accumulate sacrifices and make investments at work they come to feel that they have a lot to lose in terms of leaving the organization. Decisions to send a child to a certain school, live near a place of work, or join a pension scheme serve to bind the employee to the organization. Salancik[18] also argued that past behaviour has the effect of binding the employee to the organization and to certain courses of action. The more visible the behaviour, the more irrevocable it is and the more it is a consequence of their own volition, then the more committed they become. Mowday and colleagues[19] considered that there were three types of such commitment: *continuance* commitment (an attachment to a continued relationship with the organization); *cohesion* commitment (stemming from an attachment to social groups in the organization); and *control* commitment (when the

---

Box 8.1   Three bases of commitment

Attitudinal or affective commitment. Based on an acceptance of and belief in the goals of an organization or group. An employee's emotional attachment to, identification with, and involvement in the organization, i.e. the alignment that employees feel between their organization's and their personal value system and desires. Being psychologically synchronized with what the organization and its culture stand for. Defined by Mowday *et al.* as '. . . the relative strength of an individual's identification with and involvement in a particular organization'.[22] Measured by the Affective Commitment Scale,[23] Organizational Commitment Questionnaire[24] or British Organizational Commitment Scale.[25] Items on Affective Commitment Scale include 'I enjoy discussing my organization with people outside it'.

Continuance commitment. Being bound to the organization to the extent that the individual has to be, based on a calculation of the benefits associated with staying versus the personal costs associated with leaving. An awareness of the costs associated with leaving the organization, arising from economic and financial ties. Continuance commitment itself has been broken down into two bases.[26] *Low perceived alternative* continuance commitment based on the perception of few alternative jobs; *high personal sacrifice* continuance commitment based on the perception that leaving the organization would lead to financial hardship and other suffering. Measured using the Continuance Commitment Scale,[27] e.g., 'it would be very hard for me to leave my organization right now even if I wanted to'. Items reflect perceived exit barriers.

Normative commitment. A person's felt obligation and responsibility to the organization.[28] Based on feelings of loyalty and obligation towards continued employment brought about by events that occur before or after joining the organization. Includes general feelings of duty. Measured using the Normative Commitment Scale,[29] e.g. 'I owe a great deal to my organization', 'This organization deserves my loyalty'. Items reflect values of allegiance of loyalty.

employee believes that the norms and values of an organization represent a suitable model to guide their own actions).

Psychologists have then spent much time trying to differentiate the basis of employees' commitments to their organization and to understand the relationship that these different commitments have to other important outcomes at work, such as job satisfaction, absenteeism, extra-role behaviours and job performance. Meyer and Allen[20] are credited with the most well-known clarification of the construct of organizational commitment and its measurement. They developed a three-component model (see Box 8.1) of commitment and argue that the three components or forms of commitment are not mutually exclusive. An individual's commitment to the organization can be based on one, a combination of any two, or all three reasons. A number of studies have validated these three types of commitment.[21]

In support of existing measurements of organizational commitment it could be argued that they predict a series of important outcomes such as turnover, absenteeism and performance. Moreover, although commitment is related to other constructs such as job satisfaction, it has been shown to represent a unique construct in its own right. This said, there are still some philosophical arguments that tend to criticize the match or importance of what is being measured by commitment scales with the reality of modern organizational life. Swailes[30] argues that given the upheavals within organizations the meaning and form of commitment has changed and classical definitions do not seem to match the expectations put upon employees nor assist the design of the policies particularly well.

There is in fact still some confusion in the way that researchers study commitment. As we noted when opening the discussion in this section, commitment may be viewed as a form of employee–organization linkage (a form of psychological attachment to the organization), yet it is also commonly discussed as an outcome from – the result of – this attachment. As Swailes[31] points out, this fails to separate out the motive for commitment from its effects. Wanting to stay with an organization might best be seen as an effect of commitment.[32] However, Swailes draws attention to early discussion of commitment and the notion that 'real' commitment was evident when individuals internalized the norms and value of the organization and were:

1 more likely to remain with the job and feel attached to it whether it was satisfying or not[33]
2 more likely to maintain a behaviour even after any motivating factors for that behaviour were no longer operating[34]

In terms of different *foci* of commitment, the question has been asked whether organization commitment is just one of several different targets (among commitment, for example, to top managers, supervisor, team) or whether in fact it is a global construct that mediates the level of commitment to these local targets.[35] It appears that commitment to top management and to supervisor contributes to global organizational commitment, no local commitments appear to conflict with or diminish this global commitment, but commitment to the local workgroup is independent of it.

Research has helped explain *why* employees become committed but does not help us understand *what* this commitment should look like. Swailes draws attention to the following critical points:

1 The idea that commitment is best understood in terms of a single focus – the organization – seems outdated when organizations themselves are designed along the basis of networks and multiple stakeholders (see the discussions of organizational form in Chapter 1).
2 Goals and values differ from one part of an organization to another, commitment to the specific values of an organization is different from commitment to the organization as a whole, and commitment to one organizational value can exist independently of rejection of other values.[36]
3 Some of the existing scales actually measure some very specific and ideologically slanted behaviours or cognitions. For example, all six items on the continuance commitment scale assess 'banners to exit' based on sacrifice. Swailes[37] asks, do organizations want people who cannot see a way to leave? Are values of allegiance of good indicator of the actual commitment behaviours that a loyal employee might show (some loyal behaviours might be very dysfunctional, as, for example, at Enron)?

It is argued by many researchers that experience of the late twentieth century – with downsizing, re-engineering, outsourcing, mergers and acquisitions – placed considerable stress on the employee–organization linkages. When the increased diversity of the workforce and alternative working arrangements are added into the mix, then '... the state of employees' organizational commitment [should be expected to be] in considerable flux'.[38]

Legge points out that the attitudes and feelings that an individual holds towards their organization – attitudinal or affective commitment – has proved the most popular method for studying commitment: '... virtually all the research conducted on organizational commitment, *per se*, has used the attitudinal conceptualization'.[39] Indeed, for many years it has been assumed that affective commitment influences behaviours associated with performance, attendance and staying with the organization.[40] Meyer and Allen conclude:[41]

> ... Considerable evidence ... suggests that employees with strong affective commitment to the organization will be more valuable employees than those with weak commitment. . . [and] that employees with strong continuance commitment might be poorer performers, engage in fewer citizenship behaviours, and exhibit more dysfunctional behaviours than those with weak continuance commitment.

Higher levels of both affective and continuance commitment have been found to relate to positive outcomes such as lower turnover and absenteeism. However, only affective commitment has been shown to have a relationship to job or task performance, and what is called contextual performance (otherwise known as organizational citizenship behaviour or OCB).

However, to the surprise and frustration of many researchers, most quantitative reviews of the relationship between levels of organizational commitment and increased performance at work suggest only a moderate link. This seems to be true for each of the different bases of commitment. The level of correlation between attitudinal or affective organizational commitment and performance, for example, shows that the relationship between the two is, at best, only moderate. The true correlation between has been reported as $r = 0.13$,[42] $r = 0.21$[43] and $r = 0.13$ respectively.[44] This early evidence, gathered primarily in the early 1990s, has been questioned on a number of grounds. For example, the reviews were based on only a handful of studies that existed at the time (14), in many instances no distinction was made between the different bases of commitment, the way in which performance was measured was often very specific, and only a small range of moderator variables were used. So, with the benefit of more studies and in the light of changes in the employment relationship throughout the 1990s, has the situation changed much?

Recently the process has been replicated on a much wider range of studies.[45] Even after a decade of additional research psychologists still conclude that the link between affective organizational commitment and performance is still relatively weak: 111 samples, of which 75 per cent were gathered from the years 1990–2001, have been analysed. The meta-analysis covered 26 344 employees, the bulk of whom, however, were drawn from Anglo-American cultures. The mean corrected correlation between affective organizational commitment and performance was still only 0.20. The effect was marginally greater where self-rated performance data were used ($r = 0.24$) than for objective indicators ($r = 0.13$). The link between affective organizational commitment and behaviour that is beneficial to the organization but goes beyond formal job descriptions – called *extra-role performance* and including things such as extra hours and altruistic behaviour – was also stronger ($r = 0.25$) than the link to the behaviours required by the formal job descriptions, called *in-role performance* ($r = 0.18$).

Commitment and boundaryless workers

In Chapter 3 we noted that there is a small minority of *boundaryless temporary workers* that are emerging. The whole notion of organizational commitment is made more complex when considering employees in such alternative work arrangements.[46] Not only might they have different foci of commitment (i.e. organization, job, employment and occupation) but their commitment will vary with both their employing temporary help agency and their client organization. Marler and colleagues[47] argue that their commitment to the client is also likely to represent a cumulative experience across several assignments and several clients. The antecedents to organizational commitment – the criteria by which they judge organizations – are likely to be different too.[48]

When Marler and colleagues compared client commitment across boundary-less and traditional temporaries they found that there was in fact no difference in the level of commitment, but the boundaryless temporaries had higher levels of work and pay satisfaction, yet lower levels or task and contextual (organizational citizenship behaviour) performance. In general, the study provided empirical support for Capelli's[49] view that there is a new deal emerging at work for some groups of employee where employability and not loyalty are important. The researchers concluded that 'boundaryless tempor-aries in their prime earning years, are not pursuing careers within one organization. They preferred temporary employment relationships, which appeared to be strongly related to their perception of job opportunities and expectation of earning higher returns'.[50] They noted, however, that it is not yet clear whether such employees (already a small minority, remember, at about 20 per cent of temporary workers) are indeed really 'free agents'. They might just have an individual disposition which means that they are among the first to respond to the realities of work. While they might still have some desire for attachment to a secure institution, they are 'neither passive nor hostile bystanders, but active agents'[51] who are willing to take risks and experiment in more uncertain times.

Organizational identification

In the previous section we noted that work on commitment has suggested a general shift in the focus of commitment away from the organization towards more immediate contexts such as the team. Moreover, identification with the organization has generally been treated simply as one dimension of commit-ment,[52] or as one of the bases of commitment.[53] *Theories of social identification*, however, suggest that it should be seen as a separate construct and that there are deeper psychological processes at play that must be understood. Organizational identification similarly differs from job satisfaction from a theoretical perspective. Job satisfaction is an attitude towards specific aspects of an actual job and the tasks that the individual has to perform, whereas organizational identification is a more general cognitive and affective attitude towards the organization as a whole. It also involves the individual incorporating the organization's norms and values. Organizational identifica-tion is then essentially concerned with the ways in which people define themselves in terms of their organizational relationships.[54] It has been defined as '. . . the degree to which a person defines him- or herself as having the same attributes that he or she believes define the organization'.[55] It occurs when the individual integrates their beliefs about the organization into their own identity. Much of the current discussion of employer branding, and encourage-ment of employees to 'live the brand' has at its root the need to create deep and enduring organizational identification.

In a world or work characterized by mergers, takeovers and restructur-ings, it has become increasingly important for organizations to elicit a certain level of identification among their employees. Organizational identi-fication was first studied in the early 1970s.[56] Social identity theory, developed by Tajfel,[57] argued that part of an individual's self-concept was derived from knowledge of their membership of groups and both the value and the emotional significance attached to that membership. Individuals come to define themselves as members of social categories and ascribe characteristics typical of that social group to themselves. The more they identify with the group, the more their attitudes and behaviours become governed by group membership.[58] Ashforth and Mael argued that organiza-tional identification is a specific form of this social identification.[59] To the extent that an individual identifies with an organization, the organization provides the individual with a sense of identity. It is this cognitive process aspect to identification – the fact that it serves a self-definitional function and in part answers the question 'who am I?' – that suggests that it should be distinguished from commitment[60] (see also Table 8.2). Social identity theory reveals some important principles:

- The standing of the group with whom the individual most identifies reflects on the self.[61]
- People tend to identify more with high-status groups.[62]
- However, individuals also aim for optimal distinctiveness, balancing a desire for membership of a social category with an equal desire for individual distinctiveness or exclusiveness.[63]
- Identification with large groups implies a 'sameness', and so people are more likely to want to identify with small groups.[64]
- People are more likely to identify with a group the more similar they are to that group and the more the group's activities match their own preferences.[65]
- Some people also have an individual disposition towards group attachment.[66]
- Identification depends on the context, and the more individuals are approached on the basis of their group membership, the more salient their identification with that group becomes. Creating group identity increases attachment.[67]

Mathieu and Zajac's[68] review of the antecedents to organizational commit-ment showed that a considerable range of organizational psychology research demonstrates that individuals who feel emotionally attached to their organiza-tions subsequently show more job satisfaction, lower job change search intentions and lower actual turnover. Social Identity Theory assumes that identification with a group means that the individual incorporates the group's norms and having identified with and then seeing themselves as part of their group – and the group as part of themselves – this 'social self' acts to determine their thinking and acting.[69] The more an individual identifies themselves with the group, the more they act in accordance with the group's norms and values. Abrams and colleagues have shown that maintaining membership is one of the core norms in most organizations, and so the level of identification directly predicts the intention to leave.[70]

However, as traditional organizational forms are increasingly dismantled, hierarchies are flattened, competencies outsourced and teams empowered, then the power of organizational institutions to create an identity is being diminished.[71] The internal picture of 'what the organization stands for' increasingly resides within the heads of its employees, rather than in any externalized bureaucratic structures. Indeed, the transformations of organizational identity in modern organizational forms have recently formed the subject of a Special Issue of *Academy of Management Review*. Our identification with the organization under transition, so too is our identification with ourselves as employees. Echoing work on commitment, identification researchers have asked the question that given an employee has multiple group memberships – the organization, a department, a within-department group – which of these memberships offers the best potential for identification?[72]

Organizational identification is considered to reduce levels of alienation, to act as a precondition for job satisfaction, to increase the desire to stay with the organization and to increase the likelihood that employees will expend effort on behalf of the organization.[73] A recent study examined the proposition that workgroup identification is stronger than organizational identification by seeing which type of identification was the most predictive of job satisfaction, turnover intentions, job involvement and job motivation. The sample consisted of over 250 Dutch local government employees and university faculty. The two separate forms of – or foci of – identity could be measured reliably.[74] It was indeed the case that work-group identification was more important a predictor of important work outcomes. It is important to note that identification does not necessarily *cause* satisfaction, turnover, involvement and motivation. There is much theoretical evidence to suggest that, for example, job satisfaction and organizational identification *mutually influence* each other. Nonetheless, at a practical level, such research suggests that '... attempts to improve an organization's identification-eliciting abilities in the hope of achieving beneficial effects on organizational attitudes and behaviour might be more effective when directed at the work-group level (e.g. team building) than at the organizational level'.[75] Given what we know from social identity theory it is clear why downsizings, for example, prove so disruptive (at least in the immediate aftermath, as noted in Chapter 5). It also has implications for our discussion of how best to manage and re-engage an individual's psychological contract.

So how does such identification come about? Two theories in particular have come to dominate our understanding in this area: *social identity theory* and *self-categorization theory* (see Box 8.2). From these theories it becomes clear that any sense of connection with an organization – any feeling of 'oneness' with the organization – is actually a consequence of how individuals perceive themselves, rather than how they perceive the organization[76]. The challenge for organizations, if they wish to 'brand' themselves in the marketplace and get their employees to 'live the brand', is quite demanding. Identification involves

---

Box 8.2   Social identity and self-categorization theory

As individuals we define our self-concept through the connections we have with social groups by forming a link in our minds between the identity of the group and our own identity.[78]. We adopt some of dimensions that define the prototype target – for example, 'being a parent' – and describe ourselves along these dimensions. Social identities are cognitive constructs that define the way that our own identity overlaps with that of another group. We create this identity in two ways. First, we accentuate the similarities between ourselves and our ingroup (self-categorize) and accentuate the dissimilarities between ourselves and members of the outgroup.[79] Second, we maximize the distinctiveness of our ingroup by comparing it to other groups in ways that reflect most favourably on our ingroup (social comparison)[80]. These identifications have important consequences and satisfy needs for self-enhancement, safety and affiliation.[81] This is why if trust is broken in relation to this identification (see discussion of breach of psychological contract in Chapter 2) the implications can be quite significant.

---

more than just showing some commitment to the organization or sharing its values.[77] It involves longer term processes of changing the way the individual comes to view himself.

It should be noted that there is still relatively little empirical study in this area and the field is not even 15 years old. However, organizational identification (or the lack of it) has been shown to have important implications for both the organization and the individual. The most notable findings are that:

- Identification with positively viewed organizations increases the employee's self-esteem and status[82]
- Identification leads to greater satisfaction and motivation among employees[83]
- Identified employees are perceived by managers as having superior job performance and promotability[84]
- Identified employees show higher levels of loyalty to the organization[85]
- They see the organization as a more attractive job opportunity[86]
- They are willing to promote the organization and contribute to it financially[87]
- They will participate in more extra-role and pro-social behaviours[88]

Essentially, by developing identification among their employees, organizations can exert a degree of control by creating internal homogeneity and a motivation for employees to align the organization's outcomes with their own.

Identifying with atypical organizations

Elsbach[89] has argued, however, that while the above view of organizational identification is adequate for traditional organizational contexts – stable organizations with relatively congruent internal identities – it does not give due attention to:

1 Negative relationships with organizations, such as the identity of former members or members of opposing groups within an organization
2 Relationships with organizations that have complex, evolving or incongruent identities (such as a department store chain that moves into financial services, conglomerates that sell some neutral products but also produce cigarettes).

There is increasing evidence from social psychology that the employment relationship today presents employees with an increasing number of *individual identification dilemmas*.[90] The mental reactions that we have to such dilemmas needs to be better understood when considering organizational–individual linkages.

Organizational identity researchers have not explored negative organizational relationships – the problem of how individuals define themselves in relation to organizations that embody some values or ideals that conflict with their own identity. An individual might work for a prestigious newspaper, but know that the newspaper group also owns a pornographic or tabloid outlet. For such a journalist, claiming to be a *disidentifier* with one outlet might be as important as identifying with the other. There is a process of cognitive separation that takes place. It is not simply the organization that conflicts with the individual's identity, but the fact that the image or behaviour of the organization may be distinct in some ways but confusing in others.

Indeed, when we discussed the problems of breach of psychological contract and the challenge faced by organizations that have significant numbers of their employees disengaging from the organization, we were possibly just looking at the surface symptoms of what are much more complex cognitive adjustments taking place in the minds of employees. People are threatened by categorizations that portray them as being too distinctive or undistinctive – the psychology of interpersonal relations shows us that they seek a balance in their self-concept and maintain both connections between themselves, friends and their beliefs, as well as separations.[91] They disassociate themselves from groups that might have high status in one context, but not in theirs (Hollywood actors dissociate themselves from former soap opera actors, even though the fame of the latter might be prestigious among non-actors). Balance results not from holding a passive attitude, but by active attempts to separate either from the person or the issue. In the same manner, individuals seek to protect their self-concept at work by seeking connections and disassociations from their organization on the most important self-defining issues. People initially disidentify with a particular value or practice of an organization, but over time might come to associate an organization's name so closely with the issue at hand that they eventually disidentify with the organization itself and all its services. There is high risk to organizations in pursuing certain values. For example, while The Body Shop is identified with supporting native cultures through its use of native ingredients in products, and some will identify with this, for others it becomes a target for disidentification because they associate working with native cultures as exploitative. When social marketers align an organization with some salient issues, they risk suffering the negative consequences that accompany disidentification. Understanding both sides of the process is critically important.

The second underresearched issue is the challenge created for organizations when they create a complex and evolving relationship with their employees. We discussed the war for talent in the previous chapter. Indeed, it is clear and has been shown that people acquire a positive social identity through their association with a prestigious employer[92] and they will conform to the social norms of what is deemed to be a prestigious employer.[93] This is one reason why a war for talent image can have knock-on positive effects. However, what happens when an organization has a *hybrid identity*[94] – it embodies both positive and negative dimensions that, on the one hand, enhance but also threaten an individual's self concept? For example, the likes of Asda, Tesco and Sainsbury might be seen to support numerous charitable causes and provide local jobs, but also be considered to destroy small-town economies. As the section on trust showed, we live in a world of impaired organizational reputation, and for many employees this creates conflicting identities. We have to understand what happens when people:

- Make mental adjustments to a schizophrenic organizational identity (i.e. cope with negative or conflicting dimensions)
- Develop weak identities
- Develop intentionally neutral identities.

It might be assumed that individuals would be wary of identifying with a organization that has a conflicting identity because if they identified with it they would be accepting several negative dimensions as being self-defining. Certainly a bad press makes insiders more cautious about identifying themselves to outsiders as organizational members.[95] However, most employees have to make complex cognitive adjustments. An anti-smoker might work for a food conglomerate that in another division makes cigarettes. How does a professional, for example, who might have the opportunity to work for a more prestigious firm, justify their employment in this situation? How do they explain their job without connecting themselves to a stigmatized part of the organization's identity?

Psychologists are gaining insight into organizational identification in this context by looking at the behaviour of stigmatized groups. This shows that some group members highlight within-group variation as a means of enhancing their own status relative to the most negatively perceived group members. Stressing variation within the group serves as a *personal identity protection mechanism*, so that even if the group as a whole is seen as inferior to other groups, they can maintain their self-image.[96] Individuals stratify their 'own' according to the degree to which their stigma is apparent and obtrusive, taking up the attitudes that the 'normals' hold towards them and applying it to the others (a form of projection).[97] They use a series of tactics (called self-affirmations, identity-stands and displays of physical identity-markers) to publicly identity and disassociate themselves within the group from certain stigmatized positions. Elsbach calls this organizational schizo-identification – the challenge faced by the individual who simultaneously scores high on both organizational identification and disidentification scales:

> . . . Schizo-identification appears to be an adaptive cognitive response by committed employees who find themselves linked to an organization whose identity seemingly embodies both cherished values and the opposite of those values.[98]

There is another situation where identification becomes stretched. An individual's perception of their self-concept might fit between the identity of two or more organizations, or more commonly, between two or more stages in an organization's evolution. The individual is ambivalent and develops what is called a *liminal identity* – i.e. at the threshold of consciousness and unconsciousness. They perceive themselves as neither identifying with their organization nor indeed with their professional group. They find a space within the cultural map of the organization that has no name. Indeed, studies have shown that certain groups will use this positioning to their strategic advantage, for it allows them to selectively distance and connect themselves to dimensions of an organization's identity, enabling them to interact more easily with people from various disciplines and professions, acquiring information that might be unavailable to other participants. As Zabusky and Barley's[99] study of scientists within the European Space Agency showed, scientists were very adept at doing this. Indeed, in many organizations scientists can adopt remarkably convenient identities that enable them to justify challenging new technologies. This is then different from simply having a weak identity.

The last form of identification in atypical settings is what is known as intentionally neutral organizational relationship, or *impartial identification*. Neutrality – or a lack of connectedness – between an individual and an organization's identity might not worry a manager or an organization. In some situations, however, it should. There are certain roles – for example, individuals occupying decision-making roles such as arbitrators, non-executive directors, judges and journal editors – where being an impartial identifier is important. One has to engage with the process and topic, but not with specific parties. In such roles – and to many observers the true contribution of the Human Resource Management function in its position between the interests of the business strategy and the employees is a case is point – impartial identification is a specific state in which individuals deliberately maintain a position of balance between identification and disidentification. Individuals in these roles have to develop a self-perception based on the explicit absence of both identification and disidentification with an organiza-tion's identity (be it good or bad). They, in fact, become the target for other people's perceptions of trust and fairness (we discussed the role of trust and perceptions of fairness, such as procedural justice, in Chapter 5). When the impartial identifiers become converts, then the organization in fact has created a very unsafe environment for itself (consider the example of Enron and the role of the HR function and non-executive directors in allowing dysfunction to flourish).

Psychological ownership

We have discussed the challenges associated with managing two important individual–organization linkages – commitment and identification – in all their forms. The third and final form of individual-organizational linkage discussed in this chapter is the concept of *psychological ownership*. Neither commitment nor identification are necessary or sufficient conditions for psychological ownership to exist. There is something that exists even beyond these states of mind. Pierce, Kostova and Dirks[100] have developed a theory of psychological ownership that has much relevance to organizations today. Psychological ownership is the feeling of possessiveness and being psychologically tied to an object – it is as if the individual becomes present in the object and it becomes present in them. It is an attitudinal state of mind that reflects the extent to which an individual attaches to and invests in issues that they feel are important and that they feel are controllable by themselves. In order to understand the implications of psychological ownership, Pierce and colleagues draw upon writings in the areas of sociology, philosophy, and human developmental psychology.

Social psychologists such as Dittmar have noted that people experience a psychological connection between their self and their possessions – be it their homes, cars, or even other people.[101] These come to play an important part in an individual's identity and become an extension of the person's own personality. There is a thin line between 'me' and 'mine' in this sense. This sense of ownership can also be felt towards other entities, such as the parenting of ideas and inventions, artistic creations and other people. In general, and certainly in Western societies, the growth of possessions (defined in the broader sense relating to our ideas, creations and people and not just material goods) is considered to have positive and uplifting psychological effects, while the loss of possessions leads to a shrinkage of personality and quite emotional reactions to the invasion of what we consider to be 'ours'. With ownership comes:

- expected rights[102] (such as the right to information and a right to have a voice in decisions) and

- presumed responsibilities (a sense of burden sharing and the responsibility to invest time and energy to the advancement of the organization) for work outputs,[103] organizational citizenship behaviours, personal sacrifice and the assumption of risk[104].

This is why it is only when psychological ownership exists that formal employee ownership engendered through stock ownership, for example, ends up producing positive attitudinal and behavioural effects.[105] More to the point, psychological ownership provides insight into which individuals will both promote and resist change. For there to be a sense of psychological ownership changes have to be perceived as being self-initiated, evolutionary and additive. Without these attributions, resistance is more likely to be dysfunctional with deviant psychological behaviours such as wanting to retain exclusive control, destructive acts, or over-immersion in the target of ownership,[106] as well as feelings of loss, frustration and stress.[107] It is this loss of psychological ownership that likely underlies many of the emotional reactions to the breach of psychological contract discussed in Chapter 2.

Job satisfaction and part-time work

So far we have concentrated on the linkages between the individual and the organization. We should not ignore that the employment relationship is also influenced by the relationship between the individual and the job. We end this chapter by discussing three particular challenges in relation to the individual–job linkage:

- The creation of job satisfaction among part-time employees
- The development of individual responsibility towards the job and fostering of job-crafting behaviours
- The risks associated with overidentification with the job and workaholism.

One of the main challenges that has been discussed in this context is the issue of job satisfaction, especially for those in non-standard employment. Despite the significant rise in part-time employment outlined in Chapter 3, most of the research into important individual factors associated with important job outcomes (such as satisfaction) has been conducted on full-time employees. Back in 1982 they were described as the 'missing persons in organizational research' and this situation has changed little [108]. More recently researchers have asked questions about whether the nature of work and fairness of treatment between full-timers and part-timers might explain job attitudes,[109] or whether part-time workers might reflect a different type of individual with unique job attitudes and behaviours. Barling and Gallagher have conducted a theoretical review of the evidence on part-time employment.[110]

What explanations are used to suggest that there might be significantly different types of behaviour and different triggers for things like job satisfaction or the reason to leave the organization? We use research on the job satisfaction of part-time versus full-time employees to highlight three different explanations of differences that might be found in important work-related attitudes:

1 *Individual motivational differences*: these might mean that some people are less concerned about pay and advancement and that part-time employees are more easily satisfied.
2 *Low involvement*: people in part-time roles have other important things in their life and so their lower involvement with the organization might mean that that they have less opportunity to develop negative feelings, or more compensation for these.
3 *Reference group*: job satisfaction might be more a product of those people we chose to compare ourselves with – our reference group. If our situation compares well with these 'referent others' then we might still be satisfied despite relatively poor conditions

The above possible explanations show the complexity that lies behind any process of individualization of the employment relationship. Several subtle factors might explain an individual's response. If there are clear differences between part-time and full-time employees in terms of their attitudes and motivations to the job, this would have important implications for organizational behaviour and the sorts of interventions that organizations might design to predict and control employee behaviour. Sadly, the results across these three different explanations have been fairly inconsistent.

The low-involvement explanation was forwarded by Katz and Kahn[111]. They used the idea of *partial inclusion theory* to suggest that organizations require us as individuals to perform work roles that are typically only a part of our self-identity. Part-time employees might be assumed to be less satisfied than full-time employees because even less of their identity is included within the social systems and life of the organization. Some studies have indeed found that job involvement is lower among part-time employees, consistent with this view[112]. However, lower job satisfaction need not result from being less involved with the job. It has also been found that because part-time employees may be exposed to fewer organizational problems,[113] this may prevent them from developing fewer negative attitudes and they actually can have higher levels of job satisfaction.[114]

The referent group explanation was first suggested by Eberhardt and Shani.[115] *Social comparison theory* draws upon ideas of *equity*. It argues that full- and part-time employees can have different *frames of reference*. If employees perceive that they are being under- or over-rewarded when they compare themselves with others then this leads to a sense of dissatisfaction. Part-time employees might become more easily dissatisfied if they compared themselves to the experience of full-time employees. However, if they use a different set of 'referents' and compare themselves to other part-time workers, then they will not report lower levels of job satisfaction. This might explain why in many studies part-time employees still report similar levels of job satisfaction to full-time employees.[116] One study has found that the majority of part-time workers (82 per cent) do appear to compare themselves only to other part-time workers when making assessments of their satisfaction.[117] Another study found that it depends on the nature of the job. About half of permanent part-time employees used full-time employees as their referent, but temporary part-time workers were much more likely to use part-time employees as their referent group.[118]

Finally, researchers have asked if it is more important that the individual's work status is congruent with their desires. Coming from a marketing perspective, Wotruba[119] suggested that part-time employees might have different motivations for work, placing less priority on pay and advancement. The majority will be more easily satisfied if part-time work was their preference, being more accepting of poorer conditions. However, for those who are highly ambitious while still wanting flexible work patterns, poor job conditions for part-time employees will lower their satisfaction. The closer the fit between the individual's work desires and what the job provides (job–person fit) then the individual will adjust better and will have greater satisfaction.[120] Part-time workers who really desire full-time work will nonetheless be more satisfied with their work than full-time employees who really desire part-time work. Much of this work has actually been conducted on nurses as a profession, but it has actually shown very mixed results.[121] A large-scale attitude survey of 7279 employees in two contrasting British organizations by Fenton-O'Creevy[122] did, however, lend support to this theory.

However, a very recent meta-analysis of the results of all the major studies on job attitudes differences between full- and part-time workers has tested the strength of effect of all the major empirical findings that we have to date.[123] Thorsteinson examined all of the possible moderators mentioned above – the type of job, gender, whether the work was voluntarily engaged in or not. Thirty-eight studies were identified covering over 50 000 employees. It suggests that there is in fact very little difference between part- and full-time workers in terms of job satisfaction, organizational commitment, intentions to leave and most facets of job satisfaction (full-time workers were more satisfied with pay and co-workers, but satisfaction with promotion, supervisors and the work itself did not differ). Full-time employees are more involved with their jobs. These findings are true regardless of sex and type of job. Involuntary as opposed to voluntary employment status has a small effect on the level of job satisfaction.

The inconsistent findings noted above in fact reflect the fact that there are no simple causes for differences in job satisfaction. Not all part-time staff are the same. As they become a more prevalent part of the workforce it becomes increasingly important for organizations to understand the varied motivations and drivers of employee behaviour (this applies to all employees, not just part-time employees). The findings on low involvement also suggest that more subtle individual factors need to be examined if employee behaviour is to be managed effectively.

The desirability of job-crafting behaviours

The meaning that employees attach to work shapes their work motivation and subsequently their performance on the job. Some employees will use the work tasks and interactions that compose their workday and their lives more than others will, in order to construct and make sense of their job[124] and build up their experience of work. This has become known as a job-crafting orientation, which has recently been examined by Wrzesniewski and Dutton. They define job crafting as the '. . . physical and cognitive changes individuals make in the task or relational boundaries of their work'.[125] Individuals have latitude to define and enact their job. Individual work orientations tend to allow people to see different possibilities for how to change their tasks and relationships at work – for example, different people can view the same task as part of a job (focusing on its financial rewards), part of a career (focusing on its opportunity for advancement) or as part of a calling (focusing on the enjoyment of fulfilling socially useful work).[126] Individuals tend to revise jobs in ways that fulfil their orientations. Careerists, for example, will craft jobs to interact with people more powerful than themselves and to engage in high-visibility tasks. A job-crafting predisposition, therefore, while generally positive and proactive, can have negative consequences for the organization (this relates to some of Pfeffer's criticism of a war for talent mentality within organizations). Nonetheless, work involves increasingly the necessity for more and more employees actively to craft their own work lives.[127] It takes effort to craft a job and involves a degree of creativity in order to push, shrink or transform a task and relationships. Employees therefore need training in how best to 'grow a job' and can likely learn from those who naturally do so.

However, while the motivation to craft one's own job is clearly moderated by the opportunity to do so afforded by the organization, it is also a product of the individual's work and motivational orientations. Three individual needs are associated with the motivation to craft one's job:

1 The desire to assert personal control in order avoid alienation from work. People take control of or reframe the tasks or conditions that control the overall purpose of the work, creating new domains for mastery even in low-autonomy jobs (see, for example, the work of Braverman[128]).
2 The desire to create a positive self-image in one's own eyes and in the eyes of others. When the job makes this personal construction difficult, people are motivated to remedy this by changing such things as the pace of work, names, or demeanour (see, for example, the work of Erez and Earley[129]).
3 The need to be connected to others. People build relationships with others to reframe the meaning of work and their own identity at work (see, for example, the work of Baumeister and Leary[130]).

Wrzesniewski and Dutton point out that '... Not all employees are motivated to fulfil needs for control, positive image and connection at work. Individuals who look to fulfil these needs at work likely will look for opportunities to craft their jobs in ways that allow them to meet their needs'.[131] Crafting a job involves shaping the boundaries of a task (either physically reshaping it or reshaping it in your mind) and shaping the boundaries placed on the relationships it entails and the people with whom you interact. These actions change the frame of work for the individual, in terms of both their mental view of it and the actions they will undertake. They affect both the meaning of work for the individual and their identity (which, as we have seen, is an important part of the relationship that they have with the organization). This views individuals as agents and architects of their own jobs with discretion even in uncertain or constraining times to act in ways that will enable transformations. Job-crafters are individuals who actively compose what their job is. Cues are read about work and are interpreted (or not as the case might be) by motivated crafters. It is a creative and improvised process that captures an individual's adaptation to job changes.

Job-crafting practices therefore go beyond established ideas about job design. They address the processes by which employees change elements of their jobs and relationships with others in order to revise the meaning of work. It is also different from – but shares some similar features with – the construct of *personal initiative* which has been examined by Frese and his colleagues.[132] Personal initiative is a behavioural syndrome in which individuals self-start initiatives at work that go beyond the formal job requirements. These proactive behaviours are consistent with the organization's mission, have a long-term focus, are goal-directed and are persistent in the face of barriers. This individual difference measure, however, tends to be focused around proactive problem-solving behaviours, rather than the underlying need for control, to manage self-image and to be connected that drives a job-crafting orientation.

The extent to which the organization erodes the display of these needs for control, positive image and connection, or conversely the extent to which the individual is just overwhelmingly driven by such needs, will determine the degree to which people respond positively to the complex changes in organizational form outlined in Chapter 1. The more dynamic view painted by job-crafting theory suits the world of the new organizational forms outlined in the opening chapter. Managers, as proxies for their organization, have direct control over the incentives and material rewards that are associated with job outcomes and they can affect how the work is organized in ways that will either enhance or undermine job-crafting. Including people in strategic conversations about what they are trying to accomplish is an important part of initiating the identity-altering processes associated with job-crafting and that also are important in any renegotiation of the psychological contract.

Over-identification and engagement: workaholism

We have discussed identification earlier in this chapter. We now must consider the issue of over-identification with work as an important individual difference that might have a bearing on the psychological contract. The topic of 'workaholism' has received the attention of the popular press, but until recently there has been surprising little academic study of the phenomenon. A number of questions are now being asked.[133] Are there different types of workaholics? How prevalent is it in the workforce? What leads up to it? What consequences does it have? How best should it be managed?

Despite much popular interest, scientific understanding of workaholism remains quite limited.[134] Opinions are divided as to whether workaholism is a positive attribute[135] or should be seen as a more negative form of addiction.[136] It has also been measured in several different ways. Usually the measures comprise lists of a series of behaviours or attitudes, or adjectives, that cover habits, goals or an individual's self-concept. The habits covered include things such as waking times, hours worked per week, extra hours worked, job stress, non-delegation of duties, levels of trust and perfectionism. Conceptually, it often overlaps with other constructs such as Type A behaviour and compulsion–obsession.

One of the better known instruments for assessing workaholism, the Spence and Robbins' Workaholism Battery, however, measures three separate components:[137]

1 *Work involvement*: a generalized *attitude* of psychological involvement with work
2 *Work drive*: feeling driven to the work, an inner pressure to work maintained by a *need* for internal fulfilment rather than external pressure
3 *Work enjoyment*: the level of *pleasure* derived from work.

This has been used to distinguish workaholics from other varieties of work behaviour – work enthusiasts, relaxed workers, unengaged workers and disenchanted workers – across these three dimensions[138] (see Table 8.3). This categorization has not gone without criticism, however.[139] Workaholism represents a pattern of behaviour. An individual might have high work

Table 8.3 Five varieties of work engagement

	Workaholic	Work enthusiast	Relaxed worker	Unengaged worker	Disenchanted worker
Work involvement	High	High	Low	Low	Low
Work drive	High	Low	Low	Low	High
Work enjoyment	Low	High	High	Low	Low

Source: Burke.[133]

involvement (which is an attitude) but still not engage in workaholic behaviour. Although the two overlap, this might not be to extent that the Spence and Robbins measure assumes. Similarly, conceptualizations of workaholism that assume low enjoyment might be misleading. Although long working hours has been assumed to be a critical defining feature of workaholism (we discuss the long work hours culture in Chapter 9) the extent of relationship between the two remains uncertain. Most workaholics spend much time (working) at home so formal work hours in employment are misleading.

Does investigation into workaholism reveal something new compared to other measures of attitudes to work and general well-being? The answer appears to be yes. In a validation study on 320 New Zealand employees McMillan and colleagues[140] found that the three factors bear expected relationships with related (but different) constructs. For example, Warr, Cook and Wall's[141] Work Involvement Scale generally measures the extent to which an individual wants to engage in work, but there was only 7 per cent shared variance between this and the Spence and Robbins measure. Similarly, the work enjoyment scale shares 21 per cent of common variance with Warr *et al.*'s intrinsic Job Satisfaction Scale and the work drive scale shares 16 per cent common variance with their Intrinsic Job Motivation scale. This, of course, might mean that the measure is not very robust (the three separate elements are not found in all replications) or that it is tapping some different behaviours than the three measures used by Warr and his colleagues. For example, work involvement as measured on the Workaholism battery involves hobbies and domestic activities, and is not just restricted to work.

Most of the research has been on small samples and it has used a variety of measures and our understanding of the behaviour is therefore still limited. However, at this stage of research estimates show wide fluctuations across occupations, from 23 per cent of physicians, lawyers and psychiatrists,[142] to 21 per cent of Japanese managers,[143] 16 per cent of MBA graduates,[144] but perhaps as little as 5 per cent of the US population as a whole.[145]

Moreover, it seems clear that the extent to which an individual becomes a workaholic appears to be influenced by three important antecedents:

- *Family of origin*: the inter-generational transfer through family processes of learned addictive responses to dysfunctional family conditions deemed to represent love and reward.[146]
- *Personal beliefs and fears*: the values, thoughts and interpersonal styles that reflect a striving against others, no moral principles and desire to prove oneself.[147]
- *Organizational values and priorities*: support for work–personal life balance, limits on work hours, and weekend travelling.[148]

There is also some evidence emerging that workaholism is associated with outcomes such as lower job satisfaction, lower career satisfaction, lower perceived career prospects and higher intention to quit, all supporting the 'driven' conceptualization of the construct.[149] Workaholics have poorer well-being, evidenced through more psychosomatic symptoms, negative life-style behaviours and low emotional well-being,[150] and higher levels of depression, anxiety and anger.[151]

References

1. Herriot, P. (2001). *The employment relationship: a psychological perspective.* Hove: Routledge, p. 5.
2. *Ibid.*
3. Meyer, J. and Allen, N. (1991). A three-component conceptualisation of organizational commitment. *Human Resource Management Review, 1,* 61–89.
4. Mael, F.A. and Tetrick, L.E. (1992). Identifying organizational identification. *Educational and Psychological Measurement, 52,* 813–824.
5. Wan-Huggins, V.N., Riordam, C. and Griffeth, R.W. (1998).The development and longitudinal test of a model of organizational identification. *Journal of Applied Social Psychology, 28,* 724–749.
6. O'Reilly, C. and Chapman, J. (1986). Organizational commitment and psychological attachment: the effects of compliance, identification and internalisation on pro-social behaviour. *Journal of Applied Psychology, 71,* 492–499.
7. Mael, F.A. and Ashforth, B.E. (1992). Alumni and their alma mater: a partial test of the reformulated model of organizational identification. *Journal of Organizational Behavior, 13,* 103–123.
8. Pierce, J.L., Kostova, T. and Dirks, K.T. (2001). Toward a theory of psychological ownership in organizations. *Academy of Management Review, 26 (2),* 298–310.
9. Seligman, M.E.P. (1975). *Helplessness.* San Francisco: Freeman.
10. Gallie, D., Felstead, A. and Green, F. (2001). Employer policies and organizational commitment in Britain 1992–97. *Journal of Management Studies, 38 (8),* 1081–1101.
11. Swailes, S. (2002). Organizational commitment: a critique of the construct and its measures. *International Journal of Management Research, 4 (2),* 155–178.
12. Morrow, P.C. (1983). Concept redundancy in organizational commitment research: the case of work commitment. *Academy of Management Review, 8 (3),* 486–500.
13. Van Dyne, L., Graham, J.W. and Dienesch, R.M. (1994). Organizational citizenship behaviour: construct redefinition, measurement and validation. *Academy of Management Journal, 37 (4),* 765–801.
14. Becker, T.E. (1992). Foci and bases of commitment: are they distinctions worth making? *Academy of Management Journal, 35 (1),* 232–244.; Becker, T.E. and Billings, R.S. (1993). Profiles of commitment: an empirical test. *Journal of Organizational Behavior, 14 (2),* 177–190.

15. See, for example, Randall, D.M. (1988). Multiple roles and organizational commitment. *Journal of Organizational Behavior, 9 (4)*, 309–317; Romzek, B.S. (1989). Personal consequences of employee commitment. *Academy of Management Journal, 32 (3)*, 649–661; Cohen, A. (1995). An examination of the relationship between work commitment and non-work domains. *Human Relations, 48 (3)*, 239–263.

16. Etzioni, A. (1961). *A comparative analysis of complex organizations: on power, involvement and their correlates.* New York: Free Press.

17. Becker, H.S. (1960). Notes on the concept of commitment. *American Journal of Sociology, 66*, 32–40.

18. Salancik, G.R. (1977). Commitment and the control of organizational behavior and belief. In B.M. Staw and G.R. Salancik (Eds.), *New directions in organizational behavior.* St Clair Press.

19. See Mowday, R.T., Porter, L.W. and Steers, R.M. (1979). The measurement of organizational commitment. *Journal of Vocational Behavior, 14*, 224–247; Mowday, R.T., Porter, L.W. and Steers, R.M. (1982). *Employee–organization linkages: the psychology of commitment, absenteeism and turnover.* New York: Academic Press.

20. See Meyer and Allen (1991). *Op. cit.*; Meyer, J.P. and Allen, N.J. (1997). *Commitment in the workplace.* London : Sage

21. See Meyer *et al.* (1990). *Op. cit.*; McGee, G.W. and Ford, R.C. (1987). Two (or more?) dimensions of organizational commitment: re-examination of the affective and continuance commitment scales. *Journal of Applied Psychology, 72 (4)*, 638–642; Dunham, R.B., Grube, J.A. and Castaneda, M.B. (1994). Organizational commitment : the utility of an integrative definition. *Journal of Applied Psychology, 7 (13)*, 370–380; Hackett, R.D., Bycio, P. and Heusdorf, P.A. (1994). Further assessments of Meyer and Allen's (1991) three component model of organizational commitment. *Journal of Applied Psychology, 79 (1)*, 15–23.

22. Mowday, R.T., Porter, L.W. and Steers, R.M. (1979).The measurement of organizational commitment. *Journal of Vocational Behavior, 14*, 224–247. p. 226.

23. Meyer, J.P. and Allen, N.J. (1984). Testing the 'side bet theory' of Organizational Commitment: some methodological considerations. *Journal of Applied Psychology, 69*, 372–378.

24. Mowday, R.T. Porter, L.W. and Steers, R.M. (1982). *Employee–organization linkages : the psychology of commitment, absenteeism and turnover.* New York: Academic Press.

25. Cook, J. and Well, T. (1980). New work altitude measures of trust organizational commitment and personal need non-fulfilment. *Journal of Occupational Psychology, 53*, 39–52. For a summary of validation studies see: Mathews, B.P. and Shephard, J.L. (2002). Short research note: Dimensionality of Cook and Wall's (1980). British Organizational Commitment Scale Scale revisited. *Journal of Occupational and Organizational Psychology, 75 (3)*, 369–375.

26. McGee, G.W. and Ford, R.C. (1987). Two (or more?) dimensions of organizational commitment: Re-examination of the affective and continuance commitment scales. *Journal of Applied Psychology, 72*, 638–642; Allen, N.J. and Meyer, J.P. (1990). The measurement and antecedents of affective, continuance, and normative commitment to the organization. *Journal of Occupational Psychology, 63*, 1–18.
27. See Allen, N.J. and Meyer, J.P. (1990). Measurement and antecedents of affective, continuance and normative commitment to the organization. *Journal of Occupational and Organizational Psychology, 63 (1)*, 1–18; Meyer and Allen (1984). *Ibid.*; Meyer, J.P., Allen, N.J. and Gellatly, I.R. (1990). Affective and Continuance commitment to the organization: Evaluation of measures and analysis of concurrent and time-logged relations. *Journal of Applied Psychology, 75 (6)*, 710–720.
28. Meyer, and Allen (1991). *Op. cit.*
29. See Allen and Meyer (1990). *Op. cit.*; Weiner, Y. (1982). Commitment in organizations: a normative view. *Academy of Management Review, 7 (3)*, 418–428.
30. Swailes, S. (2002). Organizational commitment: a critique of the construct and measures. *International Journal of Management Review.*
31. *Ibid.*
32. Peccel, R. and Guest, D. (1993). The dimensionality of organizational commitment. Discussion Paper 149. London School of Economics. London Centre for Economic Performance.
33. Farrel, O. and Rusbult, C.E. (1981). Exchange variables as predictors of job satisfaction, job commitment and turnover : the impact of rewards, costs, alternatives and investments. *Organizational Behaviour and Human Performance, 28*, 78–95.
34. Scholl, R.W. (1981). Differentiating organizational commitment from expectancy as a motivational force. *Academy of Management Review, 6 (4)*, 589–599.
35. Hunt, S.D. and Morgan, R.M. (1994). Organizational commitment: one of many commitments or key mediating construct? *Academy of Management Journal, 37 (6)*, 1568–1587.
36. Gouldner, H.P. (1960). Dimensions of organizational commitment. *Administrative Science Quarterly 4*, 468–490.
37. Swailes (2002). *Op. cit.*
38. Mellor, S., Mathieu, J.E., Barnes-Farrell, J.L. and Rogelberg, S.G. (2001). Employees' nonwork obligations and organizational commitments: a new way to look at the relationships. *Human Resource Management, 40 (2)*, 171–184, p. 171.
39. Legge, K. (1995). *Human resource management: rhetorics and realities.* Basingstoke: Macmillan.
40. For reviews see: Mathieu, J.E. and Zajac, D.M. (1990). A review and meta-analysis of the antecedents, correlates and consequences of organizational commitment. *Psychological Bulletin, 108*, 171–194; Tett, R.P. and Meyer, J.P. (1993). Job satisfaction, organizational commitment, turnover intention,

and turnover: Path analyses based on meta-analytic findings. *Personnel Psychology, 46,* 259–293; Allen, N.J. and Meyer, J.P. (1996). Affective, continuance and normative commitment to the organization: an examination of construct validity. *Journal of Vocational Behavior, 49,* 252–276; Meyer, J.P. and Allen, N.J. (1997). *Commitment in the workplace.* Thousand Oaks, CA: Sage.

41. Meyer and Allen (1997). *Op. cit.* p. 37.
42. Mathieu and Zajac (1990). *Op. cit.*
43. Randall, D.M. (1990). The consequences of organizational commitment: methodological investigation. *Journal of Organizational Behavior, 11,* 361–378.
44. Cohen, A. (1991). Career stage as a moderator of the relationships between organizational commitment and its outcomes: a meta-analysis. *Journal of Occupational Psychology, 64,* 253–268.
45. Riketta, M. (2002). Attitudinal organizational commitment and job performance: a meta-analysis. *Journal of Organizational Behavior, 23,* 257–266.
46. Gallagher. and McLean Parkes (2000). cited in Marler *et al.* (2002).
47. Marler *et al.* (2002). *Op. cit.*
48. Mathieu, J. and Zajac. D. (1990). A review and meta-analysis of the antecedents, correlates and consequences of organizational commitment. *Psychological Bulletin, 108,* 171–194.
49. Capelli (1999). *Op. cit.*
50. Marler *et al.* (2002). *Op. cit.,* p. 448.
51. Smith, V. (2001). *Crossing the great divide: worker risk and opportunity in the new economy.* Itheca, NY: Cornell University Press. p. 175.
52. See, for example, Allen, N. and Meyer, J.P. (1990). The measurement and antecedents of affective, continuance and normative commitment to the organization. *Journal of Occupational Psychology, 63,* 1–18; Mowday, R.T., Steers, R.M. and Porter, L.W. (1979). The measurement of organizational commitment. *Journal of Vocational Behavior, 14,* 224–247.
53. O'Reilly, C. and Chapman, J. (1986). Organizational commitment and psychological attachment: the effects of compliance, identification, and internalisation on prosocial behavior. *Journal of Applied Psychology, 71,* 492–499.
54. Elsbach, K.D. (1999). An expanded model of organizational identification. *Research in Organizational Behaviour, 21,* 163–200.
55. Dutton, J.E., Dukerich, J.M. and Harquail, C.V. (1994). Organizational images and member identification. *Administrative Science Quarterly, 39,* 239–263.
56. See, for example, Brown, M.E. (1969). Identification and some conditions of organizational involvement. *Administrative Science Quarterly, 14,* 346–355: Hall, D.T. and Schneider, B. (1972). Correlates of organizational identification as a function of career pattern and organizational type. *Administrative Science Quarterly, 17,* 340–350; Lee, S.M. (1971). An empirical analysis of organizational identification. *Academy of Management*

Journal, 14, 213–226; Rotondi, T. (1975). Organizational identification: Issues and implications. *Organizational Behavior and Human Performance, 13*, 95–109.

57. Tajifel, H. (1978). *Differentiation between social groups: studies in the social psychology of intergroup relations*. London: Academic Press; Tajifel, H. and Turner, J.C. (1986). The social identity theory of intergroup behaviour. In S. Worchel and W.G. Austin (Eds.), *Psychology of intergroup relations. 2nd edition*. Chicago: Nelson-Hall.

58. Deaux, K. (1996). Social identification. In E.T. Higgins and A.W. Kruglanski (Eds.), *Social psychology: handbook of basic principles*. New York: Guilford.

59. Ashforth, B.E. and Mael, F. (1989). Social identity theory and the organization. *Academy of Management Review, 14*, 20–39; Mael, F.A. and Ashforth, B.E. (1992). Alumni and their alma mater: a partial test of the reformulated model of organizational identification. *Journal of Organizational Behavior, 13*, 103–123.

60. Van Knippenberg, D. and van Schie, E.C.M. (2000). Foci and correlates of organizational identification, *Journal of Occupational and Organizational Psychology, 73*, 137–147.

61. Tajifel (1978). *Op. cit.*

62. Ellemers, N. (1993). The influence of socio-structural variables on identity enhancement strategies, *European Review of Social Psychology, 4*, 27–57.

63. See, for example, Brewer, M.B. (1991). The social self: on being the same and different at the same time. *Personality and Social Psychology Bulletin, 17*, 475–482; Brewer, M.B. (1993). The role of distinctiveness in social identity and group behavior. In M.A. Hogg and D. Abrams (Eds.), *Group motivation: social psychological perspectives*. New York: Harvester Wheatsheaf.

64. Brewer (1991). *Op. cit.*

65. Turner, J.C., Hogg, M.A., Oakes, P.J., Reicher, S.D. and Wetherell, M.S. (1987). *Rediscovering the social group: a self categorization theory*. Oxford: Blackwell.

66. Mael, F.A. and Ashforth, B.E. (1995). Loyal from day one: Biodata, organizational identification, and turnover among newcomers. *Personnel Psychology, 48*, 309–333.

67. Tajifel and Turner (1986). *Op. cit.*

68. Mathieu, J.E. and Zajac, D.M. (1990). A review and meta-analysis of the antecedents, correlates, and consequences of organizational commitment. *Psychological Bulletin, 108*, 171–194.

69. Van Knippenberg, D. and van Schie, E.C.M. (2000). Foci and correlates of organizational identification. *Journal of Occupational and Organizational Psychology, 73*, 137–147.

70. Abrams, D., Ando, K. and Hinkle, S. (1998). Psychological attachment to the group: Cross-cultural differences in organizational identification and subjective norms as predictors of workers' turnover intentions. *Personality and Social Psychology Bulletin, 24*, 1027–1039; and Abrams, D. and Randsley

de Moura, G. (2001). Organizational identification: psychological anchorage and turnover. In M.A. Hogg and D.J. Terry (Eds.), *Social identity processes in organizational contexts*. Philadelphia, PA: Psychology Press.

71. Albert, S., Ashforth, B.E., and Dutton, J.E. (2000). Organizational identity and identification: charting new waters and building new bridges. *Academy of Management Review, 25 (1)*, 13–17.

72. Van Knippenberg and van Schie (2000). *Op. cit.*

73. Dutton, J.E., Dukerich, J.M. and Harquail, C.V. (1994). Organizational images and member identification. *Administrative Science Quarterly, 39*, 239–263.

74. Van Knippenberg and van Schie (2000). *Op. cit.*

75. *Ibid.* p. 145.

76. Ashforth, B.E. and Mael, F. (1989). Social identity theory and the organization. *Academy of Management Review, 14*, 20–39.

77. Elsbach, K.D. and Glynn, M.A. (1996). Believing your own PR: embedding identification in strategic reputation. In J.C. Baum and J.E. Dutton (Eds.), *Advances in strategic management, 13*, Greenwich, CT : JAI Press, pp. 65–90.

78. See, for example, Tajifel, H. (1982). *Social identity and intergroup relations*. Cambridge: Cambridge University Press; Abrams, D. and Hogg, M.A. (1990). *Social Identity theory: constructive and critical advances*. New York: Springer-Verlag.

79. Turner, J.C. (1987). *Rediscovering the social group: a self-categorization theory*. New York : Basil Blackwell.

80. Wood, J.V. (1989). Theory and research concerning social comparisons of personal attributes. *Psychological Bulletin, 106*, 231–248.

81. Pratt, M.G. (1998). To be or not to be: Central questions in organizational identification. In D.A. Whetton and P.K. Godfrey (Eds.), *Identity in organizations*. Thousand Oaks, CA: Sage, pp. 171–208.

82. Ashforth and Mael (1989). *Op. cit.*; Dutton *et al.* (1994). *Op. cit.*

83. Alpander, G.G. (1990). Relationship between commitment to hospital goals and job satisfaction: a case study of a nursing department. *Health Care Management Review, 15*, 51–62.

84. Meyer, J.P., Paunonen, S.V., Gellatly, I.R., Goffin, R.D. and Jackson, D.N. (1989). Organizational commitment and job performance: It's the nature of the commitment that counts. *Journal of Applied Psychology, 74*, 152–156.

85. Adler, P.A. and Adler, P. (1988). Intense loyalty in organizations: a case study of college athletics. *Administrative Science Quarterly, 33*, 401–417.

86. Lee, S.M. (1971). An empirical analysis of organizational identification. *Academy of Management Journal*, 213–226.

87. Mael, F.A. and Ashforth, B.E. (1992). Alumni and their alma mater: a partial test of the reformulated model of organizational identification. *Journal of Organizational Behaviour, 13*, 103–123

88. O'Reilly III, C. and Chapman, J. (1986). Organizational commitment and psychological attachment: the effects of compliance, identification, and internalisation of prosocial behaviour. *Journal of Applied Psychology, 71*, 492–499.

89. Elsbach, K.D. (1999). An expanded model of organizational identification. *Research in Organizational Behaviour, 21*, 163–200.

90. Zabusky, S.E. and Barley, S.R. (1997). 'You can't be a stone if you're cement': re-evaluating the emic identities of scientists in organizations. In B.M. Staw and L.L. Cummings (Eds.), *Research in organizational behavior, Volume 19*. Greenwich, CT: JAI Press, pp. 361–404.

91. Heider, F. (1958). *The psychology of interpersonal relations*. New York: Wiley.

92. Hall, D.T. and Schneider, B. (1972). Correlates of organizational identification as a function of career pattern and organizational type. *Administrative Science Quarterly, 17*, 340–350.

93. Pratt, M.G. and Rafaeli, A. (1997). Organizational dress as a symbol of multi-layered social identities. *Academy of Management Journal, 40*, 862–898.

94. Albert, S. and Whetton, D.A. (1985). Organizational identity. In L.L. Cummings and B.M. Staw (Eds.) *Research in organizational behavior, Volume 7*, Greenwich, CT: JAI Press, pp. 263–295.

95. Dutton, J.E. and Dukerich, J.M. (1991). Keeping an eye on the mirror: Image and identity in organizational adaptation. *Academy of Management Journal, 34*, 517–554.

96. Doosje, B. and Ellemers, N. (1997). Stereotyping under threat: the role of group identification. In R. Spears, P.J. Oakes, N. Ellemers and S.A. Haslam (Eds.), *The social psychology of stereotyping and group life*. Oxford: Blackwell, pp. 257–272.

97. Goffman, E. (1959). *The presentation of self in everyday life*. New York: Doubleday.

98. Elsbach, K.D. (1999). An expanded model of organizational identification. *Research in Organizational Behaviour, 21*, 163–200, p. 182.

99. Zabusky, S.E. and Barley, S.R. (1997). 'You can't be a stone if you're cement': re-evaluating the emic identities of scientists in organizations. In B.M. Staw and L.L. Cummings (Eds.), *Research in organizational behavior, Volume 19*. Greenwich, CT: JAI Press, pp 361–404.

100. Pierce, J.L., Kostova, T. and Dirks, K.T. (2001). Toward a theory of psychological ownership in organizations. *Academy of Management Review, 26 (2)*, 298–310.

101. Dittmar, H. (1992). *The social psychology of material possessions: to have is to be*. New York: St Martin's Press.

102. Rodgers, L. and Freundlich, F. (1998). Nothing measured, nothing gained. *Employee Ownership Report, XVIII*, No. 1. Oakland, CA: National Centre for Employee Ownership.

103. See for example, Dipboye, R.L. (1977). A critical review of Korman's self-consistency theory of work motivation and occupational choice. *Organizational Behavior and Human Performance, 18*, 108–126; Korman, A. (1970). Toward an hypothesis of work behavior. *Journal of Applied Psychology, 54*, 31–41.

104. Van de Walle, D., Van Dyne, L. and Kostova, T. (1995). Psychological

ownership: an empirical examination of its consequences. *Group and Organization Management*, 20, 210–226.

105. See, for example, Pierce, J.L., Rubenfeld, S.A. and Morgan, S. (1991). Employee ownership: a conceptual model of process and effects. *Academy of Management Review, 16*, 121–144; Pratt, M.G. and Dutton, J.E. (2000). Owning up or opting out: the role of identities and emotions in issue ownership. In N. Ashkanasy, C. Hartel and W. Zerbe (Eds.), *Emotions in the workplace: research, theory and practice*. New York: Quorum.

106. Robinson, S.L. and Bennett, R.J. (1995). A typology of deviant workplace behaviors: a multi-dimensional scaling study. *Academy of Management Journal, 38*, 555–572.

107. Bartunek, J.M. (1993). Rummaging behind the scenes of organizational change – and finding role transitions, illness and physical space. In R.W. Woodman and W.A. Pasmore (Eds.), *Research In organizational change and development, Volume 7*, 41–76.

108. Rotchford, N.L. and Roberts, K.H. (1982). Part-time workers as missing persons in organizational research. *Academy of Management Review, 7*, 228–234.

109. Fenton-O'Creevy, M. (1995). Moderators of differences in job satisfaction between full-time and part-time female employees: a research note. *Human Resource Management Journal, 5 (5)*, 75–81.

110. Barling, J. and Gallagher, D.G. (1996). Part-time employment. In C.L. Cooper and I.T. Robertson (Eds.), *International review of industrial and organizational psychology. Volume 11*. Chichester: Wiley.

111. Katz, D. and Kahn, R.L. (1978). *The social psychology of organizations. 2nd edition*. New York: Wiley.

112. Martin, T.N. and Hafer, J.C. (1995). The multiplicative interaction effects of job involvement and organizational commitment on the turnover intentions of full and part-time employees. *Journal of Vocational Behavior, 46*, 310–331.

113. Eberhardt, B.J. and Shani, A.B. (1984). The effects of full-time versus part-time employment status on attitudes toward specific organizational characteristics and overall job satisfaction. *Academy of Management Journal, 27*, 893–900.

114. Barker, K. (1993). Changing assumptions and contingent solutions: the costs and benefits of women working full and part-time. *Sex Roles, 28*, 47–71.

115. Eberhardt, B.J. and Shani, A.B. (1984). The effects of full-time versus part-time employment status on attitudes towards specific organizational characteristics and overall job satisfaction. *Academy of Management Journal, 27*, 893–900.

116. Logan, N., O'Reilly, C.A. III and Roberts, K.H. (1973). Job satisfaction among part-time and full-time employees. *Journal of Vocational Behavior, 3*, 33–41.

117. Feldman, D.C. and Doerpinghaus, H.I. (1992). Patterns of part-time employment. *Journal of Vocational Behavior, 41*, 282–294.

118. Eberhardt, B.J. and Moser, S.B. (1995). The nature and consequences of part-time work: a test of hypotheses. *Journal of Applied Business Research*, *11*, 101–109.

119. Wotruba, T.R. (1990). Full-time versus part-time salespeople. A comparison on job satisfaction, performance and turnover in direct selling. *International Journal of Research in Marketing*, *7*, 97–108.

120. Morrow, P.C., McElroy, J.C. and Elliot, S.M. (1994). The effect of preference for work status, schedule and shift on work-related attitudes. *Journal of Vocational Behavior*, *45*, 202–222.

121. See, for example, Keil, J.M., Armstrong-Stassen, M., Cameron, S.J. and Horsburgh, M.E. (2000). Part-time nurses: the effect of work status congruency on job attitudes. *Applied Psychology: An International Review*, *49*, 227–236; Krausz, M., Sagie, A. and Bidermann, Y. (2000). Actual and preferred work schedules and scheduling control as determinants of job-related attitudes. *Journal of Vocational Behavior*, *56*, 1–11.

122. Fenton-O'Creevy, M. (1995). Moderators of differences in job satisfaction between full-time and part-time female employees: a research note. *Human Resource Management Journal*, *5 (5)*, 75–81.

123. Thorsteinson, T.J. (in press). Job attitudes of part-time versus full-time workers: a meta-analytic review. *Journal of Occupational and Organizational Psychology*.

124. Gergen, K.J. (1994). *Realities and relationships: soundings in social constructionism*. Cambridge, MA: Harvard University Press.

125. Wrzesniewski, A. and Dutton, J.E. (2001). Crafting a job: Revisioning employees as active crafters of their work. *Academy of Management Review*, *26 (2)*, 179–201, 179.

126. Wrzesniewski, A., McCauley, C., Rozin, P. and Schwartz, B. (1997). Jobs, careers and callings: People's relations to their work. *Journal of Research in Personality*, *31*, 21–33.

127. Bridges, W. (1994). *Job shift: how to prosper in a workplace without jobs*. Reading, MA: Addison-Wesley.

128. Braverman, H. (1974). *Labour and monopoly capital: the degradation of work in the twentieth century*. New York: Monthly Review Press.

129. Erez, M. and Earley, C. (1993). *Culture, self-identity and work*. New York: Oxford University Press.

130. Baumeister, R.F. and Leary, M.R. (1995). The need to belong: desire for interpersonal attachments as a fundamental human motivation. *Psychological Bulletin*, *117*, 497–529.

131. Wrzesniewski, A. and Dutton, J.E. (2001). Crafting a job: Revisioning employees as active crafters of their work. *Academy of Management Review*, *26 (2)*, 179–201, p. 183

132. See Frese, M., Fay, D., Hilburger, T., Leng, K. and Tag, A. (1997). The concept of personal initiative: Operationalization, reliability and validity of two German samples. *Journal of Occupational and Organizational Psychology*, *70 (2)*, 139–161; Frese, M., Kring, W., Soose, A. and Zempel, J.

(1996). Personal initiative at work: Differences between East and West Germany. *Academy of Management Journal, 39*, 37–63.

133. Burke, R.J. (2000).Workaholism in organizations: concepts, results and future research directions. *International Journal of Management Review, 2 (1)*, 1–16.

134. See Scott. K.S., Moore, K.S. and Miceli, M.P. (1997). An exploration of the meaning and consequences of workaholism. *Human Relations, 50*, 287–314; McMillan, L.H.W., Brady, E.C., O'Driscoll, M.P. and Marsh, N.V. (2002). A multi-faceted validation study of Spence and Robbins' (1992) Workaholism battery. *Journal of Occupational and Organizational Psychology, 75 (3)*, 357–368.

135. Machlowitz, M. (1980). *Workaholics: living with them, working with them.* Reading, MA: Addison-Wesley.

136. See Killinger, B. (1991). *Workaholics: the respectable addicts.* New York: Simon and Schuster; Schaef, A.W. and Fassel, D. (1988). *The addictive organization.* San Francisco, CA: Harper and Row.

137. Spence, J.T. and Robbins, A.S. (1992). Workaholism: definition, measurement and preliminary results. *Journal of Personality Assessment, 58*, 160–178.

138. Burke, R.J. (1999). Workaholism in organizations: measurement validation and replication. *International Journal of Stress Management, 6*, 45–56.

139. McMillan, L.H.W., Brady, E.C., O'Driscoll, M.P. and Marsh, N.V. (2002). A multi-faceted validation study of Spence and Robbins' (1992) Workaholism battery. *Journal of Occupational and Organizational Psychology, 75 (3)*, 357–368.

140. *Ibid.*

141. Warr, P., Cook, J. and Wall, T. (1979). Scales for the measurement of some work attitudes and aspects of psychological well-being. *Journal of Occupational Psychology, 52*, 129–148.

142. Doerfler, M.C. and Kammer, P.P. (1986). Workaholism: sex and sex role stereotyping among female professionals. *Sex Roles, 14*, 551–560.

143. Kanai, A., Wakabayashi, M. and Fling, S. (1996). Workaholism among employees in Japanese corporations: an examination based on the Japanese version of the workaholism scales. *Japanese Psychological Research, 38*, 192–203.

144. Elder, E.D. and Spence, J.T. (n.p.). Workaholism in the business world: Work addiction versus work-enthusiasm in MBAs. Unpublished manuscript. Department of Psychology, University of Texas at Austin.

145. Machlowitz, M. (1980). *Op. cit.*

146. See, for example, Pietropinto, A. (1986). The workaholic spouse. *Medical Aspects of Human Sexuality, 20*, 89–96; Robinson, B.E. (1996). The psychosocial and familial dimensions of work addiction: preliminary perspectives and hypotheses. *Journal of Counseling and Development, 74*, 447–452; Robinson, B.E. (1996). The relationship between work addiction and family functioning: clinical implications for marriage and family therapists. *Journal of Family Psychotherapy, 7*, 13–39.

147. Burke, R.J. (1999). Workaholism in organizations: the role of beliefs and fears. *Anxiety, Stress and Coping*, in press.
148. Kofodimos, J. (1995). *Balancing act*. San Francisco, CA: Jossey-Bass.
149. See, for example, Burker, R.J. (1991). Early work and career experiences of female and male managers: reasons for optimism? *Canadian Journal of Administrative Sciences, 8*, 224–230; Greenhaus, J.H., Parasuraman, S. and Wormley, W. (1990). Organizational experiences and career success of black and white managers. *Academy of Management Journal, 33*, 64–66; Kofodimos (1995). *Op. cit.*
150. Burke, R.J. (1999). Workaholism in organizations: psychological and physical well-being consequences. *Stress Medicine*, in press.
151. Haymon, S. (1993). The relationship of work addiction and depression, anxiety and anger in college males. Doctoral dissertation. Florida State University 1992. *Dissertation Abstracts International, 53*, 5401-B. (cited in Burke (2000) *Op. cit.*).

9

Work–Life Balance

Work–life balance and the employment relationship

When we characterized the individualized work environment in Chapter 7 and some of the most pertinent individual differences that influence individual–organization linkages in the previous chapter, it hopefully became clear that work roles have become a dominant aspect of individual lives. We begin the chapter by looking at the challenges associated with balancing work with parenting and caring responsibilities and coping with a long work-hours culture. We consider the impact that work has on the home and the challenges created by gender role changes within work–life responsibilities. We introduce the main theoretical perspectives on work–life balance and review the range of employer policies and strategies. We then discuss the implications of greater diversity in the workplace and the need to understand the link between commitment, non-work obligations and the nature of family resources. We consider the pervasive long work hours culture as a block to flexible work provision and review evidence on changes in work hours. This is followed by a review of the link between work hours and well-being. Finally, we outline an agenda for change that summarizes much of the debate so far in this book.

The Future of Work Programme launched by the Economic and Social Research Council has provided support for 27 projects covering issues such as the work–life balance, the employment choices of women with pre-school children, a long work hours culture and levels of satisfaction with employment. The underlying assumption behind the research was that globalization, new technologies and business restructuring have combined to impose new burdens on families, individuals and households.

A balance is presumed to exist between the paid work that employees perform and the lives that they hold outside their job. In using the word 'balance', we have to be careful not to assume that there is a simple division between work and life, with two distinct parts of our life sitting on opposite ends of a scale, and this scale then tilting one way or the other. In summarizing the early work from the ESRC programme,[1] Taylor pointed out that in reality life and work overlap and interact and that many people give meaning to their lives through work whether they are being paid for doing so or not.

> In the experience of most people no clear-cut distinction can be established between the world of work and the world of family, friends and social networks and community. In practice, over the length of our lives it is impossible to establish neatly-constructed demarcation lines. Moreover, the word – balance – implies the existence of a settled equilibrium that can be achievable between paid employment and a life outside the job. This is highly questionable.[2]

The language used in pursuing the work–family agenda is important. In order to construct more positive discussion, the words used have ranged from balance,[3] reconciliation,[4] synergy[5] and integration.[6] These are more than just politically correct words, for each word actually touches upon different elements to the challenge to the employment relationship that must be resolved. As Taylor argues on behalf of the ESRC initiative, we face deep challenges that are to do with our understanding the implications of the changing character of employment, the pressures that more intensive business competition and technological innovation place on employees and their jobs, the issue of perceived insecurity, and finally the balance between legitimate organizational expectations and the concerns of society about social cohesion and individual well-being.

McKee and colleagues[7] note that the debate about work–life balance has arisen in relation to a series of historical shifts. In broad order, these have been: the absence of fathers from home through war, imprisonment or long working shifts; the entry of large numbers of women into the workforce; the changing composition and structure of families; expanding male unemployment; the increase in single working parents; the intensification of work hours; an ageing population and the growing number of 'cared for' groups; and the growth of equal opportunities. Today, debate takes place in the context of the changing future of work, flexible working patterns, the feminization of the labour market and the spread of telemediated businesses. Organizational policy initiatives are seen as ranging from symbolic devices intended to counteract a poor public image or to address short-term recruitment and retention difficulties, through to pioneering efforts to establish a new settlement in the workplace.

We noted at the beginning of Chapter 7 that government strategy is currently concerned with emancipating the individual in the employment relationship, but it must also be noted that there is a parallel, if not slightly conflicting, policy drive to place limits on the time that employees spend at work in order to lessen the impacts of stress, ill-health and poor quality of life. Governments and policy makers also have become concerned that the equilibrium of that balance has been disturbed. Therefore in Britain there has been a somewhat confusing drive towards US-style individualization of the employment relationship, on the one hand, and European-style regulation of the balance between paid work and life outside employment and a rules and laws set of individual or collective rights that comes when more attention is given to social partnership. For example, new legislation from April 2003 will give the parents of children under 6 and disabled children under 18 a new right to apply for flexible working. Although organizations can still not offer this where there is a business case, there will be a legal duty to consider individual requests and the threat of employment tribunals. It is estimated that the proposals will help another 375 000 new parents to work more flexibly each year.[8] The ultimate challenge, as Taylor puts it, is how to balance the protection of the perceived interests of employees without at the same time endangering business competitiveness and productivity. However, currently '. . . the gap between enlightened rhetoric about the need for a re-adjustment in the work–life balance and the reality in most workplaces remains disturbingly wide'[9]

Why is this counter-balancing focus to individualization of the employment relationship necessary? Reflecting the deeper challenges mentioned above, many writers now argue that work is now becoming too large a larger portion of life and is consequently 'colonizing' and 'displacing' non-work activities and interests[10] to the extent that it shapes our home life and even our retirement years.[11]

Hochschild[12] considers that an unacknowledged implication of the new work culture is that home life once more (for historically the separation was also minimal) is being taken over by work. Moreover, the demands of work today and in the future will call the foundations of the nuclear family into question – organizations take wonderful care of workers but not of families. As organizations respond to the pressure to take better care of workers, the cultural world of paid work grows more attractive to individuals. Yet at the same time that better care is being taken of individuals at work, worse care might be taken of families. We face a new experience in which the workplace is being changed into a more home-like environment, while the demands to accommodate work pressures mean that the home has become more efficient – a feminization of the workplace but a masculinization of the home. Hochschild talks of an enlargement of 'first-shift' work – paid employment in one or more jobs – at the expense of 'second-shift' work – which includes housekeeping, entertaining friends, volunteering, child care and spousal relationships (much of the last shift has predominantly been carried out by women, hence the attribution of gender labels to the shift). Time demands on the second shift are more malleable. Non-work time acquires an industrial tone with demands for an assembly-line of household duties. Our efforts to meet work demands mean that as parents we have no choice but to abandon, displace or defer gratification of our non-work activities. Moreover, given that both spouses work a new mutual moral commitment is created for each partner to 'match' the time at home and other activities. A new gender war can be created, the result of which is that both spouses can be tempted to use work to claim temporary freedom from, or at least defer, household duties. Hochschild's research into family-friendly policies in the USA found that women stole back time from men by committing to more overtime at work. The consequences of coping with this time bind force us to acknowledge the emotional changes and psychological coping strategies that are taking place in the home. Hochschild's description of three of these coping strategies is rather uncomfortable for many parents to accept, but realistic nonetheless:

1 Developing an emotional asceticism, minimizing how much care others need and denying their own needs.
2 Readjusting ideas about how to meet family needs, for example by detaching from having an identity as a parent and using paid services or outsourced child care to across the extended family to cope
3 Dividing their identity into a real self and a potential self, with an imaginary or deluded view of what they would do if only they had time to do so.

Increases in working time – discussed in detail later in the chapter – are not distributed equally across households. It has been greatest among members of dual-earner and professional dual-career families, with the most intense pressure arising during child-rearing years. In Britain this polarization is expressed in terms of *work-rich* and *work-poor* families.[13] Indeed it must be said that much of what we know about work–life balance is based on studies of middle-class families. How less-well-off families combine family care with underemployment or excessive demands at work and home is little understood. Therefore, the challenge for organizations is to develop approaches to work–life balance that not only fit into the new world of legislation, but also both allow expression to the ethos of individualization while fitting this into the new models of family that are emerging.

Theoretical perspectives on work–life balance

We have spent much of this book discussing various individual level factors that are associated with the changing psychological contract at work and have also in this chapter noted some of the complex individual trade-offs (in attitudes, in job priorities, in relationships and home life, in identity) that surround the uptake or not of work–life balance initiatives. We have also noted that organizations themselves have multiple motives for pursuing this as an HR strategy and are at varying levels of sophistication in their existing policies and practice.

It is not surprising therefore that one of the problems facing researchers and practitioners is that the labels 'work–life balance' and 'family-friendly policies' are ill-defined: '. . . all too often they are taken to be a loosely linked collection of assorted low-level initiatives and practices'.[14] Recent work at the Centre for Labour Market Studies has attempted to resolve this situation. Work–life balance is a broader notion than that of family-friendly policies. Potentially too the former notion has benefits on offer for a wider range of employees, i.e.

those without dependent children. Employers in essence are purchasing the employees' time and presence at work for part of the day, week or year. Employers tend to monitor, control and survey what they find important, and they monitor an employee's *attention* and *presence*. The attention of workers is similar to the notion of *engagement* introduced in Chapter 2. The presence of workers refers to the spatial location of the work. Can it be carried out on-site or off-site ?

Central to definitions of work–life balance then is the notion that the modern employment relationship is a negotiation to establish the boundaries around the attention and presence required. Employees therefore have to adopt conscious practices in order to coordinate, synchronize and integrate both the work and non–work aspects of their lives. Consequently work–life balance concerns those practices that enhance the flexibility and autonomy of the employee in this process of integration and in the negotiation over their attention and presence. This autonomy is generally achieved in two ways:

1 Practices that *increase the variety* of ways in which employees are able to relate their work and non-work spheres (by giving them choice, for example, over part-time or full-time work, flexi-hours or job-share)
2 Practices that *facilitate change or variation* in the ways in which employees relate their work and non-work spheres (by allowing them to construct their own boundaries between work and non-work through the use of returner policies, sabbaticals, long leave, parental leave and paid holidays).

The presence of these practices does not by itself constitute a policy or a strategy. Only if these policies have been designed and implemented deliberately can the employer claim to have *work–life balance policies,* and only if these policies have been adopted as part of a deliberate effort to increase the productivity or profitability of the organization can the employer can claim to have *work–life balance strategies.*

When, which and why do organizations adopt work–life balance policies? Wood's[15] research conducted for the National Institute for Economic Research draws attention to four theories to help answer these questions: institutional theory; organizational adaptation theory; high-commitment theory; and situational theory (see Box 9.1). These theories interpret common developments – such the growth in female employment – in different ways.

Employer policies and strategies

At the organizational level, initiatives within the work–life balance movement tend to be grouped together under three relatively limited sets of activity.[20]

- Attempts to combine employment with caring responsibilities and help working mothers and fathers cope with the problems of balancing paid work with parenting responsibilities.

Box 9.1   Wood's National Institute for Economic Research: four theoretical perspectives on work–life balance

Institutional theory: The adoption of work–life balance policies is predicted to vary according to size, sector, unionization and industry. Organizations conform to and reflect the normative pressures in society (changes in wider societal value systems) depending on the extent to which they have to maintain a sense of social legitimacy.[16] The organizations most likely to conform to pressures to introduce work–life balance policies are large private sector firms (because of their high visibility) and public sector organizations (because of their accountability to the electorate). Organizations that compete in the same industry come under pressure to imitate these practices for fear of damaged reputation among suppliers, customers and existing workers. Organizations with union presence are also exposed to more scrutiny and are also more likely to conform.

Organizational adaptation theory: Although organizations must respond to societal norms and expectations, how these expectations become known, recognized and taken on board by managers is more important.[17] The processes through which organizations recognize and interpret the changing world around them are important, and the perception and interpretation of societal norms is influenced by the values of senior management. Therefore, in addition to size, sector, unionization and industry as predictors of take-up, the gender composition of the workforce (more female staff employed), reliance on high-skilled workers who are difficult to replace, and work designs that already allow employees much latitude in how they carry out tasks and at what pace will all be associated with more attention to work–life balance policies.

High-commitment theory: There is a link between the organization's HR strategy and its adoption of family-friendly employment practices. Work systems and worker–management relationships that raise employee commitment to the organization revolve around the introduction of innovative HRM practices that facilitate cooperation between managers and workers,[18] and an opening up of management decisions to scrutiny by employees. Organizations can enhance commitment by showing that they understand the conflicts that occur between work and other aspects of life and can tolerate options to flexible work practices that allow employees to balance these competing demands.

Situational theory or practical response theory: Organizations act more simply and respond most to the pressures of immediate circumstances. The growth of work–life balance practices is in response to traditional pressures towards profitability and productivity, and difficulties in recruiting and retaining a high-quality labour force. Work–life balance policies are introduced where the organization sees a direct link between them and a solution to problems of absenteeism, staff turnover and unfilled job vacancies. Broader shifts in the composition of the workforce, such as more female employees, require adjustments to existing labour practices.

Source: Wood.[19]

- Attempts to reconcile the balance between paid employment and the need for time off work to deal with family emergencies and dependent relatives. For example, the extension of legal rights designed to allow parents to cope better with the pressures of work (such as the 1999 Employment Rights Act and its right to take up to 13 weeks off work to look after a child or arrange childcare).
- The pursuit of options that allow more working from home as part of family-friendly HR policies.

Box 9.2   Recent family-friendly initiatives in the UK

Lilly Industries was one of the 1996 winners of the 'Parents at Work' awards for family-friendly companies. A popular part of its life/work programme is the *'phased return to work after maternity leave or illness'* where new mothers can choose a period of part-time work before returning full-time. Some of the company's other family-friendly policies include paid paternity leave, unpaid career breaks and paid sabbaticals for childcare, eldercare or study, part-time and reduced hours work, job-share, term-time working, staggered hours and official homeworking. Lilly report that the resulting benefits to the company include staff retention, reduced over-heads and running costs from flexible working, extended business hours and increased productivity.

Ikea offers a number of services to staff who are new parents or have family commitments. Its programme was developed by 'Exploring Parent-hood', a voluntary organization, and includes:

- A two-year structured 'new parents programme' for pregnant staff and their partners, which offers support, information and help with childcare to enable staff to return to work after childbirth and to aid staff retention.
- An information and advice service to staff on any matter to prevent minor problems from escalating and affecting work and/or family. This counselling is seen as an integral part of the company's human resources and quality processes.
- A consultation service which provides managers and supervisors with advice and training on work and family issues to enable them to deal with individual members of staff.

Asda Stores have introduced the following new flexible working schemes into their existing programme:

- Childcare leave where, for a short period, parents can stop work, reduce their hours or work evenings or weekends before returning, without loss of benefits, to similar hours and a similar job.

- Shift-swapping schemes so that staff requiring time off for specific domestic reasons can swap their shifts with colleagues without needing management's permission. In this way, staff do not lose pay and departments remain fully staffed.
- Study leave which allows staff to study full-time and work at weekends or during the holiday periods. Stores try to operate this as a form of job share.
- Store-swapping schemes where staff who are studying away from home can transfer to another store for short periods.

Pricewaterhouse Coopers: launched a lifestyle intranet in 2001 aimed at encouraging its 20 000 employees to discuss work–life balance issues. The site covers flexible working, parenting, health, stress and time management and career development. It also includes a toolkit for managers on how to manage flexible workers, links to employee assistance programme and financial and legal advice.

The Automobile Association reorganized its customer services to allow a proportion of call-centre staff to work from home. Results from the initial pilot which began in 1997 were very positive: The productivity of teleworkers was, on average, 30 per cent higher than that of office-based staff. Sickness absence was very low and quality of work very high. Teleworkers cited a variety of benefits: better quality time with family, a more relaxed working environment, reduced expenses and less time wasted in commuting and the associated stress of travelling to work. Several people who could only work part-time previously because of family commitments were able to extend their hours and benefit from increased salaries. Teleworking also opened doors to a wider range of workers, including people with disabilities or unable to travel for other reasons.

Littlewoods was one of the 1999 Employer of the Year winners. It uses flexible working including part-time or reduced hours, term-time working, job shares and homeworking. Leave provision includes career breaks of up to five years, five days paid emergency family leave and 10 days paid paternity leave. Employee support includes an Employee Assistance Programme, a holiday playscheme and nursery at the Liverpool head-quarters, and wrap-around care for school-age children at the Manchester site. Information on childcare is also available to parents via an information pack. The perceived benefits of being an 'employer of choice' are increased staff loyalty and commitment, reduced staff turnover, increased productivity, reduced absenteeism, enhanced corporate image, reduced retraining costs.

Source: Cooper and Lewis[22] and Work–Life Research Centre.[23]

For most organizations the above three sets of activity tend to be combined in different ways (see Box 9.2). A wide range of websites and online resources are also now available in the area.[21] The Work–Life Policy checklist suggests innovations are needed in four areas:

1 work organization (flexitime, compressed work weeks, part-time, job share, annualized hours, telework/flexi-workplace and term-time working);
2 employee development (through personal development plans, appraisal and training);
3 leave provision (employment breaks, study leave, career leave, maternity pay, paternity leave, adoptive leave and emergency carer leave);
4 employee support (information on local childcare or eldercare, referral services, sponsorship of community care projects, own or partnership childcare services, carer subsidies and concierge or domestic back-up services).

Evidence on the impact of family-friendly policies is broadly argued by looking at the consequences of not acting in this area. Work and family issues are assumed then to have a number of potential costs for the individual, organizations, families and communities. The price paid for the conflict and stress that result from multiple roles in work and family in non-responsive employing organizations include:

• Poor physical health, job and life dissatisfaction, family conflicts and break-up[24]
• Stress-related illnesses and reduced quality of life[25]
• Higher absenteeism[26]
• 'Presenteeism' or lack of psychological availability at work[27]
• Lower engagement in suggestion schemes, attendance at quality meetings and interpersonal helping behaviours[28]
• Accidents and loss of productivity[29]
• Higher staff turnover[30]
• Lower life satisfaction[31]
• Stress on other family members[32]
• Parent mood, parent–child interaction, and children's behaviour[33].

Hillage and Simkin's[34] review for the Institute of Manpower Studies argued that cost–benefit analyses of responses to work and family issues generally demonstrate that the benefits to the organization outweigh the costs. This appears to be the case despite the fact that only a narrow range of cost measures has been used (concepts such as productivity are notoriously difficult to operationalize). Holterman[35] points out that a broader way of operationalizing costs to include wider social influences that will impact on organizations (such as family breakdown and other stressors that spill over to affect people at work) is needed. No research has yet been that ambitious. However, as Giele[36] points out, the well-being of future generations should not be treated as a trivial concern.

The above impacts – and the work of Hochschild discussed earlier – demonstrate that organizational initiatives on family-friendliness have to move far beyond the provision simply of good maternity arrangements. They have to cope with very complex social and psychological changes that are taking place in family life. The UK government's Work–Life Balance Campaign, launched in March 2000, focuses on three areas:

- tackling the long-hours culture,
- targeting sectors with acute work–life balance problems,
- providing support and guidance to both employers and employees.

Moving beyond the feminization of work

The focus of much attention on the relationship between paid work and parenting or caring is understandable. Initiatives here are designed to cope with the increased *feminization of work*. By 1997 women accounted for nearly one in every two people in paid employment with one-fifth more women working full-time than in 1984.[37] In Britain today nearly 70 per cent of mothers in two-parent households with at least one dependent child under the age of 18 are in paid work (to say that they choose to be so does not automatically follow, although for most this work is likely by free will). However, over the last 10 years the greatest rise in employment has been among women with much younger children – aged four years or less.[38] Almost half of Britain's lone mothers are in some form of paid employment, although only 1 in 5 of these are in full-time work, which is less than is found in the USA, for example, which has very high levels of female participation in paid work. Seventy-four per cent of mothers with children aged 6 to 17 are in employment in the USA and 55 per cent of women employed earn 50 per cent or more of the family salary.[39] The increased participation of women in the workforce has been linked to the issue of national competitiveness and has therefore been reinforced by legislative and social welfare initiatives such as statutory maternity pay and allowances, working families' tax credits and entitlement to unpaid maternity leave.

The message that comes out from such data is that there is immense diversity of aspiration within the workforce especially with regard to the way in which women combine their responsibilities to family and work. Reflecting the discussion of more individualized career contracts in general in Chapter 6, Hakim[40] has studied the experience of women in the labour market in particular and women's work orientations, attitudes, values and preferences. She recently examined work–lifestyle choices[41] and explains diversity through her preference theory. This theory argues that women are disadvantaged in the workplace and society because their differing needs mean that they do not face the labour market with a unitary voice. Drawing upon mainly US and UK studies of policy, practice and individual attitudes, she argues that preferences expressed in early adulthood suggest three categories of female work–lifestyle preference (see Table 9.1). These distinctions are intended to help policy makers

Table 9.1 Hakim's[42] classification of women's workstyle preferences

Home-centred	Adaptive	Work-centred
20% of women (range 10–30%)	60% of women (range 40–80%)	20% of women (range 10–30%)
Family life and children are the main priorities throughout life. Gender traditional individuals who accept the sexual division of labour in the home.	Diverse group including women who want to combine work and family without either taking a priority, as well as career drifters (women with no definite idea about the life they want but who respond to opportunities and modify goals quickly) and women with unplanned careers	Pursuing stereotypical male careers and work histories. Includes childless women, or women with children treated as a 'weekend hobby'. Main priority in life is employment or equivalent activities in the public arena: politics, sport, art etc.
Prefer *not* to work	Want to work, but not totally committed to work career	Committed to work or equivalent activities
Qualifications obtained for intellectual dowry	Qualifications obtained with the intention of working	Large investment in qualifications and training for employment in other activities
Responsive to social and family policy	*Very responsive* to all policies	Responsive to employment policies

predict which social engineering initiatives are likely to be effective and to forecast take-up rates of different types of initiatives. The basis for calculating the percentage figures for each category is not, however, clear and the adaptive category is a bit of a catch-all distinction.

Initiatives such as those at British Telecom (see Box 9.3) are often used to demonstrate the potential benefits of a broader approach to work–life balance.

However, it is clear that even when organizations offer work–life balance initiatives, there is a 'take-up' gap. A recent study by the Institute of Employment Studies[45] found that while there is latent demand for work–life initiatives a sizeable proportion of the workforce feel unable to take up the options. The main reasons forwarded for this are:

- perceived impact on career prospects;
- negative impact on earnings;
- incompatible organizational cultures that reward long work hours;

Box 9.3　Work–life balance at British Telecom

British Telecom's Work–Life Balance initiative, which has evolved over two decades of continual development and experimentation, won the Parents at Work Employer of the Year 2001 award. In 1998 the results of a staff survey revealed that 62 per cent of its managers felt that their lives were too skewed in favour of work and 33 per cent said they were not prepared to accept promotion or greater responsibilities because of the effect on their domestic life. BT has enabled 4000 employees to work from home since the early 1980s, with many in managerial positions. It is investing some of the £220 million property savings back into its core business and pursuing a flexible employment strategy. The HR team also ran a pilot 'Freedom to work' programme to give staff the chance of arranging their own work hours and patterns as long as business objectives were fulfilled. Employees can negotiate how they will make up the 41 working hours a week. The whole process is based on the psychological contract between employer and employee and creating conditions where people need to feel that they are being valued. Productivity within teams has improved, absenteeism is down, and the return rate after maternity leave has increased from 89 per cent to 96 per cent. BT decided to roll out the initiative to 8000 employees. A range of formal positions exist to support the initiative, such as a Director of Employment Policy, Social Policy Finance Manager and Manager of Employment Philosophy, and a senior executive forum helps promote the strategy. The Work–Life Balance programme is communicated through the intranet providing guidance on how to make a case submission.

Sources: Seneviratna and Turton[43] and Higginbottom.[44]

- poor infrastructure to support initiatives such as working from home;
- heavy workloads based on irreducible task sizes (so that time away from work simply increases the intensity of time remaining at work);
- a lack of supervisory understanding of how to manage the broader performance impact across a team (unfair impacts on other team members).

The potential for wider impact of current family-friendly provision is therefore limited by problems of limited access, an overtargeting of women and mothers of young children in particular, a lack of challenge to traditional organizational values, limited influence over informal practices, and the need for institutional and social change to support and reinforce organizational action.[46]

Commitment and the link to non-work obligations

We discussed the topic of organizational commitment in the previous chapter. Given the increasing demands for eldercare and the need for dual-family incomes, a number of studies have been conducted to see of there is a relationship between the increased availability of flexible work schedules and family-friendly human resource policies and important work-related outcomes such as organizational commitment.[47] There is a view emerging from studies that scrutinize work–life balance or family-friendly initiatives that suggest that they (perhaps inadvertently or perhaps through ill-judged assumptions) serve to reinforce a 'male model' of work:[48]

> Commitment tends to be regarded by management as finite and non-expandable, implying that of someone has commitments outside work, this inevitably reduces their level of commitment at work.[49]

Organizational cultures still prescribe full-time and continuous work from the end of education until retirement, without any concessions to the demands of family, and any deviation from this still leads to disadvantage in terms of career advancement, pay levels or talent development (employability) opportunities. Promotion systems within universities based on quantity of output of top journal papers are a case in point. A career break rather than a sabbatical leaves lasting damage. Much more sensitive insight is needed into the interaction between commitment at work and non-work obligations. Two avenues of work are of value here:

1 Studies examining gender attitudes at work[50] and in particular generational shifts in these attitudes.[51] The latter have shown that attitudes towards women have become more egalitarian in the USA than in other societies and that while Britain is also moving in this direction (though at a slower pace) men still remain of the opinion that children may suffer if the mother works.

2 Studies examining the link between family responsibility coping strategies and work-related outcomes such as levels of commitment.

We focus at this point on the second area of work. How do researchers define and operationalize non-work obligations and 'family responsibilities' in particular? Two approaches have been used:

1 *Kinship responsibilities*: Blegen and colleagues[52] developed the idea of kinship responsibilities, defined as an individual's obligations to relatives in the community in which the individual resides. Four components – marital status, the number of children, number of relatives living within a 50-mile radius, and number of spouses' relatives within the same radius – are added together to create a Kinship Responsibility Index. Similar indices have been used by Price and his colleagues[53] when examining turnover behaviour.

2 *Financial obligations*: Brett and colleagues[54] argue that the overall financial requirements to work can be measured by defining factors that influence an individual's need to work (marital status, spouse's employment status, young children, percentage of total household income derived from an individual's job and perception of the ability to find a comparable job).

3 *Family resources*: Tenbrunsel and colleagues[55] use a 'fixed-pie' logic to argue that time, psychological energy and physical energy act as fixed resources. Whatever is devoted to work is not available for meeting family demands and vice versa. Work involvement is limited by time devoted to children at home. As financial responsibility for others increases, the need to remain with the organization also increases, so does the need to devote time and energy to family demands. Personal costs may, however, be offset by drawing upon family resources such as relatives living close by. Adding family elements may increase or decrease overall non-work obligations.

The focus of this work has been to examine the extent to which family responsibilities moderate important outcomes such as organizational commitment. In most research to date an employee's family responsibility to work has been viewed as an additive sum – such that various obligations such as having children or parents nearby simply add up. Using the kinship responsibility approach, Blegen and colleagues found a small – only about 10 per cent of the variance – but significant moderating relationship.[56]

Mellor and colleagues note that most of the work using the kinship responsibilities or financial obligations approach have '. . . shown weak or no relationships with work-related variables of interest'.[57] They argue that a more sophisticated approach is needed. We need to understand that non-work obligations operate in quite complex ways. Spouses, parents, in-laws and other people can represent resources to an individual, not just obligations. They examined whether the separate components associated with kinship responsibilities had different impacts on affective and continuance commitment in a study of 1252 employees at communication companies and a random sample of 470 employees. Affective commitment was measured as well as continuance commitment (this was measured along two dimensions – low perceived alternatives and high personal sacrifice). Drawing upon the side-bets view of continuance commitment, the more children that one has, the more the 'sunk cost' in maintaining a relationship with the organization – financial pressures and family-friendly policies should support this decision. Affective commitment was significantly higher among married employees (but family resources only explain 5 per cent of affective commitment), and continuance commitment was linked to the number of children (be it low perceived alternatives or high personal sacrifice). Here family resources explained from 4 per cent to 7 per cent of continuance commitment.

With one exception the findings could be interpreted from the family resource perspective. There was indeed a 'trapping effect' on continuance commitment. However, the study showed that having a spouse's relatives nearby served as a family resource and weakened the relationship between having more children and continuance commitment. The personal costs associated with childcare could be reduced by assistance – continuance commitment only increased when there were no relatives. Employees' non-work obligations should be viewed as being both complex and multifaceted. However, when a family resource perspective is taken, the need for organizations to help meet their non-work obligations and minimize work and family conflicts requires flexible human resource policies. In the next section we address one of the most difficult blocking factors to this flexibility, which is a pervasive long work hours culture in the UK.

The long work hours culture

It is often stated that the UK in particular has a problem with long work hours. We begin by presenting some of the latest data and evidence on work hours and then discuss some of the cultural reasons that reinforce the problem. One way in which the work ethic is judged around the world is to consider the amount of official time off that people take. Britain and the Netherlands have the fewest bank holidays in the EU – 8 days a year – compared with 10 in Belgium, 11 in France or Sweden and from 12 to 14 in Spain or Portugal.[58] Figure 9.1 presents data from a recent analysis in *Business Week* that considers the average number of vacation days (including public holidays) taken by employees around the world. This varies from a low 13 days in the USA to 28 days in the UK and 42 days in Italy.[59] In fact the USA is famed for having an anti-vacation work ethic. Much of the developed world has cut back the annual number of hours worked per person in the last decade – for example, by 191

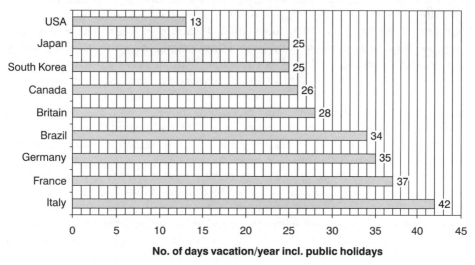

Figure 9.1 Comparative national data on holiday take-up. (After World Tourism Organization[62])

hours in Japan – but in the USA it has actually risen by 58 hours a year. In fact between 1979 and 1999 the total hours worked per person fell by only 0.1 per cent in the UK (they fell by over 1 per cent from 1960 to 1979), by 0.8 per cent in France, by 1 per cent in Germany, but grew by 0.5 per cent in the USA.[60] Americans do not even take what little vacation they are entitled to. A survey commissioned by online travel agent Expedia.com suggests that they give back an average of 1.8 days unused vacation a year, saving US business almost £19.5 billion. In Japan too, where employees still work 200–500 hours longer a year than Western counterparts, studies suggest that two-thirds of employees complain of fatigue, and *karoshi* (death from overwork) is becoming a social problem.[61]

Rubery and colleagues,[63] using Eurostat data, showed that by 1994 the UK is the only member of the EU where the number of hours worked each week has increased over the preceding data. The EU's Employment in Europe survey of the time reported that almost half of the 7 million male workers working over 48 hours a week were employed in Britain. The 1999 *Social Trends* survey reported that 42 per cent of UK employees reported that they always or often left work in a state of exhaustion.[64] In fact, the situation in terms of actual hours at work was at its worst for the UK in 1996 to 1997. Bank of England estimates showed that by late 1996 26.4 per cent of UK employees were working more than 45 hours per week compared to 24.3 per cent in 1992. Average weekly hours worked peaked at 38.9, up from 38.1 in 1992. By mid-2002, on the Bank of England time series, average weekly hours have fallen to 37.9 and the proportion of UK employees working more than 45 hours a week had fallen to 23.4 per cent.[65] European legislation – notably the Working-Time Directive – has then had some impact on work hours in the UK. A 3 per cent reduction in the average number of hours worked per employee since the introduction of the Directive in spring 1998 has cost employers around £2.3 billion a year according to the British Chambers of Commerce. Nonetheless, 4 million employees continue to work more than 48 hours a week. Other evidence suggests modest falls in working time. For example, the Labour Force Survey – a quarterly sample survey of households living at private addresses in the UK – shows that 23.6 per cent of British employees worked over 45 hours a week from February to April 2002, down slightly from 24.5 per cent two years previously. It is mainly men who work long hours – 34.4 per cent of men compared to 10.4 per cent of women work over 45 hours.[66] The Chartered Institute of Personnel and Development (CIPD) has launched its own research into long work hours culture (see Box 9.4).

The CIPD followed up the sample in 2001 with a survey on the Working Time Regulations. It showed that the Regulations have had little effect on reducing the working week of people who work long hours.[68] Follow-up interviews were conducted with 486 people who took part in the nationwide survey that was conducted in 1998. Sixty-four per cent of those who worked more than 48 hours a week before the Regulations took effect in October 1998 were still doing so, and only 2 per cent reported that their hours had been reduced to 48 or less as a direct result of the Regulations. There were some

---

Box 9.4   Factors involved in the long work hours culture

In 1998 the CIPD commissioned Harris Research to examine the long work hours culture in the UK. Telephone interviews were conducted with 7987 UK workers, of whom 823 people were found to work more than the 48 hours a week Working Time Regulations threshold (including work done at home outside of contracted hours of employment). The attitudes of the long work hours individuals were then compared with a nationally representative sample of 2053 adults. The 1 in 10 workers who admitted to working over 48 hours would equate to 2.7 million UK workers nationally. Professionals, managers and craft workers were the main occupations involved. Forty-one per cent of the employees worked long work hours willingly, 11 per cent worked the hours reluctantly all of the time, and 47 per cent were reluctant some of the time. The main reason for the hours were heavy workload. Thirty-six per cent attributed the reason to the fact that they were redoing work or solving problems that arose because their organization was disorganized and inefficient. Although 44 per cent of those with children felt that long work hours had damaged their relationship with children, 30 per cent still loved work and regarded it as a hobby and 23 per cent felt that cutting back on long work hours was totally within their own hands. One third of those who worked long hours classified themselves as 'workaholics' – with men and women being equally likely to classify themselves this way. These people were more likely to report high satisfaction with both work and life outside work.

Source: CIPD.[67]

---

positive signs, however. Although the majority of those surveyed still worked beyond the regulated hours, the 52 hours a week that they now worked compared with 58 hours a week in 1998. Nearly a third of those surveyed considered that their organization had made efforts in the last year to reduce work hours through making efficiency improvements or reorganizing work systems to help them at work (see Box 9.5 for a range of recent flexible work initiatives).

Long work hours and well-being

The more serious issue, evidenced by a number of academic reviews by Cooper and various colleagues, is that there is currently sufficient evidence to raise concerns about the risks to health and safety of long working hours.[71] These academic studies have been supported by a series of institutional studies, such as those by the London Hazards Centre,[72] Institute of Management[73] and

---

Box 9.5   Flexible working policies and confronting the long work hours culture

Barclays Technology Services: Following a high-profile campaign, in 1995, by the voluntary organization 'Parents at Work' which raised awareness among employers and individuals about the impact of long working hours on families and employees and the negative effects on productivity, Barclays Technology Services, a division of the Barclays Group, began to confront the long hours culture in which people spent longer than necessary at work in order to be seen in the workplace. Barclays already had a long-established equal opportunities programme which provided opportunities for job sharing, part-time work, career breaks and responsibility breaks. BTS went beyond this by starting a campaign in its male-dominated organization to promote the benefits of achieving a balance between work and non-work time and to challenge the belief that working long hours demonstrates commitment. Posters, hand-outs, articles in the internal newsletter and Go Home on Time Days help to raise awareness and promote good practice. BTS runs a series of management training programmes to get managers on board and employees are encouraged to work smarter not harder by using time-saving strategies and prioritizing, delegating and empowering others to act.

Swedbank: a large Swedish bank, has set up a Work Environment Fund for its staff. Managers who fail to follow overtime rules are fined and pay money into the fund. The firm contributes £211 a year per employee into the fund. Monies are used to help staff take preventive measures to manage well-being including: educational grants up to 10 per cent of salary after one year's service; stop smoking initiatives; reduced work weeks to 80 per cent for 90 per cent of salary for over-55-year-old employees; and five days paid reflection time for the top 300 managers

Sources: Cooper and Lewis[69] and *People Management.*[70]

Income Data Services,[74] which have also argued that the experience of long work hours and intense working conditions can have a detrimental impact on health, psychological well-being and family life – although from an employer's perspective the former would be seen as most problematic and the latter a more tangential concern. Such survey data is, of course, not proof of a true impact on well-being, but nonetheless it signals a general discontent among the workforce concerning the balance between the worlds of work and home.

Given the consideration of work hours under health and safety legislation, linking work hours to well-being carries important political as well as practical implications. There has been debate about the strength of evidence behind the work hours–well-being relationship for the last thirty years, perhaps stemming back to the 1960 study by Buell and Breslow[75] that demonstrated a higher incidence of coronary heart disease in men working over 48 hours a week. The tiring effect of work overload coupled with the prolonged exposure to work stressors is considered to be connected to a number of health symptoms and poor lifestyle habits such as smoking, inadequate diet and lack of exercise (which themselves have a compounded effect on well-being). A recent review of shiftwork and health suggest that the limitations suggested by EU Directives for a 48-hour working week are appropriate in the light of evidence presently available.[76]

Many of the above conclusions are, however, based on purely qualitative assessments. Research investigating the working hours–health relationship uses different health outcomes, measures and approaches and trying to draw

---

Box 9.6   The effects of work hours on health

The stress and well-being literature draws attention to limits to capacity as evidenced through either physical or psychological costs. Sparks and colleagues conducted meta-analyses on 19 previous studies and a qualitative review of existing literature on the link between working hours and health. The findings showed a small but statistically significant link between the two. The mean correlation between physiological health (somatization, headaches, work accidents, myocardial infarction, coronary heart disease and general health symptoms) and work hours was 0.0636, rising to a correlation of 0.1465 between work and hours and psychological health (hostility, depression, poor sleep, irritability/tension, problems with relationships, lack of concentration, tiredness, role strain, anxiety, frustration, exhaustion, insomnia, social dissatisfaction, mood symptoms and general mental stress). They argue that these correlations likely underestimate the true linkage. We often assume linear relationships between work stressors and outcomes but at certain levels we see breakpoints and discontinuities in the work intensity–well-being relationship. Correlational evidence also aggregates individual-level behaviour, which is both idiosyncratic and subject to numerous complex and mediating factors. The few studies conducted at group level have demonstrated higher correlations. Existing studies have also applied insufficient experimental control. More focused studies (such as those that concentrated on heart disease and mental stress) suggest a stronger link between work hours and health. A range of factors have a moderating influence on the work hours–well-being relationship, including: work task characteristics (such as attentional demands, level of physical activity); working environment (ergonomic design and equipment usage); organizational climate and culture; age; and individual choice and discretion over work hours.

Source: Sparks *et al.*[77]

firm conclusions among a series of confounding factors is difficult. Sparks and colleagues conducted a meta-analysis to see if a consistent pattern could be detected. The results clarify the situation but also reveal the considerable amount of work that has still to be done in this area (see Box 9.6).

The agenda for change

The EU has identified social partners who share responsibility for reconciling work and family life, including national and local governments, management and labour, and individuals. Lewis and Cooper point out that although the European perspective stresses partnerships, workplace change is regarded as a very important strand of activity within a collaborative process of achieving reconciliation. They argue that this is because workplaces, as we saw earlier in this chapter, are considered to '. . . remain deeply gendered in their expectations of appropriate behaviour . . . [and] Initiatives to change organizational policies and policies, and the assumptions which underpin them thus remain crucial in Europe'.[78] Despite the resistance of previous UK governments, European law has exerted some influence on UK social policy. Earnshaw and Cooper[79] note that the increased concern among employees has been associated with an increasing trend within Europe for employer litigation by workers for stress and long work hours in particular (see Box 9.7 for recent action in the UK using Working Time Regulations).

Clearly the next few years will witness considerable discussion and dialogue between all stakeholders. The hope must be that this develops a shared vision about the sort of organizations, families and society that we wish to develop

---

Box 9.7   Use of Working Time Regulations against employers

Indeed, there is also increasing evidence that employees will use the Working Time Regulations to prosecute organizations. Hours limits are seen as an implied term of the employment contract. The first case under the legislation was brought against Forbuoys Newsagents in August 2002 where an employee was found to have worked 71 hours a week over a 17-week reference period and Safeway were found guilty of unfair dismissal of an employee who had been recruited before the Sunday Trading Act 1994 and had refused to work on Sundays. From April 2003 the Employment Act 2002 gives working parents the right to make formal requests for working arrangements and organizations must give serious consideration to such requests.

Source: Daykin and Baldwinson.[80]

and support. Lewis and Cooper highlight a number of significant steps that are needed:[81]

1 There needs to be continued proactive attempts by organizations to integrate work–family issues into their core thinking and strategic planning.
2 Organizations must question traditional ways of working to reflect the needs of today's more diverse and complex workforce. Those with the power to ensure questioning – found still to be men with non-career wives or women without family commitments – need to exercise considerable insight into the lives of others.
3 We must rethink our notions of time. Currently men's time tends to be market-valued economically as being more important than women's time. A more critical evaluation of how value is assigned to time is needed and the ways in which time contributed is considered to be symbolic of productivity, commitment and value needs to be challenged. Genuine flexible working can only be achieved once time is revalued and atypical workers will only be truly valued once this is done.
4 Career stages have to be separated from assumptions about age – different types of work are needed at different times both within individual careers and organizational work processes.
5 Management control systems have to continue to shift towards a trust and collaboration basis rather than a control philosophy, and performance management systems have to find mutually acceptable ways of achieving goals.
6 Notions of equality – our definitions of equal opportunities – have to be divorced from assumptions about social roles. Diversity does not mean enabling women to act like men or men to act like women, but requires an honest reassessment of the legitimate concerns of individuals without regard to gendered assumptions about their commitment to work, family and society.
7 The meaning of long-term impacts and what we define as 'success' – be it profits and responsibilities of shareholders or attributions of personal career success and worth for individuals – have to be deconstructed and reflected upon. More inclusive definitions have to be applied to organizational and individual action.
8 Finally, public policy makers have to recognize the implications of changes in family structure and institutional arrangements have to reconcile the needs to ensure equal employment protection with legitimate needs for organizational competitiveness.

In conclusion, the challenge presented to the employment relationship by the need for work–life balance is made more complex by many long-standing assumptions about work and family. These assumptions are little more than social and historical constructs. In order to meet current needs they need to be renegotiated and reconstructed in order for us to reconcile work and family. This process is slowly taking place. However, in the next chapter we introduce one final important consideration. We cannot conduct this dialogue based purely on our understanding of current needs and priorities. We must also consider, first, whether the needs and desires of the future generation are likely to be in line with those that we are reconciling now, and second, whether the challenges that they will face will introduce the need for new values and new flexibilities for which even future generations might not be well equipped.

References

1. The work summarized by R. Taylor draws upon several emerging outputs, including research by: M. White at the Policy Studies Institute and S. Hill from the London School of Economics on attitudes to paid employment and pressures faced at work; J. Hyman from Glasgow Caledonian University on call-centre and software firm employees; survey work by the Institute of Employment Research at Warwick University and IFF on work–life balance; S. Himmelweit and M. Sigala at the Open Univerity into the work experience of mothers with pre-school children; I. Bruegel from South Bank University looking at educational and employment experiences of young Pakistani and Bangladeshi women; and D. Houston and G. Marks at Kent University on employment choices of young mothers.
2. Taylor, R. (2002) *The future of work–life balance*. Swindon: Economic and Social Research Council, p. 17.
3. Hall, D.T. (1990). Promoting work/family balance: an organizational change approach. *Organizational Dynamics*, *18*, 5–18.
4. Moss, P. (1996). Reconcilary employment and family responsibilities: A European prospective. In S. Lewis and J. Lewis (Eds.), *The work–family challenge: rethinking employment*. London: Sage, pp. 20–33.
5. Fletcher, J. and Rapoport, R. (1996). Work–family issues as a catalyst for organizational change. In S. Lewis and J. Lewis (Eds.), *The work–family challenge: rethinking employment*. London: Sage, pp. 20–33.
6. Greenhaus, J.H. and Parasuraman, S. (1999). Research on work, family and gender: current status and future directions. In G.N. Powell (Ed.), *Handbook of gender in organizations*. Newbury Park, CA: Sage.
7. McKee, L., Mauthner, N. and MacLean, C. (2000) 'Family-friendly' policies and practices in the oil and gas industry: employers' perspectives, *Work, Employment and Society*, *14 (3)*, 557–571.
8. Walton, P. (2002). The flexibility take-up gap. *Flexible Working Briefing*, Issue No. 105, 4–5.
9. Taylor (2002). *Op. cit.*, p. 15.
10. Boje, D., Gephart, R.P. and Thatchenkery, T. (Eds.) (1996). *Postmodern management and organizational theory*. Newbury Park, CA: Sage.
11. Shavinshinsky, J.S. (2000). *Breaking the watch: the meaning of retirement in America*. Ithaca, NY: Cornell University Press.
12. Hochschild, A. (1997). *The time bind: when work becomes home and home becomes work*. New York: Henry Holt and Company.

13. Brannen, J. and Moss, P. (1998). The polarisation and intensification of parental employment in Britain: Consequences for children, families and the community. *Community, Work and Family, 1*, 229–247.
14. Felstead, A., Jewson, N., Phizacklea, A. and Walters, S. (2002). Analysing the opportunity to work at home in the context of work–life balance policies and practices. *Human Resource Management Journal, 12 (1)*, 54–76, p. 55.
15. Wood, S. (1999). Family-friendly management: testing the various perspectives. *National Institute for Economic Research*, No. 168, April 2/99, 99–116.
16. See DiMaggio, P.J. and Powell, W.W. (1983). The iron cage revisited: institutional isomorphism and collective rationality in organizational fields. *American Sociological Review, 48 (2)*, 147–160; Oliver, C. (1991). Strategic responses to institutional responses. *Academy of Management Review, 16 (1)*, 145–179.
17. Goodstein, J. (1994). Institutional pressures and strategic responsiveness: employer involvement in work–family issues. *Academy of Management Journal, 37 (2)*, 350–382; Ingram, P. and Simons, T. (1995). Institutional and resource dependence determinants of responsiveness to work–family issues, *Academy of Management Journal, 38 (5)*, 1466–1482; Morgan, H. and Milliken, F.J. (1992). Keys to action: understanding differences in organizations' responsiveness to work–family issues. *Human Resource Management, 31 (3)*, 227–248.
18. Gallie, D., Felstead, A. and Green, F. (2001). Employer policies and organisational commitment in Britain, 1992–7, *Journal of Management Studies, 37 (6)*, 1081–1101; Osterman, P. (1995). Work/family programs and the employment relationship. *Administrative Science Quarterly, 40 (4)*, 681–700; Wood, S. (1999). Getting the measure of the transformed high-performance organization. *British Journal of Industrial Relations, 37 (3)*, 391–417.
19. Wood, S. (1999). Family-friendly management: testing the various perspectives. *National Institute for Economic Research*, No. 168, April 2/99, 99–116.
20. Felstead *et al.* (2002). *Op. cit.*
21. People Management (**www.peoplemanagement.co.uk/work-life**) provides a series of useful links. Long-term research is accessible at **www.employersforwork-lifebalance.org.uk**. The Work–Life Balance Centre (**www.worklifebalancecentre.org**) has links to the Cabinet Office resources at **www.diversity-whatworks.gov.uk** and the Women Returners' Network at **www.women-returners.co.uk**. The Work–Life Research Centre provides a forum for the exchange of information between researchers and practitioners at **www.workliferesearch.org**. The Work Foundation (formerly Industrial Society) publishes the Work–Life Manual at **www.the-workfoundation.com**. The DTI's work–life balance team (**www.dti.gov.uk/work-lifebalance**) disseminates good practice alongside legislation on flexible working.
22. Cooper, C.L. and Lewis, S. (1998). *Balancing your career, family and life*. London: Kogan Page.

23. Examples taken from 1999 Employer of the Year Awards conducted by PARENTS AT WORK in association with Lloyds TSB, at http://www.workliferesearch.org

24. Lewis, S. and Cooper, C.L. (1987). Stress in two earner couples and stage in life cycle. *Journal of Occupational Psychology, 60,* 289–303; Neal, M., Chapman, N., Ingersoll-Dayton, B. and Amlen, A. (1993). *Balancing work and caregiving for children, adults and elders.* London: Sage Publications; Bacharach, S.B., Bamberger, P. and Conley, S. (1991). Work–home conflict among nurses and engineers: mediating the impact of job stress on burnout and satisfaction at work. *Journal of Organizational Behavior, 12,* 39–53.

25. Frone, M.R., Russell, M. and Cooper, M.L. (1992). Antecedents and outcomes of work–family conflict: testing a model of work–family interface. *Journal of Applied Psychology, 77,* 65–78.; Jones, F. and Fletcher, B. (1993). An empirical study of occupational stress in working couples. *Human Relations, 46,* 881–903.

26. Goff, S.J., Mount, M.K. and Jamison, R.L. (1992). Employer supported childcare, work–family conflict and absenteeism: a field study. *Personnel Psychology, 43,* 793–809.

27. Cooper, C.L. and Williams, S. (1994). *Creating healthy work organizations.* Chichester: Wiley.

28. Lambert, S.J. (2000). Added benefits: the link between work–life benefits and organizational citizenship behavior. *Academy of Management Journal, 43 (5),* 801–815.

29. Ganster, D.C. and Schaubroeck, J. (1991). Work stress and employee health. *Journal of Management, 17,* 65–78.

30. Grover, S.L. and Crooker, K.J. (1995). Who appreciates family responsive human resource policies: the impact of family-friendly policies on the organizational attachment of parents and non-parents. *Personnel Psychology, 48,* 271–288.

31. Judge, T.A., Boudreau, J.W. and Bretz, R.D. (1994). Job and life attitudes of male executives. *Journal of Applied Psychology, 79,* 767–782.

32. Cartwright, S. and Cooper, C.L. (1994). *No hassle: taking the stress out of work.* London: Century Books.

33. Barling, J. (1994). Work and family: in search of more effective workplace interventions. In C.L. Cooper and D.M. Rousseau (Eds.), *Trends in organizational behavior, Volume 1.* Chichester: J Wiley.

34. Hillage, J. and Simkin, C. (1992). *Family friendly working: new hope or old hype.* IMS Report 224. Brighton: Institute of Manpower Studies.

35. Holterman, S. (1995). The costs and benefits to British employers of measures to promote equality of opportunity. *Gender, Work and Organization, 2,* 102–112.

36. Giele, J. (1995). Women's changing lives and the emergence of family policy. In T. Gordon and K. Kauppinen-Toropainen (Eds.), *Unresolved dilemmas: women, work and the family in the United States, Europe and the former Soviet Union.* Aldershot: Avebury.

37. McRae, S. (2001). *Mothers' employment and family life in a changing Britain.* Economic and Social Research Council Report 000223137. London: ESRC.

38. Taylor (2002). *Op. cit.*

39. Hochschild, A. (1997). The time bind: when work becomes home and home becomes work. New York: Henry Holt and Company.

40. See Hakim, C. (1987). Trends in the flexible workforce. *Employment Gazette,* 95, 549–560.; Hakim, C. (1991). Grateful slaves and self-made women: fact and fantasy in women's work orientations. *European Sociological Review, 7,* 101–121.; and Hakim, C. (1996). The sexual division of labour and women's heterogeneity. *British Journal of Sociology, 47,* 178–188.

41. Hakim, C. (2000). *Work-lifestyle choices in the 21st century: preference theory.* Oxford: Oxford University Press.

42. *Ibid.,* p. 6.

43. Seneviratna, C. and Turton, S. (2001). Dependants' day. *People Management, 7 (24),* 38–40.

44. Higginbottom, K. (2001). Flexible working policy rings in rewards for BT. *People Management,* 27 September, 11.

45. Kodz, J., Harper, H., and Dench, S. (2002). *Work–life balance: beyond the rhetoric.* Institute for Employment Studies Report 384. Brighton, Sussex: IES.

46. Lewis, S. and Cooper, C.L. (1995). Balancing the work/home interface: a European perspective. *Human Resource Management Review, 5 (4),* 289–305.

47. See, for example, Campbell, D.J., Campbell, K.M. and Kennard, D. (1994). The effects of family responsibilities on the work commitment and job performance of non-professional women. *Journal of Occupational and Organizational Psychology, 67,* 283–296; Grover, S.L. and Crooker, K.J. (1995). Who appreciates family human resource policies: the impact of family-friendly policies on the organizational attachment of parents and non-parents. *Personnel Psychology, 48,* 271–288; and Honeycutt, T.L. and Rosen, R. (1997). Family-friendly human resource policies, salary levels, and salient identity as predictors of organizational attraction. *Journal of Vocational Behaviour, 50,* 271–290.

48. See, for example, Brewer, A.M. (2000). Work design for flexible work scheduling: barriers and gender implications. *Gender, Work and Organization, 7 (1),* 33–44; Bruegel, I. and Perrons, D. (1995). Where do the costs of unequal treatment for women fall? An analysis of the incidence of the costs of unequal pay and sex discrimination in the UK. *Gender, Work and Organization, 2 (3),* 113–124; Jones, C. and Causer, G. (1995). 'Men don't have families': Equality and motherhood in technical employment. *Gender, Work and Organization, 2 (2),* 51–61; Lewis, S. (1997). Family friendly employment policies: a route to changing organizational culture or playing about at the margins? *Gender, Work and Organization, 4 (1),* 13–23; Waldfogel, J. (1995). The price of motherhood: family status and women's pay in a young British cohort. *Oxford Economic Papers, 47,* 584–610.

49. Lewis, S. (1997). Family friendly employment policies: a route to changing organizational culture or playing about at the margins? *Gender, Work and Organization, 4 (1),* 13–23, p. 16.

50. Spence and colleagues developed the Attitude towards Women Scale to examine sex-role ideologies in the USA and Parry developed a UK version. See Spence, J.T., Helmreich, R. and Stapp, J. (1973). A short version of the Attitudes towards Women Scale (AWS). *Bulletin of the Psychonomic Society*, 2 (4), 219–220; Parry, G. (1983). A British version of the Attitudes Towards Women Scale (AWS-B). *British Journal of Social Psychology*, 22, 261–263.

51. Scott. J., Alwin, D.F. and Braun, M. (1996). Generational changes in gender-role attitudes: Britain in a cross-national perspective. *Sociology*, 30 (3), 471–492.

52. Blegen, M.A., Mueller, C.W. and Price, J.L (1988). Measurement of kinship responsibility for organizational research. *Journal of Applied Psychology*, 73, 139–145.

53. Brooke, P.P. Jr, Russell, D.W. and Price, J.L. (1988). Discriminant validation of measures of job satisfaction, job involvement, and organizational commitment. *Journal of Applied Psychology*, 73, 139–145; Price, J.L. and Mueller, C.W. (1981). A causal model of turnover for nurses. *Academy of Management Journal*, 24, 543–565.

54. Brett, J.F., Cron, W.L. and Slocum, J.W. (1995). Economic dependency on work: a moderator of the relationship between organizational commitment and performance. *Academy of Management Journal*, 38, 261–271.

55. Tenbrunsel, A.E., Brett, J.M., Maoz, E., Stroh, L.K. and Reilly, A.H. (1995). Dynamic and static work-family relationships. *Organizational Behavior and Human Decision Processes*, 63, 233–246.

56. Blegen *et al.* (1988). *Op. cit.*

57. Mellor, S., Mathieu, J.E., Barnes-Farrell, J.L. and Rogelberg, S.G. (2001). Employees' nonwork obligations and organizational commitments: a new way to look at the relationships. *Human Resource Management*, 40 (2), 171–184, p. 172.

58. O'Brien, L. (2001). Unions seek big break in bank holiday drive. *People Management*, 13 September, p. 12.

59. Brady, D. (2002). Rethinking the ratrace. *Business Week*, 26 August, 142–143.

60. Wolf, M. (2002). Wasting time at the workplace. *Financial Times*, 10 April, 19.

61. See, for example, Ono, Y., Watanabe, S., Kanocko, S., Matsumoto, K. and Miyako, M. (1991). Working hours and fatigue of Japanese flight attendants. *Journal of Human Ergology*, 20, 155–161; Shimonitsu, T. and Levi, L. (1992). Recent working life changes in Japan. *European Journal of Public Health*, 2, 76–96.

62. Graph plotted from data taken from Brady (2002). *Op. cit.*, pp. 142–143.

63. Rubery, J., Smith, M. and Fagan, C. (1995). *Changing patterns of work and working time in the European Union and the impact on gender provisions*. April. Brussels: European Commission

64. Office for National Statistics (1999). *Social trends*. London: Office for National Statistics.

65. *The Economist* (2002). Time is money. *The Economist*, 364, No. 8290, 35.

66. Data taken from Labour Force Survey homepage on **http://www.statis-tics.gov.uk/**
67. Chartered Institute of Personnel and Development (1999). *Living to work?* London: Chartered Institute of Personnel and Development.
68. Chartered Institute of Personnel and Development (2001). *Working Time Regulations: have they made a difference?* London: Chartered Institute of Personnel and Development.
69. Cooper and Lewis (1998). *Op. cit.*
70. *People Management* (2002). Bank invests in well-being of staff. *People Management, 8 (13)*, 12.
71. See, for example, Sparks, K., Cooper, C.L., Fried, Y. and Shirom, A. (1997). The effects of hours of work on health: a meta-analytic review. *Journal of Occupational and Organizational Psychology, 70*, 391–408; Spurgeon, A., Harrington, J.M. and Cooper, C.L. (1997). Health and safety problems associated with long working hours: a review of the current position. *Occupational and Environmental Medicine, 54 (6)*, 367–375; Spurgeon, A. and Cooper, C.L. (2000). Working time, health and performance. In C.L. Cooper and I.T. Robertson (Eds.), *International review of industrial and organizational psychology, Volume 15*. London: Wiley; Sparks, K., Farragher, B. and Cooper, C.L. (2001). Well-being and occupational health in the 21st century workplace. *Journal of Occupational and Organizational Psychology, 74 (4)*, 489–510.
72. London Hazards Centre (1994). *Hard labour*, London: London Hazards Centre.
73. Institute of Management (1995). *Survival of the fittest: a survey of managers' experience of, and attitudes to, work in the past recession*, Kettering: Institute of Management.
74. Incomes Data Services (2000). 24-Hour Society. *IDS Focus 93*, London: Incomes Data Services.
75. Buell, P. and Breslow, L. (1960). Mortality from coronary heart disease in Californian men who work long hours. *Journal of Chronic Diseases, 11*, 615–626.
76. Harrington, J.M. (1994). Shift work and health – a critical review of the literature on working hours. *Annals of Academic Medicine (Singapore), 23*, 699–705.
77. Sparks, K., Cooper, C.L., Fried, Y. and Shirom, A. (1997). The effects of hours of work on health: a meta-analytic review. *Journal of Occupational and Organizational Psychology, 70*, 391–408
78. Lewis and Cooper (1995). *Op. cit.*, p. 292.
79. Earnshaw, J. and Cooper, C.L. (1996). *Stress and employer liability. Law and employment series*. London: Chartered Institute of Personnel and Development.
80. Daykin, S. and Baldwinson, L. (2002). The long-awaited wake-up call. *People Management, 8 (21)*, 20–21.
81. Lewis and Cooper (1995). *Op. cit.*

10

New Generations: New Expectations and New Problems?

Introduction

In this chapter we consider the question of whether or not there have been any significant changes in behaviour in relation to the employment relationship, both between the different generations and across the equivalent generations over time. If there have been changes, are they relatively minor matters of taste and preference, or might they affect deeper aspects of behaviour and mindset? Sparrow[1] has asked some questions that will arise if there has been a shift in values across the generations. Are higher levels of insecurity associated with a shift in the acceptable timeframe for rewards, with a tendency for more immediate reward and less deferred gratification? As employees make choices about the exchange of free time for consumerism, will they automatically trade off or exchange more free time for less pay? What will be the impact of the increasing attractions of, cost of losing touch with, but desire to stay in touch with, a consumer society? Will the creation of increasingly productive households and processes of wealth creation outside employment (through the value of housing, inheritance of wealth from previous generations and so forth) lead to strategies of income substitution and blunt the value and incentives created by rewards from employment? Will the pursuit of job pauperizing economic growth mean that traditional careers, progression systems and rewards expectations become the interests of an ever narrower range of people, given that young employees enter the organization later and older employees leave it earlier? Are changes in many areas of employment leading to large segments of the population becoming estranged from traditional social expectations of advancement and the historically validated exchange of financial security for compliance at work?

What might be the impact of repeated exposure to people with transactional assumptions about their employment contract? Murphy and Jackson conclude that if there is a continued and widespread erosion of the foundations of trust and relational expectations in the employment contract, then '... at the societal level, such an effect could cause the psychological landscape of work to be so fundamentally altered that employment structures based on relational contracts may become increasingly difficult to retrieve'.[2] Psychologists have also become concerned about the impact of inequality and social exclusion *within* organizations – defined as access to important resources, social networks, and intangible career opportunities – and argue that there are new patterns of social exclusion being created within organizations which may also bring unexpected consequences. Barker[3] outlines the new behaviours being generated by the increasing differentiation between different layers of citizenship within an organization, and the associated privileges and exclusions that are embedded within each of these layers, in terms of access to facilities, training, or career-enhancing experiences. She argues that those with lower levels of citizenship accumulate deficits over their employment contract, and very probably new value sets that might shock those remaining in the core: '... contingent work may be the solvent that dissolves older forms of workplace privilege'.[4] Current models of socialization, commitment and organization culture identification may eventually have limited utility for those organizations that will have a greater reliance on the contingent workforce.

It will become evident that in order to address the questions above we have to adopt a range of perspectives from the social sciences. If there are any generic, cross-individual changes taking place in attitude, behaviour and mindset, then they lie hidden within complex and often contradictory patterns of change. Despite the rhetoric, there is much continuity in the employment relationship. We therefore perhaps need to use the tools of a historian more than those of a psychologist. Historians are more prepared to pronounce on patterns of continuity and discontinuity between the present and the past than are psychologists, and historians tend to make such pronouncements with more insight than management gurus. The problem, however, with trying to detect patterns in what are recent events is that it is the hardest part of history to analyse. As Hobsbawm[5] points out 'there is a twilight zone between history and memory: between the past as a generalized record which is open to relatively dispassionate inspection and the past as a remembered part of or background to one's life'. Two forms of history exist side by side – the archival and personal memory. The archivists fear interviewing someone today and being told 'but it wasn't like that' while those who gather personal narrative understand that there are deeper economic, political and cultural patterns that might also mean that it also wasn't just like the individual's memory, post-rationalization and nostalgia. We have seen throughout this book how often there is a large gap between objective data on changes in the employment relationship, individual perceptions of what is happening to them, and actual behaviour in the workplace.

Moreover, the challenges facing the future employment relationship are contentious. We have avoided speculating on future impacts as best we can but in this chapter we must rely on a rather disparate set of analyses, ranging from socio-cultural histories to detailed economic and social analyses and forecasts. We address the difficulties of establishing whether there really is a sustainable change in the attitudes and values of future generations at work (i.e. values that will not just be socialized away) by examining longitudinal data on values. We then consider whether younger workers indeed face a new and different employment relationship from that of their forefathers by examining data on job entry experiences and analyses of the school-to-work bridge experienced by different cohorts. We also consider whether there is any evidence that parental experiences of the employment relationship have had any lasting effect on the perceptions of younger workers. We return to the issue of trust that has featured in so many chapters in the book by exploring the consequences of recent corporate scandals and the signals that they have sent about control, fairness and equity. Finally we consider the new challenges that will likely shape the attitudes and behaviours of all future employees. Here we rely primarily on various reports in the economic and business press and explore two challenges that will be created by changing demographics: the problems of financing and sustaining a longer employment relationship for the older generation; and the challenges faced by immigration of skilled and unskilled labour to lessen the burden on the young generation.

Generational research on work values

The argument that we may see new patterns of employee behaviour rests on three observations:

1 Employees now work in a state of permanent flux. Changes have no beginning or end point, and there is no opportunity for individuals to internalize the usual sequence to transitions. There is no period of foreclosure and no refreezing of change. Consequently, the value systems intended to support organizational changes and supposedly generated by them do not necessarily become internalized.
2 The traditional period of engagement and disengagement with work and careers, beginning in the 1920s and ending in the 1960s, is now constricted to a shorter age range, and subject to several stratified layers of employment contract. The needs and principles of motivation, value-sets, sources of satisfaction that applied to a life-long employment relationship should not be assumed to apply to this new pattern.
3 Many employees have now entered the workforce since changes to the employment relationship began in the 1980s – commonly referred to as Generation X. For this generation, there are no 'former realities' to change.

Generations are considered to be groups that can be identified on the basis of shared birth years, age, location or significant life events that occurred at critical stages of their development.[6] The effects of these historical and social factors are relatively stable over each cohort's lifetime and also serve to distinguish one group from another in terms of important feelings, desires or stated plans in relation to work. Such discussion has been confined, however, in the main to popular articles and has only recently begun to receive attention in scientific study.[7] Although individual differences are still fundamentally important, membership of the generational wave is felt to be predictive of sufficient common variance in behaviour to make it a viable source of investigation. The most commonly accepted definitions are shown in Box 10.1. Clearly, such groupings may serve as much to stereotype as constructively to inform understanding (especially in the eyes of an 'I am an individual' cohort). It is important therefore at this stage to remember the following:

1 When noting that desires or plans might have some shared qualities, previous distinctions between expectations and obligations made in relation to the psychological contract and between expectations, feelings, and intentions made in relation to attitudes apply here. We are talking about generational influences on subtle aspects of work behaviour.
2 The causal factors are a complex pattern of social and historical contextual influences. Specific aspects of this context may resonate more or less across individuals within the cohort but they nonetheless result in a common pattern of behaviour.

Having noted the necessary 'health warnings' associated with this work, we can now note some of the possibilities for analysis that it opens up. First, it might help to explain whether there are manageable differences in actual observed work behaviours, or in important underlying causal components (such as values, psychological contract elements, or attitudinal dynamics). Second, it alerts us to the need for a more sophisticated understanding of human behaviour at work. If we accept that a complex jigsaw of societal and historical influences shapes important work behaviours then even if this currently is not associated with any radically different behavioural dynamics between the generations, it becomes clear that the removal of just one or two pieces more of the jigsaw just might be enough to change the behavioural dynamics of one generation, while still leaving another generation's behavioural integrity intact.

It is evident that it will be very hard to consider such issues with certainty. Short of having measured each generation's attitudes at birth and tracking them all through life's events, we have to rely on proxy experimental designs to try to test some important assumptions. One example of an attempt to compare both inter-generational differences in work values and changes in the same values over time as each generation matures is outlined in Box 10.2. The authors of the study, Smola and Sutton, conclude:[9]

Box 10.1   Defining the generations

Four generations have been identified in relation to current workforce and soon-to-be-realized workforce at the turn of the millennium. Each generation is considered to have three waves, divided by periods of five to seven years, and called first wave, core group and last wave.

Traditionals: Anglo-Saxon individuals born from 1909 to 1933 or 1934 to 1945. Parental or early childhood experiences shaped by the First and Second World Wars respectively. Latter waves now reaching retirement.

Baby Boomers: Born between 1946 and 1964. Grew up within a psychology of entitlement. Formative years influenced by Vietnam War, civil rights riots, political assassinations, scandals and foibles of political, religious and business leaders, and the sexual revolution. Limited respect for and loyalty to authority and social institutions. Pressures to care for ageing parents and children. Protesting against power in their youths, now entered or entering positions of corporate and national power. Driven by material success.

Generation X: Less agreement over birth years but generally reported from the early 1960s and ending by 1975 to 1982, depending on nationality. Early development years characterized by more family, financial and social insecurity. A sense of individualism over collectivism. Insight into dual-earner family structures but also work–life balance dysfunctions, divorces and so forth. Seek social support from small like-minded enclaves, seek mentoring and more immediate feedback and rewards. Untrusting and cynical having seen parents experience recessions and downsizing. Influenced by and sensitive to global popular culture and phenomenon (MTV, AIDS, global warming). Higher levels of educational attainment and technical competency, but also wider socio-economic divisions and levels of family wealth.

Millennials, Generation Y, next generation: Born from 1975 to 1994 and now entering or just entered the workforce. In the UK, the Thatcher generation or in the USA Reaganites and Economic Bubble influence. The first generation born into a highly computerized world, sharing a greater sense of connection to virtual communities rather being confined to their own socio-economic/regional/local identity. Highly influenced by the individualism of their parents, and competitive or value-for-money ethos of societal structures. Higher levels of wealth or property attained before work careers being.

Source: Smola and Sutton.[8]

Box 10.2   Replicating within-generation value changes over time

In 1974 Cherrington and colleagues[10] gathered data on workers' attitudes to jobs, their companies, communities and work in general in 53 US organizations. In 1999 Smola and Sutton replicated the study using a slightly modified questionnaire. A snowball sampling technique was used to generate a broadly equivalent sample in the South Eastern states of the USA. During this time significant shifts had taken place in the US workforce. From 1974 to 1999 the proportion of US employees aged over 25 holding at least a bachelor's degree increased from 16 per cent to 26 per cent. The proportion of female employees had increased from 39 per cent to 49 per cent. Blacks had increased from 10 per cent to nearly 18 per cent of the workforce, and Hispanics from an unrecorded basis to 10 per cent of the workforce. The data from the two surveys were divided into generational cohorts, i.e. Traditionals, Baby Boomers, Generation X'ers and Millennials. There were sufficient individuals to compare the Baby Boomers and Generation X cohorts. The 1999 groups were divided into groups so that those who were, for example, 27 in 1974 were compared to those who were 52 in 1999. This quasi-longitudinal design (between-person) revealed some interesting changes. Looking at today's employees, those from Generation X report a significantly stronger desire to be promoted compared to the Baby Boomer generation. There were no differences in Pride in Craftmanship values. Generation X employees were more convinced that working hard makes one a better person, while the Baby Boomer generation were more convinced that work should be the most important part of one's life. Such values clearly reflect the different age and career stages of the two cohorts today. However, when today's employees were compared to the age groups that they would have been in in 1974 there were clear differences in both Pride in Craftsmanship and the moral importance of work. Compared to their birthmates, the older employees today had become less likely to believe that work makes you a better person, that an individual's worth is influenced by how well they do their job, that a worker should feel a sense of pride in their work.

Source: Smola and Sutton.[11]

> . . . work values are more influenced by generational influences than by age and maturation . . . The overriding influence seems to be a move away from company loyalty and an association of self-worth with one's job.

Dose[12] demonstrates that work values act as evaluative standards by which individuals either discern what is 'right' or assess the importance of their preferences relating to work or the work environment. It is generally accepted that many of these work values change as individuals pass through career stages[13] and even as they pass through different stages of the educational system.[14] One of the most documented work values has been what is called Protestant Work Ethic (PWE). This is a set of beliefs that values hard work, dedication, frugality and perseverance. Furnham[15] notes that it is somewhat inappropriate to use the word Protestant because the value set is found across cultures and religions. These values co-vary at least with age. The balance of evidence suggests that there is a curvilinear relationship, with PWE increasing until around the age of 60 and then declining again. The values co-vary with other factors such as wealth, conservatism and perceived control.

What of the generation whose perceptions are first being formed now? What of future generations? The issue of inter-generational differences in work values and in the meaning of work has only just begun to receive serious study (popular attention to the topic has existed for years).[16] An important area of debate has been whether or not we will see generic adaptations in the way that people adjust to the new employment relationship, and whether or not a changed psychology across generational cohorts and across the work–life divide, might occur in the future. In order to answer the last question, we need to be able to disentangle whether work values are influenced more by:

- shared experiences within generations, or
- maturation and development of people over time.

Put simply, while young employees might have different attitudes today as they enter the workforce than the older generation, by the time they themselves are older will they have been socialized back to the same attitudes as the older generation have now, or did the older generation when they were themselves younger have similar attitudes? Even if there are some different attitudes that do seem to reflect the reality of the world today, if today's older generation were taken back to their youth themselves and were now being released onto the labour market, would they have the same attitudinal response as today's younger employees if faced with the same novel situation, i.e. with a degree of empathy they ought to be able to see and predict the behaviour of the younger generation? Or are today's young generation so unique, socialized into a very different way of seeing the world, and faced by a totally novel situation? Is there no reason at all to assume that their reactions and behaviours to the new world of work will reflect any previous experience base with which the older generation might empathize? As might be imagined, unravelling such a range of possible situations with any degree of certainty presents an immense challenge to researchers.

The work values, attitudes and behaviours of 'young workers'

Another ultimately more defensible way of gaining insight into new patterns of behaviour at work is to study young workers. Barling[17] noted that developmental and work and organizational psychologists have spent time looking at how family influences the work attitude and behaviours of young workers, but have generally ignored the impact that their own work experiences have. This is a strange oversight given that the teens and early 20s still represent impressionable years and a critical period for later development.[18] Moreover, there is no ample opportunity to examine the work experiences of younger workers. Loughlin and Barling[19] recently reviewed the evidence. United Nations data show that youth employment (aged from 16 to 24) has become the norm in North America and Europe. The proportion employed in this age group ranges from, for example, 63 per cent in Sweden, 67 per cent in Austria and 75 per cent in Denmark.[20] In North America almost 80 per cent of high school students work part-time for pay before they graduate and 70 per cent are employed more than 20 hours a week during the summer.[21]

Certainly it appears that young workers face a different employment context than did their parents or grandparents. For example, Pollock[22] conducted a longitudinal analysis of data from the British Household Panel Survey. If one considers the proportion of each generational cohort that experienced four or more employment statuses from the ages 15 to 30, then this figure has more than doubled for the 1920s cohorts to the 1960s cohorts. Eight per cent of young people experienced more than four employment statuses in the 1920s. By the 1960s this figure had grown to 19 per cent. Cappelli[23] notes that in the USA too there has been a 10 per cent increase in the number of job changes for younger workers. Statistical analysis appears to confirm and support the thesis that young employees entering the labour market today face an increasing individualization of their labour market experience and uncertain employment futures that will combine unemployment, government schemes, self employment and part-time employment, with diminishing experience of full-time employment.

Industrial sociologists and vocational education and training specialists have also demonstrated that the changing socio historical context has had an impact on teenage aspirations for future careers and work outcomes. Schoon and Parsons[24] report on a longitudinal follow-up study of over 17 000 British teenagers (aged 16) born 12 years apart. The study used data from the two richest resources for the study of British human development – the 1958 National Child Development Study and 1970 British Cohort Study. The subjects were all children born in Britain between 3 and 9 March 1958 (followed up at ages 7, 11, 16, 23 and 33) and children born 5–11 April 1970 (followed up at ages 5, 10, 16 and 26). The loss of manufacturing and textile occupations,[25] the virtual disappearance of a youth labour market,[26] the pressure for continued full-time education, and the appearance of educational achievement as a significant predictor of employment outcomes[27] meant that the socio-historical context was found to play a key role in influencing aspirations and predicting occupational outcomes. There were increases over time between the two cohorts in parental social class, exam scores, teenagers' job aspirations, but decreases in school motivation at age 16, parental expectation of age to leave education and actual occupational attainment. Individual aspirations were a good predictor of actual attainment for both cohorts, but the later born cohort experienced more complex and varied education, training and employment choices. The earlier born cohort had better opportunities for career development and were less dependent on their academic achievements – aspiration and academic achievements were much more closely linked for the 1970s cohort whereas for the 1958 cohort an individual desire to excel could counterbalance educational limitations. The impact of parental social class on occupational attainment remained the same and there was an increase in social inequality. The aspiration – to career attainment link has indeed changed for the different cohorts, perhaps explaining shifts in values. Bynner and Parsons[28] argue that experiences associated with full-time and discontinuous employment among these two cohorts are influencing the degree of work commitment as a personal value. A similar conclusion has been reached in Germany where studies of early careers show similar destabilizing career patterns and increased interruptions during the period of job entry.[29]

Family influences and imaging inertia theory

As we have seen, there has been much popular discussion of generational differences in work values and claims that the youngest cohort of workers have learned from their parents' experiences. In particular, the 1980s and 1990s meant that many young workers saw their parents experience downsizing exercises, and as a result are said to have inherited sceptical, mistrustful and self-reliant behaviours.[30] What is the evidence for such an assertion? It comes from studies of two types: those that have examined how children's understanding of work and employment develop; and those that use ethnographic techniques to see how children are uniquely affected by their family experiences. Although some of the generational research must remain speculation, there are mechanisms through which value change can occur. Children's understanding of work and employment appears to be influenced by their parents' employment and economic circumstances in quite significant ways[31] and their understanding of the world of work increases steadily from the ages of 4 and 11. Notable findings are that:

- Children can accurately report on their parents' level of job satisfaction by the age of 7 or 8 years[32]
- The attitudes of children to unions are shaped by parental attitudes and beliefs.[33]

Although there is still some debate, a growing number of researchers argue that: 'children's perceptions of parental work attitudes and experiences shape the development of their own work beliefs and attitudes'.[34] Empirical work by

Barling and colleagues has shown that parental experiences of layoffs and job insecurity significantly predict late adolescents' perceptions of parental job security, and this in turn predicted their own work beliefs and work attitudes such as alienation and cynicism.[35]

Cappelli[36] supports the conclusion that employment structures based on relational contracts may become increasingly difficult to retrieve. His *imaging inertia* theory, based on the assumption that altered perceptions endure throughout generational cohorts, argues that employees do not make decisions or judgements purely on the basis of a rational cost–benefit model. They rely instead on recalling previous experiences in similar situations – imaging – and basing their decisions on what happened then. Elder's[37] study of the Great Depression showed that people who experienced the hardships often felt insecure throughout their lives even when they had become wealthy. The generation that grew up assuming their employer was responsible for careers may similarly never forget the waves of downsizing. Their children, the next generation of workers, may also never forget. Employers may find it difficult to go back to the old model because the new generation of employees will not go back to the old model. Their images of work may have been forever altered. There is, however, a question as to how long such negative influences might play a role in the behaviour of young people. Elder's[38] study of the influence of the Great Depression on children of the affected also demonstrated what was called the 'downward extension hypothesis' whereby adolescents whose fathers became unemployed suffered initially in terms of their own adjustment, but ended up significantly better adjusted in later life. The current generation of younger workers might eventually end up having benefited from their early family experiences.

There is some emerging evidence to support at least the front end of this process – more negative and inertial attitudes. Work on the impact of layoffs on childrens' values[39] and the impact of layoffs on third-party perceptions[40] suggests that a shift to more transactional contracts might indeed be taking place. Research into job loss also suggests that employees are adopting new beliefs or perceptions regarding their careers.[41] Individuals who have experienced job loss believe that all subsequent employment opportunities are less secure and adopt a more transactional stance. Recent ethnographic research into the home–work interface in economic sectors characterized by 'institutionalized instability' also appears to support this scenario. McKee and colleagues[42] studied oil and gas families from three Scottish communities over a couple of years. Reflecting Cappelli's imaging inertia theory, when examining the experience of 'instability survivors who surf the threat', the researchers found that the severe 1980s recession had become a turning point and had permanently altered the mindset and family culture. Determined to 'never again be left so vulnerable', families had more instrumental values. While they still had short-term labour market power and good times, they were using the income to buy a big house and race towards safety in the future. The culture was one of never again becoming attached to the job.

Will the next generation trust in business?

One of the major concerns for many individuals today is that they find it hard to believe that there is a link between their actions and the consequence of such actions upon the success (or otherwise) of their employing organization – and therefore any long-term benefit for themselves. HRM academics see this as a problem of decreasing 'line of sight'. Having discussed the role of images creating inertia in previous generations, has the stock market collapse of 2002 after various corporate scandals in the USA created some powerful new inertia images? Do employees believe that it makes sense to place trust in the actions of their employers? Does it make sense to work hard for the interests of the organization in order to satisfy one's own interests?

The whole question of trust in business – and indeed trust in the American economic model – has itself recently been called into question. We noted in Chapter 5 that in the eyes of the public, trustworthiness lies in the triple bottom line of social, environmental and financial factors. Trust in the social factors has already been eroded. What seems to have happened now is that trust in another root – stated financial performance – has also been challenged. For example, the number of restatements of US corporate results was on an upwards trend long before the Enron, WorldCom and Xerox crises, increasing from a figure of around 35 a year in 1990 to over 200 a year by 1999.[43] Between 1997 and 2002 almost 1000 US companies had to restate their earnings '. . . admitting in effect that they had previously published wrong or misleading numbers . . . phoney accounts mean that much of the profit growth of the late 1990s, the ostensible justification for Wall Street's bubbling up to its ephemeral heights, was equally phoney'.[44] The pay of US executives of the S&P 500 fell by from 2.9 per cent to 4 per cent from 2001 to 2002 while after-tax profits fell by 50 per cent and redundancies rose from 614 000 to 2 million, but board compensation as a total rose by 10 per cent. Fifty-eight per cent of chief executive reward is now based on stock option grants exercised over 10 years, begun as part of a deliberate strategy to align the goals of managers with the interests of the company's owners.[45] Indeed, the shares allocated for options at America's top 200 corporations grew to 16.4 per cent of all shares outstanding by the end of 2000. These outstanding options amounted to an average of 19.7 per cent of profits of US firms. Had stock options been treated as an expense, then by 1997 rather than 2000 it would have been apparent that the boom in US company profits had come to an end.

What appeared to really hit home was the fact that the senior executives in most of the misreported organizations made significant financial gains themselves at the expense ultimately of their employees (see Box 10.3).

> . . . On the whole, Americans suffer neither envy nor egalitarian yearnings when gazing at the fortunes of their business leaders. But they do like to think that their market-based system works fairly. The collapse of Enron, Andersen and other once-prestigious companies has rocked that faith.[47]

Box 10.3   Fairness at the top? Stock options and reward arrangements

There has been much controversy about the level of executive pay in recent years and especially in the aftermath of a series of high publicity corporate collapses in the USA. The average tenure of chief executives is relatively short – they change jobs every 5.7 years – but rewards have been very high regardless of performance. Watson Wyatt found that in 60–70 per cent of top US companies it is the company (and thus ultimately the chief executive) and not the board that chooses and employs the pay consultant. For example, the chief executive of Qwest made $75 million from options exercised in the year before the collapse of share price and $27.1 million in salary. Over $680 million was paid to 140 executives of Enron in 2001, its chairman received $67.4 million in salary, bonuses and stock options and its chief financial officer made more than $40 million between 1999 and 2001 in the off-balance sheet partnerships that lay at the heart of the financial collapse. The chief executive of WorldCom borrowed $341 million from his firm at 2 per cent interest before the bankruptcy. Even in organizations where no financial impropriety was involved, arrangements seemed unduly generous. For example, the Time Warner executives who had to forgo bonuses after very poor performance still each collected stock options valued at $40 million per head. Pension and post-tenure arrangements are also relatively generous. Under the terms of his termination contract, Jack Welch, the retired boss of General Electric, is 'required' to consult for the company for the rest of his life at the rate of $17 000 a day. After 8 years' service at IBM, Lou Gerstner retires on £1 million a year and 10 years' consultancy work.

Sources: Various articles in *The Economist*.[46]

Moreover, in a globalized economy the actions of the few can influence the fortunes of many. At one time the situation in the US stock market would have had little impact on European stock markets, but the increased interdependence of business globally means that such images have a wider impact than before. Between 1976 and 1999, for example, the correlation between US and European stock markets was low, ranging from 0.24 for Italy and 0.5 for Britain. However, since late 2000 correlations are as high as 0.9.[48] The outcome for many European employees is that their lifetime financial position has been adversely affected by the activities of a few in a distant land.

Demography as destiny?

A number of more predictable events are also likely to have a significant impact on our experience of the employment relationship. In the last half of the chapter we draw upon evidence in the business and economic press that examines some significant social challenges. The ninetenth-century French philosopher Auguste Comte pointed out that demography is destiny. The effects of demographics endure for longer and have a wider impact that any other social or economic force. Drucker[49] states that the shrinking of the younger population is very significant for nothing on this scale appears to have happened since the dying centuries of the Roman Empire. In every single developed country but also in developing countries such as China and Brazil the birth rate is now below the replacement level of 2.2. He notes that we should beware demographic changes in that they can quickly reverse. Between 1925 and 1935 the US birth rate halved and dipped below the replacement level leading to confident predictions that the US population would stop growing by 1945. An explosion in the birth rate led to the Baby Boomer generation described earlier, a further baby-bust cycle in the 1960s as people feared nuclear holocaust and a 'Baby Boom echo' in the late 1980s as economic confidence grew. However, Drucker concurs that '. . . population predictions for the next 20 years can be made with some certainty because almost everybody who will be in the workforce in 2020 is already alive'.[50]

So what can we be sure will happen? Consider the following data. In Britain, the Office for National Statistics estimates that our population of 59.8 million in 2001 is expected to grow to 64 million by 2021, despite a fertility rate of only 1.64 (down from 2.5 in the 1960s).[51] This is largely the result of an influx of 135 000 immigrants a year. In Scotland, the fertility rate of 1.48 will lead to a fall in overall population. In both instances, the population continues to age. In Europe fertility rates continue to fall below the 2.1 needed for population stability – from just below 1.9 in the mid 1980s to less than 1.4 now (they are as low as 1.1 and 1.3 for Spain, Italy and Greece). The number of children aged under 15 has shrunk by 23 per cent in Europe since 1970. In Germany, for example, by 2030 people aged over 65 will account for almost half the adult population and unless the birth rate recovers from its present 1.3 the proportion of under-35-year-olds will shrink twice as fast as the older population will grow. In South Korea too a sharp plunge in the birth rate has seen births per woman fall from 4.5 to 1.4 in three decades. The elderly population is expected to double by 2019.

Beyond this directly predictable term, unless there is a dramatic change in social behaviour very soon, the shifts become more marked. The United Nations Population Division calculates the average age of the world today is 26. By 2050 it is anticipated to be 36 – rising to a figure of 55 years in Spain, for example.[52] The ageing rate (measured as the percentage of population aged 65 and older) for the developed region as a whole accelerated from 2 per cent in 1950 to 5 per cent by 2000 and is projected to accelerate to 15 per cent by 2050. In Japan, these figures are 5 per cent, 17 per cent and 32 per cent respectively.

Table 10.1 Child and elderly populations as a percentage of the total in the USA and Western Europe

	Western Europe child population (aged under 15)	US Child population (aged under 15)	Western Europe adult population (aged 60 and over)	US adult population (aged 60 and over)
2000	18%	22%	20%	17%
2050	11%	23%	40%	23%

Source: Data derived from US Census Bureau. US middle projection.

European fertility rates are projected to decline for another ten years. In North America – despite the shift explained next – the ratio falls from 5 to 1 today to 3 to 1 by 2050 (see Table 10.1), in Asia from 11 to 1 today to 4 to 1 by 2050, with a similar ratio change in Latin America.

However, a remarkable change appears to be taking place that potentially will set the USA and Europe on very different paths in terms of the employment relationship.[53] America is the demographic outlier among the industrialized nations – it will soon start getting younger (see Box 10.4). The recovery in fertility rates in the USA has implications for the discussion in the previous chapter of family-friendly policies. The demand for this will be sustained but will also apply across longer episodes of family life with women requiring and taking career breaks later in their career and sustained pressure on men to share in the responsibilities that this entails.

Who will pay my pension?

There are three main options that might be pursued to deal with this last challenge to the employment relationship:

- increased productivity
- extending the working life
- an expanded labour force based on imported labour

In order to put some relative scale on these options, consider the following analysis of the economic impacts of global ageing by the Centre for Strategic and International Studies in Washington. If immigrants were not to be allowed into advanced economies, then Europe for example faces the task of boosting its productivity by two-thirds before 2020 just to keep its economy from shrinking (this, of course, assumes that regions will still seek to expand their economies). Given that the trend growth in productivity as measured by GDP per hour worked was only around 2 per cent per year in Italy, Germany, the UK and France (1.5 per cent per year in the USA) from 1979 to 1999, or that total growth in GDP per person of working age over the same period ranged from

Box 10.4   A different future for the USA?

In the USA the 2000 Census showed that the population is rising much faster than anyone expected. In 1950 Western Europe (the countries that were not Communist after the Second World War) had twice the population of the USA. Even now just the European Union's 15 countries have a population that is 100 million larger than the USA. By 2050 the USA will be twice the size that it is now. By 2040 – and possibly as soon as 2030 – it will overtake Europe in population – negating the European Union's boast that global firms should concentrate on Europe as it is the world's largest consumer market. Given that Americans are about one-third richer per head than Europeans, the US economy will be twice the size that of Europe with 400–550 million rich consumers, and US business practices could become even more dominant. The USA will actually become younger because of:

- The *social confidence* factor: The fertility rate of its native-born white population is rising. From 1960 to 1985 US fertility rates fell faster than those in Europe but by the 1990s it had rebounded to 2.1. Women merely delayed childbirth by half a generation to start families in later life, but start them nonetheless.
- The *immigration* factor: US immigration (at 11 million legal and 7–8 million illegal immigrants over the past decade) outstrips that of Europe. The US Census Bureau forecast for immigration 2000–2050 suggests 77.6 million immigrants to Western Europe and the USA with 72 per cent going to the USA. The US immigrant population is reproducing faster than native-born Americans (the fertility rate for non-Hispanic whites is just over 1.8, for blacks is 2.1 and for Latinos is nearly 3.0)

Source: *The Economist*.[54]

1.1 per cent per annum in Germany to 2 per cent per annum in the UK, then this is a tall order.[55] Such productivity improvements would require a massive investment in labour-saving machinery and new plants, intensified deregulation of labour markets, and change on a scale that would make the experience of the last decade seem relatively mild.

These broad demographic shifts then have quite profound implications for work. Not least for Europe the question is who will do the work to support a less productive and aged population? There are still currently four people of working-age to support every citizen aged 65 or older in Europe, but by 2050 this figure falls to two people. The ageing countries of Europe face an unsustainable gap between future tax revenues and commitments to spend and to service government debt. In fact both Europe and the USA face fiscal problems in the near future providing pensions and healthcare as their post-war baby boom generation retire. To sustain current social systems some estimates point out that by 2050 government debt will represent 100 per cent of national income in the USA, 150 per cent in the EU as a whole and over 250 per cent in France and Germany.[56] The burden is much heavier in Europe.

Another option then is to extend the retirement age. In Europe, the level of economic activity among the older workforce is relatively low – only 40 per cent of people aged between 55 and 64 are economically active. Expanding the number of older workers represents a significant challenge, especially given the current trend to more early retirement and the fiscal pressures faced by the older generation. Their situation is made more difficult because there has also been a shift from defined benefit to defined contribution pension funding. This signals two trends:

1 a shift in risk from the employer to the employee in terms of the final scale of benefits provided
2 a reduction in the contributions made by employers in any event.

The number of UK employees belonging to defined benefits pension schemes in the UK fell from 5.6 million to 3.8 million over the 1990s.[57] Contributions made by employers to defined contribution plans are typically only around half of the contributions that they made to defined benefits plans. Two other related issues make the situation more challenging. More people are retiring early, and this is increasing the length of pension payments. Life expectancy in the UK is now 10 years longer than it was in 1950. By 2020 there will be another 800 000 non-working over-55-year-olds in the UK, supported by a smaller working population. The net result is that there is a £27 billion shortfall between what the working population is saving for retirement and what it should be saving.

One of the implications of this is the need for organizations to educate employees about the issues involved. It is estimated that 16 per cent of UK companies now make online benefits projection tools available to employees as part of this education process. Drucker[58] points to some of the managerial implications of this new society. Historically the workspan of most manual employees was less than 30 years but in the society we are moving into people can expect to remain productive (and will have a need to maintain earnings) over a period of up to 50 years. The shifting age structure will mean that, for politicians and organizations alike, winning the support of older people will become an imperative. In the USA discussion of 'second careers' has become quite normal. A growing number of people over 50 will participate in the labour force in new and different ways – as temporaries, part-timers, consultants, special assignments. Drucker argues that in the USA within 20 years' time up to half of the people who work for an organization will not do so on a full-time basis and this will especially be the case for older people. New ways of working at arm's length will become the norm. Subsequent to his analysis US Labor Department data seemed to support this contention. From

September 2000 to September 2002 the year-on-year percentage point change in the share of the population that was working fell for every group except for the 55–64-year-olds.[59] For example, 55–64-year-old women grew by 2.7 per cent as a proportion while each of the 20–24, 25–34 and 35–44 age groups fell in proportion by 1 per cent. In the more age discriminatory environment of the UK facilitating a shift towards sustained employment of older workers will represent a very significant challenge.

Immigration as opposed to a longer working life?

Difficult industrial relations issues will also need to be faced in relation to the third option, which is to increase immigration levels to sustain social welfare systems. In the UK there has been concern about the impact that recruitment of trained South African nurses will have on the donating country. Is it right to suck talent from a developing country? The current figures are shown in Table 10.2 but they will soon become a thing of the past.

Either we prepare for a very different future and working life, or we prepare for a very different society. Box 10.5 details some of the trends that characterize the market for global talent. The challenge is to buy youth, but whose youth, with what skills and with what relaxation of procedures or controls? The cost of settling asylum seekers in the UK is £1 billion, or one-third the official

Table 10.2 Foreign population as a percentage of the population and labour force, 1999

Country	Foreign population as a % of total population 1999	Foreign employees as a % of the labour force 1999
Australia	24.0	24.6
Canada	17.0	19.2
Sweden	11.5	5.1
United States	10.2	11.7
Netherlands	9.9	3.4
Austria	9.3	10.0
Germany	9.0	8.8
Belgium	8.8	8.8
Denmark	5.5	4.4
France	5.2	5.8
Britain	3.9	3.7
Ireland	3.0	3.4
Finland	2.4	1.5
Italy	2.0	3.6
Spain	1.9	1.0
Portugal	1.8	1.8
Japan	0.9	0.2

After: OECD figures reproduced in *The Economist* Survey of Migration.[60]

foreign aid budget. Whereas the case for attracting highly skilled people has become accepted economic wisdom, a more difficult challenge is what to do with unskilled labour. Immigrants tend to cluster at the upper and lower ends of the skill spectrum.

> . . . Because the difference in earnings is greatest in this sector, migration of the unskilled delivers the largest global economic gains. Moreover, wealthy, well-educated, ageing economies create lots of jobs for which their own workers have little appetite.[61]

The economic impacts of this brain drain highlighted in Box 10.5 are complex although generally negative on the sending country. However, it does appear to act as a further stimulus to globalization and interconnection in the employment relationship. Overall the sums that migrants send home to

---

Box 10.5   The market for outward bound global talent

Some 36 per cent of New York's present population is foreign born, a figure only reached before in 1910. Of the 1 million Indians living in the USA more than three-quarters have a bachelor's degree or better. These individuals account for 0.1 per cent of India's population but earn the equivalent of 10 per cent of India's national income. Twenty-one per cent of all legal immigrants to the USA have at least 17 years of education, implying some post-graduate study, compared to 8 per cent of native-born Americans. Britain's Department for International Development estimates that three-quarters of Africa's and roughly half of Asia and South America's immigrants have higher-level education. This can create major challenges for the sending countries. About 30 per cent of highly educated Ghanaians live abroad. The USA has proved to be a particular magnet for highly educated immigrants. Seventy-five per cent of all Jamaican and 12 per cent of all the Mexican higher-educated population live in the USA. In the case of Mexico, 12 per cent of their total labour force is in the USA but 30 per cent of Mexicans with PhDs are there. The USA educates one-third of all foreign students. About half of the students who get PhDs are still in the USA five years after graduating, rising to 60 per cent of those with PhDs in the physical sciences or mathematics. The OECD found that around 60 per cent of Indian, Chinese and British students in the USA have definite job offers there, and 80 per cent of students of this nationality have plans to stay in the USA. When Germany tentatively introduced a green card system in 2000 and issued 20 000 visas for information technology staff it found that only 12 000 were taken up as skilled Indian workers decided that they would rather go to the USA.

Source: The Economist.[62]

developing countries represent $60 billion through official channels and a further estimated $15 billion in various unreported ways. Overseas remittances to developing doubled between 1989 and 2000 and already represent 20 per cent more than official development aid. A Canadian analysis found that for every 10 per cent increase in the number of immigrants from a given country there was a 1 per cent rise in exports to that country and a 3 per cent increase in imports from that country. Entrepreneurs travel back and forth and transfer of knowledge can be high. Of the 312 companies in the Hsinchu industrial park in Taipei, Taiwan, 113 were started by US-educated engineers with professional experience in Silicon Valley, where 70 per cent of the Taiwanese companies have offices to pick up new recruits.

Scaling the different options

Are there going to be different options in this area? It seems unlikely. The question has been asked if it would help to increase the proportion of working age population actually at work or to raise the retirement age. The answer is a little, but not enough:

> . . . Even if everyone of working age were in work, support ratios in 2050 would still drop below three even in the US. Only by raising the retirement age to 75 could current support ratios be maintained.[63]

However, immigration too would also not be a sufficient solution. As noted in Box 10.5, the USA has been importing immigrant labour on a relatively massive scale for the last 20 years at both the upper and lower ends of the labour market – around 1 million immigrants a year including illegal immigrants. Even if it maintains current inflows at the same level as this, by 2010 it will experience labour shortages. A growing number of European governments now accept that there is an economic case for large-scale immigration. Gaps in income per head between sending and receiving countries have enabled quite accurate forecasting of expected flows of labour to be made. For example, the German Institute for Economic Research (DIW) confidently estimate that EU enlargement will lead to 335 000 people moving west each year, falling to 150 000 people a year in 10 years' time as income differentials reduce. However, research for the manpower agency of Watson Wyatt Worldwide demonstrates that in Germany immigration would have to be boosted by a factor of 20 and in Japan by a factor of 50 just to offset domestic population reductions.

The United Nations Population Division has also tried to establish what levels of immigration are needed to prevent a population decline in Western countries and to maintain the existing ratio of workers to those needing support. Their findings on the challenge of immigration produced an international uproar.[64] The EU would require an annual inflow of nearly 3 million migrants a year – roughly twice the present level of legal and estimated illegal immigration – to prevent future support ratios of 15–64-year-olds to over-65-year-olds dropping from the present 4:1 to below a 3:1 ratio. Britain, for example, needs over 200 000 net migrants per million population, Germany 600 000 and Italy 650 000. The implication for industrial relations let alone social attitudes are immense. It is interesting to note that even in the successful US social experiment, the opposition to large-scale immigration from US trade unions puts them in the anti-globalization camp during the violent protests at Seattle.[65] Yet, the length of our working lives and the level of financial resources that we believe that we need access to during the employment relationship will depend on how such issues are resolved.

Clearly there is a gulf between the economic arguments that are marshalled to support changes in the employment relationship and the social impact that such changes will have. There are also difficult organizational, social and political questions that will have to be answered. As Drucker concludes, we can be sure that the society of 2020 will be very different from that of today and that the greatest changes in the employment relationship still lie ahead of us. As we look towards this future it is clear that the existing workforce, future generations coming into the workforce, organizations and indeed society as a whole will have little option but to reconcile themselves with the need to manage a very challenging employment relationship.

References

1. Sparrow, P.R. (2000). The new employment contract. In R. Burke and C.L. Cooper (Eds.), *The organization in crisis*. London: Basil Blackwell.
2. Murphy, P.E. and Jackson, S.E. (1999). Managing work role performance: challenges for twenty first century organizations and their employees. In D.R. Ilgen and E.D. Pulakos (Eds.), *The changing nature of performance: implications for staffing motivation and development*. San Francisco: Jossey-Bass, p. 358.
3. Barker, K. (1995). Contingent work: research issues and the lens of moral exclusion. In L.E. Tetrick and J. Barling (Eds.) *Changing employment relations: behavioural and social perspectives*. Washington, DC: American Psychological Association.
4. *Ibid.*, p. 50.
5. Hobsbawm, E. (1987). *The age of empire*. London: Abacus Books, p. 3.
6. Smola, K.W. and Sutton, C.D. (2002). Generational differences: revisiting generational work values for the new millennium. *Journal of Organizational Behavior*, 23, 363–382.
7. Loughlin, C. and Barling, J. (2001). Young workers' work values, attitudes and behaviors. *Journal of Occupational and Organizational Psychology, 74 (4)*, 543–558.
8. Smola and Sutton (2002). *Op. cit.*
9. *Ibid.*, p. 379.

10. See Cherrington, D.J., Condie, S.J. and England, J.L. (1979). Age and work values. *Academy of Management Journal*, 22, 617–623; Cherrington, D.J. (1980). *The work ethic: working values and values that work.* Amacom : New York.
11. Smola and Sutton (2002). *Op. cit.*
12. Dose, J. (1997). Work values: an integrative framework and illustrative application to organizational socialization. *Journal of Occupational and Organizational Psychology, 70,* 219–241.
13. Rhodes, S. (1983). Age-related differences in work-related attitudes and behaviour: a review and conceptual analysis. *Psychological Bulletin, 93,* 328–367.
14. Walsh, B.D., Vacha-Hasse, T., Kapes, J.T. (1996). The values scale: differences across grade levels for ethnic minority students. *Educational and Psychological Measurement, 56,* 263–276.
15. See, for example, Furnham, A. (1982). The Protestant work ethic and attitudes to unemployment. *Journal of Occupational Psychology, 55,* 277–285; Furnham, A. (1990). *The protestant work ethic: the psychology of work-related beliefs and behaviours.* Routledge : London; Furnham, A., Bond, M., Heaven, P., Hilton, D., Lobel, T., Masters, J., Payne, M., Rajamenikam, R., Stacey, B., and Van Daalen, H. (1993). A comparison of Protestant work ethic beliefs in 13 nations. *Journal of Social Psychology, 133,* 185–198.
16. Gephart, R.P. Jr (2002). Introduction to the brave new workplace: organizational behavior in the electronic age. *Journal of Organizational Behavior, 23,* 327–344.
17. Barling, J. (1990). *Employment, stress and family functioning.* Chichester: Wiley.
18. Krosnick, J.A. and Alwin, D.F. (1989). Aging and susceptibility to attitude change. *Journal of Personality and Social Psychology, 57,* 416–425.
19. Loughlin, C. and Barling, J. (2001). Young workers' work values attitudes and behaviours. *Journal of Occupational and Organizational Psychology, 74 (4),* 543–558.
20. United Nations (1996). *Demographic yearbook. Issue 46.* New York: United Nations.
21. Runyan, C.W. and Zakocs, R.C. (2000). Epidemiology and prevention of injuries amongst adolescent workers in the United States. *Annual Review of Public Health, 21,* 247–269.
22. Pollock, G. (1997). Uncertain futures: young people in and out of employment since 1940. *Work, Employment and Society, 11 (4),* 615–638.
23. Capelli, P. (1999). *The new deal at work.* Boston, MA: Harvard Business School Press.
24. Schoon, I. and Parsons, S. (2002). Teenage aspirations for future careers and occupational outcomes. *Journal of Vocational Behavior, 60,* 262–288.
25. Bynner, J., Elias, P., McKnight, A. and Pan, H. (2000). *The changing nature of the youth labour market in Great Britain.* Rowntree Foundation Report. York: Rowntree Foundation.

26. Banks, M., Bates, I., Breakwell, G., Bynner, J, Emler, N., Jamieson, L. and Roberts, K. (1992). *Careers and identities*. Milton Keynes: Open University Press.
27. See Shavit, Y. and Müller, W. (Eds.). (1998). *From school to work: a comparative study of educational qualifications and occupational destinations*. Oxford: Oxford University Press; Bynner, J., Joshi, H. and Tsatsas, M. (2000). *Obstacles and opportunities on the route to adulthood*. London: The Smith Institute.
28. Bynner, J. and Parsons, S. (2000). Marginalization and value-shifts under the changing economic circumstances surrounding the transition to work: a comparison of cohorts born in 1958 and 1970. *Journal of Youth Studies, 3*, 237–249.
29. Heinz, W.R. (2002). Transition discontinuities and the biographical shaping of early work careers. *Journal of Vocational Behavior, 60*, 220–240.
30. Zenke, R., Raines, C. and Filipczak, B. (2000). *Generations at work: managing the clash of the Veterans, Boomers, Xers and Nexters in your workplace*. Washington, DC: American Management Association.
31. See, for example, Berti, A.E. and Bombi, A.S. (1988). *The child's construction of economics*. Cambridge: Cambridge University Press; Dickinson, J. and Emler, N. (1992). Developing conceptions of work. In J.F. Hartley and G.M. Stephenson (Eds.), *Employment relations: the psychology of influence and control at work* (pp. 19–44). Cambridge, MA : Blackwell.
32. Abramovitch, R. and Johnson, L.C. (1992). Children's perceptions of parental work. *Canadian Journal of Behavioural Science, 24*, 319–332.
33. Barling, J., Kelloway, E.K. and Bremermann, E.H. (1991). Pre-employment predictors of union attitudes: the role of family socialization and work beliefs. *Journal of Applied Psychology, 76*, 725–731; Kelloway, E.K. and Walts, I. (1994). Pre-employment predictors of union attitudes: Replication and extension. *Journal of Applied Psychology, 79*, 631–634.
34. Loughlin and Barling (2001). *Op. cit.*, p. 545.
35. See, for example, Barling, J., Dupre, K.E. and Hepburn, C.G. (1998). Effects of parents' job insecurity on children's work beliefs and attitudes. *Journal of Applied Psychology, 83*, 112–118.
36. Cappelli (1999). *Op. cit.*
37. Elder, G.H. (1974). *Children of the Great Depression*. Chicago, Il: University of Chicago Press.
38. *Ibid.*
39. Barling, J., Dupre, K. and Hepburn, C.G. (1998). Effects of parents' job insecurity on children's work beliefs and attitudes, *Journal of Applied Psychology, 83*, 112–118.
40. Sharlicki, D.P., Ellard, J.H. and Kelln B.R. (1998). Third-party perceptions of a layoff: procedural, derogation, and retributive aspects of justice, *Journal of Applied Psychology, 83*, 119–127.
41. Leana, C.R. and Feldman, D.C. (1994). The psychology of job loss. In G.R. Ferris (Ed.), *Research in personnel and human resource management, Volume 12*. Greenwich, CT: JAI Press; Shore, L.M. and Tetrick, L.E. (1994).

The psychological contract as an explanatory framework in the employment relationship. In C.L. Cooper and D.M. Rousseau (Eds.), *Trends in organizational behavior, Vol. 1*. Somerset, NJ: John Wiley; Cavanaugh, M.A. & Noe, R.A. (1999). Antecedents and consequences of relational components of the new psychological contract, *Journal of Organizational Behaviour, 20 (3)*, 323–340.

42. McKee L. Mauthner, N. and Maclean, C. (1999). Organisational culture and change; a study of the male model of work and the psychological contract in the oil and gas industry. Paper presented at the British Academy of Management Conference, 1–3 September, Manchester.

43. *The Economist* (2002). Face value: called to account. *The Economist*, Volume 364, Number 8278, 74.

44. *The Economist* (2002). An economy singed. *The Economist*, Volume 364, Number 8220, 13.

45. *The Economist* (2002). Executive pay: An expense by any other name. *The Economist*, Volume 363, No. 8267, 12.

46. See *The Economist* (2002). Executive pay: Wallowing in wages. *The Economist*, Volume 363, No. 8267, 65–66; *The Economist* (2002). Special report into American Companies: Chief executives, churning heads. *The Economist*, Volume 364, Number 8220, 80.

47. *The Economist* (2002). Executive pay: Wallowing in wages. *The Economist*, Volume 363, No. 8267, 65–66.

48. *The Economist* (2002). Stop this dream. *The Economist*, Volume 364, No. 8282, 65–66.

49. Drucker, P. (2001). The next society. *The Economist*, 361, No. 8246, 3–22.

50. *Ibid.*, p. 7.

51. *The Economist* (2002). Scottish population: Bairns needed. *The Economist*, Volume 364, No. 8286, 26.

52. Baker, S. (2002). The coming battle for immigrants. *Business Week*, 26 August, 138–140.

53. *The Economist* (2002). Special Report: Demography and the West: Half a billion Americans? *The Economist*, Volume 364, No. 8287, 21–23.

54. *Ibid.*

55. Wolf, M. (2002). Wasting time at the workplace. *Financial Times*, 10 April, 19.

56. *The Economist* (2002). Special Report: Demography and the West: Half a billion Americans? *The Economist*, Volume 364, No. 8287, 21–23.

57. Brown, D. (2002). A change in fortune. *People Management, 8 (14)*, 12–13.

57. Coy, P., Conlin, M. and Thornton, E. (2002). A lost generation? *Business Week*, November.

58. Drucker (2001). *Op. cit.*

59. Coy, P., Conlin, M. and Thornton, E. (2002). A lost generation? *Business Week*, 4 November, 34–36.

60. *The Economist* (2002). Special report: A survey of migration. *The Economist*, Volume 365, No. 8297, 3–16.

61. *Ibid.*, p. 14.
62. *The Economist* (2002). Outward bound. *The Economist*, Volume 364, No. 8292, 27–29.
63. *The Economist* (2002). Special report: A survey of migration. *The Economist*, Volume 365, No. 8297, 3–16, p. 13.
64. *Ibid.*
65. Drucker (2001). *Op. cit.*

Name index

Subject index